THE
EVERYTHING

HOME-BASED
BUSINESS BOOK

Everything you need to know to start and run
a successful home-based business

Jack Savage

Adams Media Corporation
Holbrook, Massachusetts

An Everything® Series Book.
Everything® is a registered trademark of Adams Media Corporation.

Published by Adams Media Corporation
260 Center Street, Holbrook, MA 02343. U.S.A.
www.adamsmedia.com

ISBN: 1-58062-364-6

Printed in the United States of America.

J I H G F E D C B

Library of Congress Cataloging-in-Publication Data
available upon request from the publisher.

Illustrations by Barry Littmann

This book is available at quantity discounts for bulk purchases.
For information, call 1-800-872-5627.

Visit our exciting small business Web site: www.businesstown.com

Acknowledgments

Thanks to Pam Liflander for overseeing this project, to Erin Clermont for her stellar editing, and to Bob Adams for his support. Jere Calmes helped keep things in perspective.

I'm hugely indebted to Cheryl Kimball for her help and encouragement. Thanks to Terrie Harman, Henry Isaacson, and others who provided their professional expertise. Thanks also to home businesspeople everywhere, but especially Todd LeFevre as well as Keith and Kathy Chick. I will always be inspired by the hard work and enthusiasm shown by Jon Richert.

I also extend thanks to Jean Kerr, Spencer Smith, Andy Bangs, and the other Upstarts from whom I learned so much about small business.

Contents

Part II
Starting Your Home
Business / 61

Chapter Six
Steps to Starting Your Business . . 63

Chapter Seven
Creating a Business Plan 77

Chapter Eight
Setting Up Your Home
Business Office 103

Introduction

Americans like to think of their country as a land of opportunity. With a little gumption and a good idea, anyone can hitch a ride on the gravy train. Our society supports a resilient middle class, many of whom run their own businesses.

For many more Americans, running their own business is an intimidating prospect. Collecting a regular paycheck for showing up on time and working for someone else seems a lot less risky than generating their own income.

Yet the lure of independence remains. When employees find their work life less than satisfying, they dream of a day when they can start their own business, call the shots, take the risks, and enjoy the rewards of entrepreneurship.

Home-based businesses have long been a fundamental part of our economy. In fact, it's actually the concept of leaving the home to go to work is relatively new, a product of the industrial age. Today, as office workers flee the confines of their workday cubicles in exchange for running a business out of their home, they are returning to an older lifestyle. Technology's advances have, to a certain extent, made this possible. The information age is one of specialization, and specialization makes independence possible for more workers.

Economic gain is rarely the sole motivation for home-business operators. Instead, most are looking for balance in their lives, a reasonable combination of commerce and family. Whether your home business income is meant to be supplemental or a living wage, you choose to run a business out of your home on purpose.

This book is intended to help introduce you to the elements of a home business. In its pages you will find the guidance you need to plan a home business start-up. It will help you decide what kind, how, and when to start your home business. From figuring out whether your current home personal financial situation is appropriate for a home business to creating a marketing and business plan, to finding ways to stay focused and motivated in the sometimes isolated world of the sole proprietor, the *Everything® Home-Based Business Book* explores every choice you need to make. And, it will point you in the direction of additional, specific planning for the future.

A lot of suggestions and advice appear in the following pages. Following all of it will enhance your chances of success—but it won't guarantee it. Conversely, you may break all the rules and be fabulously successful. One of the great advantages to being on your own is that you get to decide how you're going to run things. And, I'll be the first to admit, as a home-based businessperson myself, that I don't always follow my own suggestions, even when I know I should.

You may read this entire book and conclude that a home business is not for you. But for many of you, owning this book is the first small step toward a longtime goal.

PART I

Is a Home Business Right for You?

CHAPTER ONE

Can You Run a Home Business?

If you're trapped in a cubicle or behind a counter in an unchanging nine-to-five routine, there's a good chance that the idea of running your own business out of your home will seem ideal. Set your own hours and your own salary. Make your own decisions. Determine your own priorities. Face the daily challenge of succeeding or failing. It has to be better than toiling away endlessly in order to make someone else rich, right?

For many years, business pundits have talked about the high failure rate of small businesses. More recently, this conventional wisdom has been challenged. Small businesses may cease to exist, but this does not mean they actually fail—rather, their owners decide to get out. For one reason or another, running a small business simply didn't suit their lifestyles, their work habits, or their personalities.

Which is one reason that it's so important, if you're contemplating starting your own small home-based business, to be honest with yourself about your goals and reasons for thinking this might be a good idea. It's not for everyone.

Qualities of a Successful Home Businessperson

There's nothing wrong with working for someone else. For the right kind of person, at the right time of life, and for the right reasons, salaried employment may be just the right path to your brand of contentment.

Similarly, self-employment with a business run from the home might be just the right thing—for the right kind of person, at the right time of life, for the right reasons. But what is the right kind of person?

To get a sense of the personal qualities that would indicate you might be the right person, ask yourself these questions:

1. Do you currently maintain a household budget, and keep to it?
2. Do you track household expenses monthly, project your needs, and save regularly for large purchases?
3. Are you comfortable with change, unpredictability?
4. Do you enjoy the challenge of needing to reach a financial revenue goal each month, or does the thought make you tense and uncomfortable?

5. Are you energized by the challenge of solving problems, or does encountering problem after problem leave you tired and discouraged?
6. Do you enjoy being on your own, not missing the company of coworkers?

If you answered yes to all these questions, great.

The ability to plan ahead, postpone gratification, roll with the punches, and set and reach for goals while deftly outmaneuvering obstacles are good characteristics to have (But on the other hand, they won't guarantee your success, either.) as a home business entrepreneur. If you were honest with yourself and answered no to these questions— you see yourself as a poor planner with little self-discipline who panics at the thought of missing a paycheck—then a full-time home business is probably not right for you at this time.

Good Reasons to Start a Home Business

There are any number of good reasons to start a home-based business. The best overall is simply that you want to. Still, it's worth thinking through the reasons behind that desire. What is it about a home business that appeals to you? And does your home business idea match any of the scenarios here?

- *You have a good idea in a good market.* This doesn't have to be a new or brilliant idea, just a match for the market. For example, you realize that 75 percent of the households in your area own pets, the owners are in an above-average income bracket and often travel, but there's no kennel or pet-sitter around. Get busy!
- *You have a marketable skill.* You're a great carpenter. Everywhere you turn, people are asking you if you would do a project for them. There are other carpenters around, but you sense that you can do a better job than they typically do.

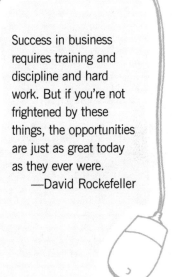

Success in business requires training and discipline and hard work. But if you're not frightened by these things, the opportunities are just as great today as they ever were.
—David Rockefeller

- *You want a change of lifestyle.* This is a common reason for starting home businesses and is a good one as long as the lifestyle you seek involves working hard. Running a home business does not mean lounging around watching soap operas. It does mean taking charge of your life and determining your own goals and being responsible for your own achievements.
- *You're determined to be successful.* The drive to succeed—and having a clear idea of what you mean by "success"—will be invaluable to you. Now analyze the market and find a match between what you can and want to do and what there's a market for.
- *You believe in your own abilities and like to challenge yourself.* Dissatisfied employees often cite a lack of challenge as one of the reasons for their unhappiness. Well, a home business will certainly be challenging.

Bad Reasons to Start a Home Business

As you contemplate starting a home-based business, try to take stock of the real reasons behind your interest. Sometimes we hop the fence in search of greener pastures only because we're unhappy. The solution may lie in addressing the reason for your discontent, which may be unrelated to how you earn a living. Starting a home business won't automatically lead to contentment—it must be something you actively want to do. Are your reasons for wanting to run a business out of your home similar to one of these?

- *You hate your boss.* Well, welcome to the club. Everybody struggles with his or her supervisor at one time or another, and you need to evaluate what's really bothering you. If you like your work, believe in the company you work for, enjoy and respect your coworkers, then opening up your own business may not be the key to happiness.
- *You never find the time to do what you really want.* If you long for the flexibility a home business would give you, sorry. If you don't find time for what's important now, you won't as a

home business entrepreneur either. However, if you can schedule and manage your time reasonably well and a home business would give you more flexibility within that schedule, you're on track.

- *You want to get rich.* Monetary rewards can be a good motivator, but most ongoing home-based businesses yield only a modest income. Exceptions might be businesses that can grow over time and then be sold at some point or businesses based on high-tech products or processes, inventions, or new products. But in those cases, the riches often come when it's time to get out of the business.

- *The cost of day care is outrageous.* Well, guess what, it's still going to be expensive. Raising children is a full-time job, and a home business can be almost as demanding. In order to focus on a home business full-time, you're likely going to have to make some arrangements for day care, at least part of the time. Of course, if you're planning on opening a day care business, the solution may be at hand!

- *You have a better mousetrap.* Sure, you could sink your life savings into a business based on one invention. Or then again you could play the lottery. Just get ready to face rejection, huge market barriers, copycats, and any number of shady characters who are more than happy to take your money. If you can find your way through those forests, then go for it!

- *Aunt Matilda left you $50K.* Having a modest chunk of capital is helpful. But you need to want to start a home business. Desire without money often succeeds; money without desire rarely does.

- *You saw on cable TV where you can make $1,000 in just a few hours a week.* Yes, that may be true—if it's by starting a company that promises other people $1,000 in just a few hours a week and you then take their money. If it sounds too good to be true, then it probably is.

- *All your current employer ever thinks about is the bottom line.* With your own home business you won't have to think about money all the time. Hello? As a small businessperson, tracking the comings and goings of cash will become one of your

What's It Like, I Mean Really?

If the idea of running your own home-based business appeals to you, but you're not sure that you'd be as enthusiastic about the reality of it, ask somebody who has a home business, or at least has a friend who in turn knows someone. Ask if he or she would be willing to spend an hour talking with you about what it's really like to run a business out of the home.

Ideally you'll be invited to visit, so you can see and get a feel for the home business environment. Then ask every question you can think of: Does he get lonely? Does she worry about not being able to pay the bills?

If you find yourself starting to ask logistical questions—how do I file for an EIN number, or what kind of phone is best?—then you're hooked.

priorities. Yes, you can set your own mission and be a caring business that considers more than the bottom line in making decisions. But the only time you'll be able to stop thinking about money is when you have too much of it.

- *The idea of taking a walk whenever you want is so appealing.* Do you want to take walks or run a business? Yes, you'll be able to make your own schedule. But you also need to want to run a business. Home businesses are usually more work than a regular job, not less.
- *All my friends have their own businesses.* OK, so what? Are they happy? Are you happy? You need to figure out what you want to spend your time doing, and then do it! Don't let other people's lives define your wants and needs.

Don't Make Excuses for Yourself

It is important to be clear that you're starting a home business as a means toward fulfilling a personal goal, but don't let other goals stand as excuses not to act. Making the decision to invest hard-earned savings or quit a job is difficult—we all worry that it might be a mistake. Here are some common excuses people sometimes use to avoid making these tough choices:

- *I need to keep working so my children can go to college.* Yes, large, looming financial obligations can keep you rooted in your job. But isn't it possible that your children will also benefit from watching and participating in a home business? If you're afraid to take a risk, won't they likely hold back from trying to achieve their dreams, too? Make a college fund an important goal of the home business, and go after it!
- *I need my current job because of the health benefits.* Believe it or not, you can get health insurance as a self-employed person. It's possible that, depending on your personal circumstances, it

will cost more. But as a home business entrepreneur you might be able to earn more than you do in your current job. Don't let the health care issue scare you off—investigate what it would cost, build that expense into your business plan, and see if it works.

- *I'm worried about not having enough money for retirement.* A legitimate concern. But how secure is your current job anyway? And are you making yourself miserable today—your best years from a health standpoint—just so you can be comfortable in 10, 20, or 30 years? You can run your own business and plan for retirement. And you might be happier along the way!

- *My current employer just couldn't get along without me.* If that's true, then they should be offering you some equity in the business! More likely, while they would miss you, the truth is that everyone is dispensable. If you got hit by a bus tomorrow, they'd find someone to replace you. Think of yourself first.

- *My husband wouldn't like it/my wife wouldn't stand for it.* In a healthy relationship, partners support each other's goals and dreams and want the other to be happy. Talk to your spouse. If starting a home business is something you really feel strongly about, find out why your spouse is opposed and see if there isn't some compromise. Who knows, you might be surprised to find out that he or she isn't so dead set against it after all!

- *I just couldn't afford it.* OK, if you're up to your armpits in credit card debt and the mortgage payment is a challenge each month, you might not be the greatest candidate for taking a flyer on an unproved home business idea. But you can still tackle your business as well as a personal financial plan to get out of your current predicament. Challenge yourself to be in a position to start your business in three or five years—stick to the plan, and make it happen!

> ### Words to the Wise
>
> Home businesses are, above all, businesses. The most important decision you have to make is whether the advantages of a home-based business will make you happy.

If you find yourself coming up with a new excuse every time you think about starting a home business, then maybe entrepreneurship isn't for you. There's no shame in coming to the conclusion that, in fact, you're happier working for someone else, leaving your employment worries behind when you head home at night.

TEST YOUR HOME BUSINESS POTENTIAL

Scale your answer to the following questions with a number from 1 to 5, a 1 being the least and 5 being the most.

1. I prefer to get my way.

2. I like to experiment.

3. Mistakes are good learning experiences.

4. I am determined to succeed.

5. I rarely get lonely.

6. Without risk, life would be pretty boring.

7. I don't like when others have authority over me.

8. I like setting goals and accomplishing them.

9. I rarely give up.

10. I like to solve problems—the more the better.

11. If I don't know something, I just go find out about it.

12. People who know me might say I'm stubborn.

13. Failure makes me more determined.

14. If somebody says it's impossible, then I'm determined to prove them wrong.

15. I don't worry too much about what others think about me.

16. I'd call myself a confident person.

17. When I'm interested in a project, I work long hours to finish it.

18. I have a clear view of where I want to be in 10 years.

19. I like other people, but I'm happy to be by myself.

20. Financial security is a goal, but I'm comfortable with risk.

Score:

20–50:   You'll likely be happier keeping your day job or sticking to a hobby business.

51–75:   Look before you leap, but give yourself a chance, plan carefully and a home business could work for you.

76–100:   Figure out what you want to do, pick the right time, and go for it.

CHAPTER TWO

What Kind of Home-Based Business Do You Want?

A home-based business can take any number of forms. For some, it will be a full-time replacement for an office or factory job. For others, it will be a natural outgrowth of a hobby or a part-time retirement business after a successful career working for someone else. And certainly the latter can grow into the former. But it's helpful if you can plan your home business based on whether you want it to be full-time or part-time.

What Is a Home Business?

Seems like a simple question, doesn't it? But as you begin your search for information on starting and running a home business, you'll find that different businesses start from different points of view. And you'll have different needs depending on your own view of a home business.

A home business is, among other things, a business run by one or more people out of someone's residence. The business operator is also the business owner who calls the shots, takes the risk, and enjoys the success of the business. This does not include those who work out of their home as employees of another business, such as telecommuters—though many of the issues discussed in this book apply to telecommuters as well as home business owners.

Home businesses can be further broken down into several different categories. Many magazines and books focus on the late-twentieth-century version of a home-based business: an office in a home where the proprietor offers a service to clients, such as a tax preparer, resume writer, or book editor. Walk-in customer traffic is at a minimum and is usually by appointment.

There are also more retail-oriented home businesses, in which the product or service requires a customer visit. This might be a retail craft shop, hair salon, day care, kennel, or automotive repair business. Parking and a business space apart from the home are usually requirements of this kind of home business.

And then there are the contractors, such as plumbers, electricians, landscapers. These home businesspeople administrate their

business out of their homes but actually do the work off-site, at the customer's home or business.

Hobby Businesses

Hobby businesses are one of the most common home businesses in America today. What do we mean by a hobby business? Well, simply that you have a hobby—knitting, woodworking, photography, or gardening—that grows from a casual way to pass your time into an organized home business that generates revenue and incurs expenses. You may do little more than sell your products or services to friends or neighbors, or you may be regularly promoting and advertising your hobby business to garner more and more customers, but your primary motivation is likely to be an enjoyment of the business activity.

Advantages of a Hobby Business

There are a number of advantages to a hobby business. You may already have a reputation for quality work among your neighbors or among other hobbyists. That reputation can be helpful as you seek to build your business in the beginning. It's built-in "goodwill," an important asset for any successful business.

Another advantage is that you are likely to already own many of the tools, machinery, software, or other necessary items required for your business, which will minimize the initial capital outlay needed to start up. While for some businesses, commercial grade equipment will be necessary for more frequent usage, what you have on hand will likely get you started.

Jim, for example, had for a number of years enjoyed fixing and customizing golf clubs in his basement. When he was laid off temporarily from his factory job, he put up notices at several golf courses in the area and soon had a steady flow of business. He already had the basic equipment he needed, so he could get going without spending a lot of cash he didn't have or using credit cards. His work was good, and after a local golf pro commissioned him to do all the repair work for the pro shop, he was able to upgrade

Does a Hobby Business Have to Make Money?

One seeming advantage of a hobby business is that when tax time comes around, you might be able to write off certain expenses related to your hobby. But it shouldn't surprise you that the IRS is well aware of this ploy and has set specific standards.

As a sole proprietor, you'll be filing Schedule C (or Schedule C-EZ), "Profit or Loss From Business." While the IRS recognizes that you may show a loss, you are expected to be running your business in an effort to make money. That means generating revenue, which is offset by appropriate expenses. As a general rule, the IRS expects your business to show a profit three years out of five.

his equipment to keep up. When the factory called him back to work three months later, his business had grown to the extent that he turned them down!

Another advantage of the hobby business is that you can be content working at it part-time. Since it's your hobby, and presumably a pleasure, it can generate modest income as a part-time activity. And that's a big advantage if the alternative is getting a second, part-time job to help cover expenses.

Of course, hobby businesses often grow into full-time businesses, and therein lies another advantage. With a hobby business, you can slowly build up the business until you're ready to make the switch from hobby to full-time. It can lessen the risk if you're contemplating giving up a steady job in favor of your home business. You'll have a sense of the cash flow requirements and the overall rhythm of the business. By the time you make the leap, it may seem more like a relief than a risky proposition, because you can finally concentrate on the home business without having to run off to work 40 hours a week for someone else!

Keeping it a hobby business for a while allows you to learn whether this is something you would like to do on a full-time basis. If you build your hobby into a business while still employed elsewhere, but then find out that you really preferred the enjoyment of your hobby without the added pressures of making a profit, you can always back away without having given up your regular job.

Retirement Businesses

A retirement home business is just that, a business you start or operate after retiring from another career. Today, millions of Americans are operating retirement businesses for reasons ranging from financial need to just wanting something to do to keep them active, alert, and engaged.

A retirement home business could be full-time, but might more likely be part-time and meet other needs of the proprietor, like time flexibility. Priscilla, a retired beautician in Iowa, opened her own one-chair salon in a converted garage in her home. She has a set

Warning:
This Seems Too Much Like Work!

Most of us engage in hobbies to pass time pleasantly while getting a sense of satisfaction and accomplishment. Whether it's the pleasure of passing a leisurely afternoon in your woodworking shop creating furniture from raw wood or the expression of creativity that is satisfied behind the lens or in the darkroom, your hobby is usually a relaxing escape from the daily grind of the rest of your life.

But once a hobby becomes a business, with all of business's usual issues such as deadlines, collections, cash flow, bookkeeping, and customer service suddenly intruding, it may seem more like work than pleasure. If you're planning on making your long-loved hobby a business, make sure that the accompanying pressures stay in perspective and that you can continue to enjoy the activity that is the core of the business. You don't want to end up hating your hobby as you attempt to make it your business.

Bill, a retired shipyard worker in Maine, had long enjoyed tinkering with old lawnmowers, weedwackers, and other small engines. He'd often fix his neighbors' mowers and rarely charged them for more than parts. Once Bill retired, he figured that it was a perfect home business, and he put an ad in the local newspaper.

Soon, however, Bill was swamped. Many of the repairs that customers brought him were just not the kind of work he enjoyed, but he took it on anyway because he didn't want to disappoint anyone. Before long, he was finding himself spending 10 to 12 hours a day bent over his workbench in order to get a lawnmower fixed by a certain day or time. As a hobbyist, he often salvaged parts off old machines to fix his neighbor's mower, but his new customers insisted on new parts, which required carrying inventory to avoid delays.

Bill found he no longer enjoyed what he was doing. It wasn't that he couldn't do the work, but the pleasure he experienced previously whiling away an afternoon, listening to a Red Sox game and doing a favor for a neighbor, was replaced by stress, worry, and demanding customers. It was all just too much like work!

How Much Can You Earn?

As of April 2000, the law determining how much you can earn while collecting your Social Security benefits changed. But you still will be looking at some reduction in benefits if you earn "too much money" in the eyes of the Social Security administration until you reach full retirement age (currently age 65).

Here's how it works under the new law:

- If you are under full retirement age when you start getting your Social Security payments, $1 in benefits will be deducted for each $2 you earn above the annual limit. For 2000, that limit is $10,080.

- In the year you turn full retirement age, $1 in benefits will be deducted for each $3 you earn above a different limit, but only counting earnings before the month you reach the full benefit retirement age. For 2000, this other limit is $17,000.

But now the good news, and the reason for the new law. Starting with the month you reach full retirement age, you will get your benefits with no limit on your earnings. However, you should note that starting with those born in 1938, the legal definition of "full retirement age is defined as age 67. To get more information on the impact of home business income on your Social Security benefits, they maintain a highly informative Web site at *www.ssa.gov*.

As you plan your retirement home-based business, consider your overall financial picture, including Social Security benefits.

clientele, who know that she spends at least six weeks in Florida each winter and that they have to make appointments early around the holidays, when her children and grandchildren come to visit. Priscilla's retirement business generates some welcome added income, but more important, gives her a real sense of satisfaction and ongoing accomplishment as she grows wiser (not older!). Plus, she still keeps up on all the gossip!

For some, retirement businesses are a way to pay the bills. Sometimes life throws us curves, and retirement nest eggs just don't turn out to be enough to get by or else get quickly used up in medical or other emergencies. And sure, there are service-sector or other jobs out there for those on their second or third career, but they're not for everybody.

John, a former maintenance man at a school district, wanted to supplement his income after retirement. He realized that many of the vacation homeowners in his area of Wisconsin frequently needed work done on their property, but weren't able to be there to supervise or check the work when done. So John started a home business helping these absentee homeowners maintain their homes—he would do drive-by checks on the vacant property in the off-season, hire specialists such as plumbers or electricians, and oversee the work when repairs were needed or simply charge a fee to open up and prepare the house prior to the owner coming back for some rest and relaxation. For John, it was perfect—he worked 20 to 25 hours per week, setting his own hours for the most part, and he was able to use the knowledge gleaned in 30 years of his previous career.

Retirement businesses are so popular in Florida that one gentleman retired only to start a retirement business brokerage. Retired friends of his would ask if he knew of any small businesses for sale that they could run on a part-time basis. For the most part, they weren't as interested in putting in the energy to start a business from scratch as they were in buying an ongoing concern. As this clever retiree looked into it, he discovered that there was a healthy business to be made out of brokering such deals.

Full-Time Home Businesses

With a full-time home business, the presumption is that you plan to live, save, send the kids to college, and retire off the proceeds. It's your bread and butter, and success is critical. Many of the functions of running a full-time business may not be different from a hobby business or retirement business, but the attitude may be just a little bit more serious because there's more at stake for the owner.

The most important part of starting your full-time home business will be planning. While you won't be able to predict every challenge that's due to come your way as a home businessperson (how boring if you could!), you can improve your chances of success by setting goals, creating a plan to reach those goals, and analyzing your progress to make sure you're moving toward achieving those goals. By planning on paper before you invest your savings into an entrepreneurial venture like a home business, you give yourself the opportunity to make mistakes on paper—and correcting them before you start.

The next three chapters will help you identify some of the hoops you'll need to jump through on the way to starting your home business. Once you've determined that your home and family will tolerate a full-time business under the roof, make sure that the business will let you reach your financial goals. The idea of puttering around the shop fixing televisions may appeal to you, but the realities of the market may be that a home TV repair business just won't generate the kind of income you want or need.

But don't despair! Being a home business entrepreneur is all about putting your creativity and business acumen to use. If your first plan doesn't work, use what you learned to come up with a second plan. Somewhere there's a business you can operate out of your home that will satisfy your needs—after all, computer giant Hewlett-Packard started as a home-based business years ago by a couple of guys named Hewlett and Packard. Your home business could grow the same way if you want it to!

Deciding the Future of Your Home Business

As you start your home business, it can be helpful—although not necessary—to have an idea of what you want to happen to your home business in the future. If you decide to discontinue as the proprietor of the business, what will happen to it? Will it simply disappear? Do you hope that a son or daughter will want to take over the business? Would you ever sell your business? Like many small businesspeople, perhaps you're hoping to build the business and then retire from the proceeds of selling it.

If this is a hobby or retirement business that will simply live and die with its proprietor, then you needn't think much more about it. But if you hope to sell it someday, it's never too late to begin preparing for that eventuality.

For example, consider the name of your business. Many sole proprietors use their own name in the name of the business. The credibility of the business rests on their personal credibility. Customers don't just call your business for help, they call you personally.

But if you hope to sell that business, will your name go with it? Part of the value of a business is its goodwill, or reputation. Are you comfortable with someone else using your name as they run the business their way after you sell it? And if you don't sell the use of the name, your business may not be worth as much.

The solution is to start with a business name that isn't quite as personal. Instead of Raymond Jones Plumbing, consider a more generic name, like Quick 'n' Clean Plumbing Services.

You Can Sell Any Part of a Business

It is possible to sell a business without selling the business name or the property on which it's located. If you've run an automotive repair business for years out of a building in your backyard, you can sell the tools, the contracts you have for ongoing work with other businesses, the client list, the receivables, and even the building itself if it can be moved. It's worth thinking about these issues when you first start out.

Home Business Ideas

Here are examples of businesses that typically work well when operated out of the home. Some require special training or licensing.

Accountant
Adoption Consultant
Advertising Agency
Antiques Dealer
Architect
Beauty Salon/Barber
Bed and Breakfast
Bicycle Repair
Boat Repair/Restoration
Bookkeeping Services
Business Broker
Candy Maker
Car Body
   Repair/Detailing/
   Mechanic
Carpenter
Carpet and Tile
   Installation
Carpet Cleaning
Caterer
Chiropractor
Clock Repair
Computer
   Consultant/Repair
Cooking Teacher
Country Store

Craft Shop
Data Entry Specialist
Day Care Center
Desktop Publisher
Direct Mail Service
Dog Groomer/Trainer
Driving Instructor
Elder Care
Electrician
Farm Stand
Feed Store
Financial Planner
Fitness Trainer
Florist
Forestry Consultant
Freelance Editor/Writer
Furniture Maker/Repair
Genealogist
General Contractor
Gift Baskets
Glass Installation/Repair
Graphic Designer
Heating Contractor
Horse Stables/
   Riding Lessons
House Inspector

House Painter
Housecleaning Service
Insurance Broker
Interior Decorator
Janitorial Services
Kennel
Knife Sharpening Service
Landscaping
Lawn Care
Lawyer
Literary Agent
Locksmith
Marketing Services
Massage or
   Aroma Therapy
Online Retailer
Party Clown
Party Planner/Consultant
Pest Control Specialist
Pet Sitting
Photographer
Pick-Your-Own Farm
Plumbing Contractor
Pool Maintenance
Property Management
Psychiatrist

Public Relations
   Consultant
Real Estate
   Agent/Assessor
Resume Writer
Sales Representative
Secretarial Services
Septic Installation/
   Cleaning
Sewer Pipe Cleaning
Shoe Repair
Sign Maker/Painter
Small Engine Repair
Specialty Retail Sales
Tack Shop
Tax Preparer
TV & VCR Repair
Thrift Store
Travel Agent
Truck Driver
Vacuum Repair
Veterinary Services
Web Site Designer
Wedding Consultant
Well Drilling Service

Selling a business is a critical decision for home businesses, especially if the location is an important element of the business and it means selling your home as well. For example, if you open a country store in your barn along a busy road, the location will be a big factor in the value of that business. Such a scenario might work out well for you—between the appreciation of the real estate, and the added value of the business located on the property, you may be able to retire well by selling out when the time comes.

But if you live in a homestead that's been in your family for generations, and you plan to live there until they carry you out feet-first in a box, you're not likely to want to sell your home as part of a business. Consequently, you may want to start your business as a home business in order to keep costs down, but include moving the business elsewhere in your future plans. That way, when you're ready to get out, you can sell the business for its full value without giving up your home.

Look Before You Leap

Some entrepreneurs may stumble onto success. But most who've found the way of life and standard of living they wanted did so by setting goals and then following a planned path to those goals. Whether it's a hobby, retirement, or full-time business, you'll find your own version of success comes a lot faster if you spend some time thinking about what you want before you jump into anything.

For more information on this topic, visit our Web site at businesstown.com

CHAPTER THREE

Is Your Home Right for Your Business?

For many of us, our home is a personal hideaway from the cares of the world. For others, it's a place to entertain friends and relatives, and someone is always stopping by. If you enjoy your time at home, for these or other reasons, make sure you think carefully about bringing a home business into the mix.

Many people who start their own business do so because they want to be their own boss. That's a fine motivation on the surface of it, but as any small business entrepreneur can tell you, success often means that the business, and the customers who come with it, are in fact your new boss. By setting up a business in your home, you run the risk of giving up the sense of separation between your personal life and your business life. The feeling of respite and retreat that your home always provided is now invaded by the realities of the business world, especially if the house itself isn't set up properly. This isn't true for every kind of business, but certainly for plumbers, electricians, furnace repair technicians, and the like, calls will come from customers around the clock, on holidays, and while you're in the shower. Businesses that market across the country or around the world can expect calls and faxes throughout the day and night.

Setting up a home office is discussed in more detail in Chapter 8, "Setting Up Your Home Business/Office," but here are issues you will have to consider as you decide whether your home is right for the home-based business you have in mind:

- Zoning
- Dedicated space used exclusively for the business
- Storage
- Parking
- Location and signage
- Phone lines and utilities
- Taxes

Zoning

Home businesses aren't welcome just anywhere. And in some neighborhoods, they aren't welcome at all! In most communities,

the zoning ordinance regulates home businesses, and it's important to know what the rules are before you begin. Business licenses are required for certain kinds of home businesses as well.

Your first stop to find out about zoning will be city or town hall, where you'll want to get a copy of the zoning ordinance. Buried in it somewhere will be a section on what's permitted within the residential zone. If your community prohibits business use of a home within a residential zone, it's not advisable to proceed anyway hoping that you won't get caught. This may be particularly difficult to abide by if you're expanding a hobby that you've been enjoying for years.

When you look into the permitted uses within the residential zone of your community, make sure that your property is in fact zoned residential. Most zoning ordinances have been applied to existing towns, and it may be that your house is in fact part of the commercial zone. If so, you're all set—just abide by the regulations established for businesses within that zone.

Variances

Even if the written zoning rules prohibit your business, don't give up right away. It is possible in many cases to get permission to proceed with your business under certain conditions by requesting a *variance*. A variance acknowledges that the rules don't always make sense when applied to every situation, and a low-impact home business (no noise, few or no in-person customers, no environmental hazards) may be welcome despite the rules.

If you purchase a home that already had a business of the type you plan to continue—for example, you've purchased a home with a commercial-grade garage to perform automotive repair, as did the previous owner—and the owner had already established the business for "permitted use" or had obtained a variance, then typically the use is grandfathered (a variance goes with the property, not the person) and you can continue to operate the same kind of business on the same spot. However, expansion of the business in such a case is usually prohibited without another variance.

Assuming that home businesses are permitted in your residential zone, look carefully at what limitations there may be. You may be limited to a certain number of nonfamily employees, for example. You

Deeded Covenants

Even if a home business is a permitted use within the residential zone of your community, you may be prohibited from establishing a home business by your deed or by the rules of a condo or neighborhood association. Sometimes the developer of a subdivision will have included covenants in the deeds of all the lots, prohibiting home businesses. Similarly, if your property is part of a common neighborhood association, the rules may prohibit home businesses. In both cases, the rules are meant to preserve the character of the neighborhood. Make sure the venture you're about to launch won't get shut down prematurely by your neighbors.

may be required to provide adequate parking space, a certain width driveway, or any number of details. Discuss these with the building inspector or code enforcement officer in your town to make sure that you understand them correctly. It's always better to know ahead of time what the restrictions are. You don't want to find out 18 months down the road that you have to spend an unplanned $10,000 making changes to your home in order to comply with the zoning ordinance.

Dedicated Business Space

The ideal home business setting will include space that can be dedicated exclusively to the business. Although it makes a good story to tell friends how you started your business years ago sitting at your kitchen table, the realities of business are such that you'll want a separate space. Customers don't like invoices splashed by last night's spaghetti dinner. And if your home business is a full-time occupation, you'll want and need to be able to shut it out of your personal life on occasion. Being able to close the office door or shop and be off the clock is important. You'll be in danger of burning out if your home business demands your attention 24 hours a day.

If your home business is office-based without the need to host customers, a spare bedroom may be ideal. If that isn't available, consider whether you might be able to rearrange the house to provide dedicated space. Do you have a formal living room as well as a family room? Perhaps by making the living room into the family room you can create space for your home office.

Finished basements can also provide the space you need. But check with your building inspector first. To use your basement as a living or working space, you may need to put in a separate fire exit or other safety items.

If your business will require you to meet with customers on-site, then a separate entrance would be preferred. A walk-in basement or converted garage may provide this for you. Or perhaps you can set up your house so that an existing side or back door can be used—either for the business or for your family—in order to avoid having customers parade through your living room.

Storage

Will your home business require storage for inventory or parts? Even space for business records can be at a premium for the home businessperson. Does your house provide enough dry space for your projected storage needs?

If not, you may want to consider renting storage space. Storage space is a lot cheaper to rent than office space or retail space, running from about $35 monthly and up, depending on where you live. Consequently, running your business out of your home and then driving once a week to a storage facility nearby may be the ideal storage solution.

Parking

If your customers will be visiting you on-site, you'll need to provide appropriate parking. Again, this is an issue that the zoning ordinance will likely address, and you may be required to provide a minimum number of spaces and be prohibited from having more than a certain number.

Employees also present a parking issue. If you plan to hire people, make sure they have a safe place to park that won't interfere with the comings and goings of the household or with customers.

Location and Signage

Small business consultants like to talk about the cost of a business location being equal to rent plus advertising. Especially for a retail business, location is key. Opening up a retail pottery shop in your home may seem like a great way to save on what it costs to rent a retail location—but what will it take to get customers in the door? Which makes more business sense: $600 a month to rent space downtown where walk-by or drive-by traffic will flow in the door or a $1,500 a month advertising budget and no rent?

Are you counting on bringing in business via a sign in front of your home? No matter where you're zoned, there are likely specific regulations spelling out how big your sign can be, whether or how

If They Say No to a Variance Request ...

You can still appeal to the zoning board or in court. At this point, of course, you'll need a real estate attorney or a specialist in zoning to assist you. If your request concerns a proposed new structure or addition—say, a sign you want to put at the end of your driveway—you will have to show why the sign will not adversely impact the character of your neighborhood, that you cannot do business without it, and that denial of your request means financial loss.

If you are applying for changes in use of existing property—for example, converting your garage into a retail pottery studio—it's harder to win an appeal. You will have to prove that the zoning rule is preventing you from using your property to its full value, that you bought the house to eventually use the garage for a business, and that the business will not disrupt the neighborhood in any way.

Security Check

Remember to be security conscious when it comes to bringing customers into your home. Do you know much about the people doing business with you? Is it possible that they're "casing the joint" as they discuss business—and are planning to come back when you're not around to burglarize your home? You won't be able to do a background check on everyone who knocks at your home business door, but you can minimize your exposure by separating your business from your home. If possible, use a separate entrance that leads only to the business area of your home.

it can be lighted, and where it can be located. Make sure you know what's allowed and that it will meet your needs.

Consider, too, your customers' needs. When you give directions to your house, is it easy to find? Where could you place a sign to help the customer find you? Will the sign be visible through all four seasons of the year, or might it be obscured by leaves in the summer or knocked down by the snowplow in the winter? Is it clear which driveway is yours? For safety as well as customer satisfaction reasons, make sure it's easy to find your business and easy for customers to know where to park.

Phone Lines and Utilities

Bringing multiple lines into a residence shouldn't prove to be a major obstacle. Phone companies large and small have been rising to the challenge of the demand for more lines created by the emergence of the Internet. But it would be wise to make the call to your local phone service provider to find out what it will take to bring in the lines you need. If you're a long way off the road or in an area where demand for new lines is high, you may be facing a delay.

Will your current residential electric service meet the needs of your business? How about heating? Water? A home-based catering business might need significant upgrades—converting from electric to gas stove, for example—over your current facilities. Are you planning to use an outbuilding on your property? Is it up to the current building code for the use you're planning? Will you need electricity, heat, or water brought in to the building? Consider your business needs, check the local building codes, and get quotes from contractors on what it will cost to get what you need.

Insurance

Read through your home insurance policy carefully. There's a good chance that your current policy does not cover certain losses when the property is used in a commercial activity. If you have customers coming on to the property, you may find yourself liable for damages

Americans with Disabilities Act

If your home business is a "place of public accommodation," such as a doctor's office, day care center, or retail shop, then the portion of your home used in the operation of the place of public accommodation is covered by Title III of the Americans with Disabilities Act (ADA). Included are sidewalks, driveways, and other portions of your home used by customers or clients. Basically this means that you may be required to remove barriers and make reasonable changes to accommodate the disabled.

The ADA requirements shouldn't be something that prohibits you from using parts of your home as a business. But if you expect significant customer traffic, you will need to consider how you might make access possible for someone in a wheelchair, for example. For more specific information, contact the U.S. Department of Justice (*www.usdoj.gov* or call 800-514-0301 voice; 800-514-0383 TDD).

This aspect of planning only reinforces the point that your home will change once you create a business in it. You may or may not be called upon to build a ramp into your home business, but if that were the most reasonable solution, would you be willing to do it? How would others in your family feel about the aesthetics of it? Take all of this into consideration as you decide whether or not your home is a good place for your business idea.

in the event of an accident, but without insurance coverage. Check with your insurance agent.

Taxes

Using your home for a business presents opportunities and pitfalls with regard to taxes. Fairly well documented are the pros and cons of taking a "home office deduction" on your income tax return. This is discussed in more detail in Chapter 12, "Taxes and the Home Business." Suffice it to say here that when it comes to the IRS, you're best off when the space allocated to your home business is used exclusively for the home business. This includes work space as well as storage.

Discuss thoroughly with your accountant the short-term and long-term consequences of locating a home business in your home in your particular area—there may be hidden disadvantages. For example, in New Hampshire, when your home is used for business, it becomes, in part, an asset of the business. When that asset is sold (even years after you may have closed the business), the state expects you to pay business profits tax on the proceeds.

If you make improvements to your home to accommodate a home business, you may find your real estate taxes going up. That's not necessarily a bad thing—it means your home, an important asset, is worth more. You will also be able to deduct as business expense what you spend on improvements specific to the business. As you weigh the pros and cons of siting a business on your home property or elsewhere, this is worth thinking about.

CHAPTER FOUR

The Home Business Family

Unless you live alone, running a business out of your home will affect other members of the household. It's important to have their cooperation in order to make the business run as smoothly as possible. When children, spouses, or other relatives are involved, it's easy for resentment to develop when a business intrudes into home life.

Communicate First

The best way to minimize potential conflicts is to discuss them ahead of time. As you investigate and consider starting a home-based business, take time to sit down with your spouse and your children and talk about what you're doing and why it's important to you.

Don't be surprised if you encounter a lack of enthusiasm among one or more of your family members. While you may be excited and are looking forward to the satisfaction and sense of accomplishment that comes from running your own business, a spouse may be dreading the idea of having customers or vendors coming to the house. Children may be concerned that you will be paying less attention to them.

To be fair to you and your family both, help them understand exactly why a home business is important to you. To the best of your ability, paint them an accurate picture of what life will be like with that business under the home roof. Be honest. If you need them to answer the phone once in a while, tell them up front. If you're expecting to meet with clients in the living room and will need them to keep it neat and clean at all times, let them know. Be sure, too, to ask them what their biggest concerns would be.

The Naysayer Spouse

In an ideal relationship, upon hearing of your dreams of a home-based business, your spouse will jump up, give you a congratulatory hug, and ask how he or she can help. But ideal relationships are a rare commodity—more likely you have a very human relationship, which by its nature is charged with emotions, insecurities, and baggage from past experiences.

Whatever your motivations for starting a home-based business, you're likely to be proud of your initiative and excited about the potential. And even the most entrepreneurial personalities harbor doubts and a certain fear of failure. What you may be wanting from your spouse—without even knowing it, perhaps—is the moral and emotional support that only a loved one can offer. In fact, your own struggles with self-esteem may be such that the only person you've dared to tell about your home business dream is your husband, wife, or partner!

So it can be a crushing blow when your spouse reacts with anything less than your own enthusiasm. You announce this life-changing event, and your soul mate gives it the old "yeah-yeah-yeah, whatever" treatment. Or worse than not taking you seriously, he or she reacts negatively, immediately launching into a litany of reasons why your hare-brained scheme will "never work."

Though the temptation may be to take a baseball bat to his new car or weed-whack her flower garden to nubs, you need to think of this as your first obstacle to be overcome. You're sure to encounter many more roadblocks in starting a business—so take a deep breath and focus on winning over your spouse.

Familiar Issues

In many ways, these kinds of conflicts are nothing new. When two people decide to spend their lives together, each will come to the union with their own vision of the personal partnership. Very traditional men may see a wife's home business as an affront, a not-so-subtle way of saying that the household needs more money, for example. Traditional women, used to being the homemaker, may pale at the idea of having hubby home all the time—as well as worry about the absence of a reliable income.

In other, less traditional relationships, jealousy may play a role—perhaps your spouse has always wanted to start a home business, too, but hasn't acted upon his or her dreams. Watching you make the leap may make your partner feel inadequate, left behind.

Whether or not these feelings are appropriate for a mature adult is somewhat irrelevant. If the feelings exist, it's important to address

It's Going to Be All Right!

You may discover that your children have a skewed idea of what a home business will be like. One mother recalled that her seven-year-old cried unmercifully when she told him that she wanted to start a home business in the family room. After buckets of tears, she discovered that his idea of a "business" was when Dad took him to work one day—at a meat-cutting plant—and that he thought dead cows would take the place of the Nintendo game.

them. People can adapt, get comfortable with change, and even change their minds. But it takes communication.

Talk . . . and Listen

If your spouse is unhappy about or unsupportive of your home business idea, you need to talk about it. Help him or her understand your reasons for wanting to do this. Is it a lifestyle decision? Well, you and yours need to come to some agreement, or at least compromise, about what kind of lifestyle you want together. Then discuss how and if a home business fits that picture. Perhaps you're simply tired of working for someone else and want to build a business on your own. You want and need challenge. Express those feelings.

And, perhaps more important, *listen.*

If you discover that the love of your life is a Negative Nelly, try to understand the real reasons behind the reticence. This may be difficult—after all, they may not understand it themselves. There may be deep-seated control issues, or it may be as simple as not wanting to hear another phone and fax ringing off the hook. If together you can narrow down the real source of the discomfort, you may find ways to alleviate the problem.

A Case Study: Lisa B Graphic D

Lisa Baillargeron was desperately burned out on her job in the marketing department at a large insurance company. She longed for the calmer confines of a home office and believed strongly that she could make it as a freelance graphic artist. She thought she could get her current employer to let her design a few newsletters, and she had contacts with numerous advertising agencies that liked her work and often used freelancers. She and her husband Bob had a spare bedroom, the kids were school-aged, and with Bob's middle-management job relatively secure, they could comfortably get by while she built up the business to match her previous steady income. In fact, she was confident she could double her income within two years. She was fired up and ready to act and already had the paperwork filled out to register the business name: Lisa B Graphic D.

When Lisa told Bob about her idea, his heart sank. He just knew what it would mean—more work for him, since Lisa would be on deadline and working into the evening. The pressure at his own job was high—he often had to work late himself, and the last thing he wanted was feeling obliged to come home and make dinner because Lisa had to do a rush job for an important client. Almost worst of all, Bob considered their home a sanctuary away from the pressures of work life. No way he wanted to listen to a fax machine go off in the next room at 11 o'clock at night. He couldn't understand why Lisa would want to make their life miserable this way. What was wrong with the way things were? Weren't they doing fine financially? Weren't the kids happy, well fed, doing well in school? OK, nothing's absolutely perfect, but why complicate your life with a home business?

Lisa couldn't believe how self-centered Bob was acting. She needed this, wanted this, and felt betrayed when he couldn't understand that. His objections were so lame! She'd be able to set her own schedule and would be able to spend more time with the kids than ever. She longed to go to their son's after-school ball games, something she could never do while working her regular job. Your kids are only young once! How could Bob care so little about her to let a few rings of the phone get in the way of her happiness? Their first discussion of Lisa's idea ended in an argument.

As they'd done after past conflicts, they decided to discuss it further over dinner that weekend. In the meantime, Bob told a few of his buddies at work about Lisa's crazy plan. He was surprised to find out that some of them thought it was a great idea. "I wish I had the guts to try something like that myself," said one, "tell Lisa congratulations." Bob found himself feeling proud of his wife's independence and remembered that it was one of the qualities he always admired in her. Still, a home business could be a huge headache, he thought.

Lisa decided to prepare for their talk. She worked up a preliminary pro forma income statement. She whittled her expenses to the

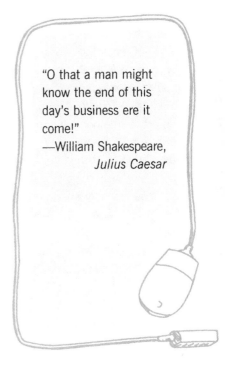

"O that a man might know the end of this day's business ere it come!"
—William Shakespeare, *Julius Caesar*

Don't Be a Workaholic

For entrepreneurial types who are driven to succeed in any venture, it's easy to get swept up in launching a home business. You think, now's the time! If this business fails, it won't be for lack of trying, you assure yourself.

There's nothing wrong with working hard, and you're likely to face some long days if you're starting up a full-time home-based business. But a few long days is different than an obsessive need to spend all your waking hours working or worrying about your business—it's just not healthy. Don't forget the variety of reasons that you decided to

(continued on next page)

bone so that she could prove to Bob that she could make a profit right away—no rent, she'd use some old furniture in the garage, and she could get by at first by sharing the computer they got for the kids. She mapped out a work schedule that allowed her to spend time with the kids as well as time with Bob in the evenings. She was convinced she could talk Bob into it. And even if he didn't agree, well then . . . tough.

When it came time to talk, they both apologized to the other. Bob said he was trying to understand, but had severe reservations. Lisa told him about how she spent her workday at her current job, how little time she spent actually working opposed to going to meetings or writing reports and memos. For 40 or more hours a week, she was unhappy, she said. She loved Bob, loved her family, but felt she needed something more challenging and satisfying in her work life. She asked Bob if he sometimes felt the same.

Bob thought about it and said that while his job came with the usual bureaucratic nonsense, he enjoyed his coworkers and felt that he would be able to rise in the company. He confessed that he'd never really thought about Lisa's happiness at her job—it was just a job that brought in a needed second income. But he didn't like the idea of sharing his house with a business. It was an invasion of privacy, he said.

Lisa showed Bob her initial revenue and expense forecast and work schedule. Bob was impressed, but worried that she might be shortchanging herself on the expense side. Wouldn't she need a better computer than what they now had? What about a proper desk and work area? Lisa agreed, but said she was trying to have as little financial impact on the family as possible.

It was then that Bob realized that he was bothered more by the idea of having Lisa's work spread out on the kitchen table than he was by the temporary loss of a second income. He suggested a compromise. He'd be supportive of Lisa's home business if she agreed that they would spend the money to convert the room above the garage into a home office and acquire the furniture and equipment she needed to run it properly.

Lisa was stunned. She'd assumed that if Bob was against her idea it was because of the money. But here he was excited as he helped her figure out whether to bring in one phone line or two into a new office space. It occurred to her that she'd always admired his sense of appropriate priorities. Maybe she wouldn't have to divorce him and move to Mexico after all!

Home Businesses and Kids

On the one hand, running a home business with one or more children in the household seems like a recipe for disaster. Raising children can certainly be a full-time job in and of itself. Adding entrepreneurship to your routine might be just enough to drive you around the bend.

On the other hand, it's been done for thousands of years. While the modern concept of a home business or home office may seem relatively new, people have been mixing trade and family life for a long time. Certainly the traditional family farm is a mix of home and business, as are any number of other trades and retail stores. Kids can learn a heck of a lot about life from having a business right there in front of them. Valuable lessons about trust, responsibility, work ethics, and human interaction are available on a daily basis.

Many kids get involved in the home business. Over time, it may grow into less of a "home-based" business and more of a midsized "family business." Or you may find your kids taking the entrepreneurial lessons they've learned from Mom or Dad and putting them to use—the proverbial lemonade stand, a lawn care business, or, in this high-tech age, a teenage computer consultant! (If your kids are really sharp, you might want to get them to sign a noncompete contract before you let them in on any of your secrets!)

Whether running a home business is right for you and your family is a matter of personal choice and will be influenced by the kind of business and the nature of your personal values.

Don't Be a Workaholic

(continued from previous page)

be a home-based entrepreneur in the first place. A flexible schedule allows you to spend more time with your family, right? Well, make sure you set aside that time—it's part of the job.

In addition to family time, don't forget to make time for yourself. It's easy, as a home-based businessperson, to spend all of your personal time on your business. Everybody needs a break, including yourself. It will keep your mind clear and your outlook fresh, allowing you to make the best decisions possible in your business.

Keys to Being a Successful Home Business Parent

Running a home business and a household with children will require you to be a time-management expert. You'll need to schedule your work time and stick to your schedule. The older the kids, the easier it will be, but kids and businesses have at least one thing in common: both are very demanding.

Many home businesspeople work out of their home so that they can spend more time with their children. In that case, you've probably picked a home business conducive to stop-and-start activity.

Others, however, may consider using day care just as they might if they were employed full-time at a traditional job. Having even a few hours a day to yourself during which you can concentrate exclusively on your business or arrange to sit down with an accountant can make a world of difference.

If you aren't comfortable with formal day care, you may be able to form an alliance with a few other home businesses nearby to share baby-sitting chores. Perhaps three of you will agree that one person will look after all the kids one day a week—which gives you each two days a week without the children to focus on your business. Running a home business is all about finding creative ways to make things work.

Undoubtedly there will be times when you have to juggle the kids and the business simultaneously. Let your kids know what's expected of them ahead of time. If your business will require having clients and customers on the premises, let the kids know how they need to behave during the business visit. Where are they allowed to go and what are they allowed to do? You'll also want to warn your customer ahead of time that the kids may be underfoot—some people are comfortable with that, others may prefer to reschedule the appointment.

However you handle the children issue—a rigid schedule, day care, help from neighbors—you need to make some plans to accommodate the kids before you jump into the business. But, remember, it is possible!

Kids As Assets

Years ago when the most common home business was the family farm, children were considered a valuable asset. They could and did do countless chores to help out, from milking the cows and churning butter to weeding the garden and filling the woodbox. The chores may have changed for most of us, but including your children in your home business can be a great idea.

Whatever your business, there is some task that can be the responsibility of an appropriately aged child. Look for those opportunities to include your children in the business. By making them a part of it, they'll have a better appreciation for the time and attention you spend on the business. And, as mentioned earlier, children can learn valuable lessons by being involved in a home business.

Respect the Family's Time and Space

Children and a spouse can get as enthusiastic as you are about the business, are often happy to help out, and, like you, find the business a source of pride. But in the end the business is your activity, not theirs, and may conflict at some point with their wants or needs.

Of course, if the home business is paying the mortgage and putting dinner on the table, you have the option of telling the rest of the family to quit whining. But though the business will take priority sometimes, a "like it or leave it" attitude isn't going to bring peace to the household. It's your business, but it's everyone's home, and being sensitive to that may help keep things running as smoothly as possible.

There may be times during your home business career when a project grows too big for your home office or workspace. The dining room table may be perfect for the task at hand—does the family mind if you take over the dining table for a day or a week? Ask them! By giving them a chance to object, you acknowledge

It's All in the Attitude

An active family in the house will certainly present ongoing challenges. But your attitude toward those challenges, and your ability to prepare ahead of time and communicate can make all the difference. A family shouldn't be a barrier to a home business, but your ally.

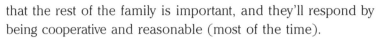

that the rest of the family is important, and they'll respond by being cooperative and reasonable (most of the time).

Nobody likes to have his or her time wasted. You'll want to manage your time well in order to operate your business efficiently, certainly, but also in order to respect your family's time. If you've established the family dinnertime as 6:00 P.M., make sure you're ready to sit down with them at 6:00 P.M. Don't make them wait until 6:45 so that you can finish up work you didn't get finished earlier in the day. If you do need to work late, let the rest of the family know ahead of time so that they can plan to eat later or go ahead without you.

Similarly, you want to maintain a schedule that your family can depend on. Granted, some home businesses involve emergency calls, periods of intense work and a certain amount of unpredictability. But to the extent you're able, stick to whatever schedule you've established for the day. If you promised Susie you'll come to her piano recital at 3:00 P.M., then do it. If you repeatedly let your home business force you to break promises made to your loved ones, they're likely to begin resenting the business. Given that the business is located in their home, you want those around you to appreciate what you do and respect its importance—which can only be done if you offer the same to them.

Telephone Wars

One area of potential conflict among family or household members is the telephone. Even without a home business thrown into the mix, complaints about unfair use of the phone by one or more members of the family can generate problems, especially in today's world of dial-up Internet access. Add a home business using a home line and you've set the stage for World War III.

As suggested previously, a separate business phone line can be a big help. But make sure your housemates understand the rules for its use. Are they permitted to call you on the business line? If not, do you answer the home phone when you're in your home office? Are they allowed to call out on the business phone in the evening

if the home phone is busy? Are they allowed to use it for the Internet if Tommy the lovesick teenager is chatting up his latest girlfriend on the home line? If the business phone rings when you're not home, should they answer it? Answer these questions and any others the family has before the telephone becomes an issue.

Confidentiality

Make sure that your family understands what's appropriate to talk about outside of the home business. If you run a residential cleaning business and your kids are running around town telling everyone how filthy Mrs. Harrison's house is, you won't be in business long. Customers may cluck disapprovingly about Mrs. Harrison's housekeeping, but they'll be quick to find a new cleaning service that knows how to keep quiet.

How to Handle Friends and Neighbors

Your family members aren't the only ones who may need some guidance and limits once you set up your home business. Once the chatty neighbors understand that you're home all day, stopping by to say hello seems like such an easy, friendly thing to do. Especially when you first open your business, you'll find many people will stop in to see what you're up to. At first, this will be a great opportunity to get the word out about your product or service. Tell them all about it. Show them your home office or work area. Tell them all about the advantages of doing business with you. Ask them to send business your way.

But you'll also want to mention your hours of operation (hint, hint). Talk a little bit about how busy you are setting up the business. "Things are going so well already, I have to keep at it in order to keep up!"

If subtle reminders don't work, don't be afraid to simply say, "Listen, I'll let you get home—I've got a ton of work to do." If you've got a hard-core gossip hound on your hands who won't throttle

Looking for Mr. Goodneighbor

If you know that some of your neighbors are leery of having the traffic or noise of a home business in the area, find ways to point out the advantages of having a home business in the neighborhood.

For example, having someone around all day is a deterrent to theft and vandalism. Lower crime rates can lead to lower insurance rates. Home businesspeople can help out by letting a dog out when the owner is unexpectedly delayed getting home from their traditional job. A home business can serve as a "safe house" for schoolkids who find themselves sent home early from school unexpectedly.

back on the chitchat and won't take a hint, then get politely direct: "I'm sorry, I have to get back to work. I'll catch up with you later."

You'll have the same challenge with the telephone. Friends with time on their hands will give a call "just to say hello." Don't be afraid of finding a kind way of letting them know that you are running a business and have things to do.

That said, use your ability to set your own schedule to build those friendships in ways you couldn't when working full-time. Can you take some time for lunch? Invite your chatty friend to come over then—or go off to a local restaurant and treat yourselves to lunch. In many cases, a home business is all about living a lifestyle that keeps your priorities in balance.

Neighboring Needs

Some home businesses have the potential of making neighbors a bit feisty. An automotive body shop or woodworking shop can be noisy, for example. You'll want to do your best to keep your neighbors supporting your desire to run a business out of your home. If your

municipality has restrictions for the operation of a home business, such as hours of operation, abide by them. Talk to your neighbors and ask them if they have any concerns. If you often do noisy work on Saturdays, tell them you'll always be happy to keep it quiet on a day when they're planning a big family barbecue.

As you deal with your neighbors, try to remember that they may be one of your best sources of customer referrals. Thinking of it in those terms may make it easier to hold your tongue if a complaint surfaces.

For more information on this topic, visit our Web site at businesstown.com

CHAPTER FIVE

Are Your Finances Right for a Home Business?

Many businesses fail every year because they're undercapitalized. A brilliant idea, excellent timing, and thousands of hours of hard work can end up on the scrap heap because there just wasn't enough money for equipment, inventory, or to cover the inevitable dry spells during the delicate start-up months.

Which is not to say that you can't start a business on the proverbial shoestring. Your odds for success are just better if you've got enough cash at the get-go.

But how much is enough? And how much needs to be in cold hard greenbacks and how much in credit or loans?

Determining Your Current Financial Needs

A good place to start is to figure out how much money you or your family need each month to live. Use the worksheet to estimate your monthly expenses.

Adjusting Your Lifestyle

If money is an issue as you consider starting your home business, look carefully at your lifestyle. It's easy to get comfortable on a regular salary. Restaurants, new cars, boats, home improvements, even daily coffee and a bagel on the way to work add up. Can you alter your lifestyle slightly in order to improve your chances of success as a home business entrepreneur? See if you can whittle your monthly "nut" down as low as possible. Pay off those credit cards and then shelve them until a true emergency arises. Rent a video and make your own popcorn instead of going out to the movies.

Someday, when your business is successful, you'll be able to enjoy those perks again. In the meantime, think of the adjustments as "buying your life back." What's more valuable to you—a new car every couple years, purchased on credit, or the chance to be your own boss and the satisfaction of building a business from the ground up?

Trimming the extras from your lifestyle can be a good way to economize and make a home business start-up viable, but you can still treat yourself! Just do it on a budget. Small treats can be as

MONTHLY EXPENSES

Housing

    rent or mortgage

    taxes

    insurance

    maintenance

Car

    monthly payments

    registration

    insurance

    maintenance

    gas

Food

    groceries

    eating out

Utilities

    gas and/or electric

    telephone

Savings

    rainy days

    college funds

    large purchases

Retirement plan

Entertainment

    movies

    cable TV

    gym

TOTAL MONTHLY EXPENSES $

meaningful and rewarding as large stress-buster ("I deserve this 'cause I work so hard") purchases.

Determining What You Really Need

After you've done an initial estimate of your monthly expenses and thought about how much money you might save, look again. If you're really willing to change the way you live, can you get by on less? How much less? Don't make yourself miserable by giving up too much, just try to make an honest assessment.

Assessing What You Owe

So now that you know how much you need to live, how much do you owe? If you bought a house, you'll recall making a fairly accurate assessment of your overall net worth. That exercise will be helpful in determining your financial health and will help you make a good decision as to whether you should consider starting a home business.

First, the good news—add up the value of your assets. These will include:

Value of your home
Value of other real estate
Value of your car(s)
Value of household goods
Amount of savings
Amount of retirement savings
Cash on hand (checking account)
Value of stocks or bonds
Value of collectibles or other valuables
TOTAL ASSETS $

Make sure that you're honest as possible in making these calculations. It's easy to put down how much you have in your savings account, but estimating the value of your household goods or collectibles is more of a guesstimate. Use figures that represent what you think you could get if you needed to liquidate (sell) the assets today.

Now add up your liabilities. These will include:

Outstanding principal on mortgages

Outstanding principal on auto purchases

Outstanding credit card balances

Other loans or liens

TOTAL LIABILITIES $

Subtract the total liabilities from your total assets to get your net worth. Are you in the black or the red? If you're better off than you thought, great! Equity in a home or other asset may come in useful as you try to finance your home business. If things look a little grim, don't be discouraged—many a great entrepreneur has built an empire out of little. For the small business person, cash flow is king!

The most important part of this evaluation is to have a clear understanding about how you stand financially so that you can make informed decisions. You may decide, for example, that though starting a home-based business continues to be a goal, you would be more comfortable continuing collecting a regular paycheck while reducing your debt and increasing your cash-on-hand savings.

The Apple Choice

A home business can lead to any level of financial reward. Steve Jobs and Steve Wozniak started Apple Computer in Jobs's garage. It made them wealthy men. But their vision was entrepreneurial—they were interested in finding a way to improve the way computers were used, not in the lifestyle associated with running a business from home. They built a factory as soon as they could.

Determining Your Financial Goals

OK, now you have a good idea of where you are financially, but where do you want to be? Do you dream of the lifestyles of the rich and famous-because-they're-rich? Or are your goals more modest—a comfortable living with reasonable provisions for future

FISCAL FITNESS QUIZ

This quiz will help you determine how well you're taking care of your financial health.

Answer the following questions, keeping score as you go along:

1. Do you have emergency reserves equal to 4–6 months of living expenses? If so, give yourself 2 points.
2. If you have had your insurance policies reviewed within the last three years, give yourself 1 point.
3. If you keep a budget and monitor your family's spending on a monthly basis, give yourself 2 points.
4. If you have long-term disability insurance coverage, give yourself 1 point.
5. If you have a life insurance plan, give yourself 1 point.
6. If your will has been reviewed in the past two years, give yourself 1 point. If you don't have a will, subtract 1 point.
7. If your will designates a guardian for your minor children, or your children are all grown, enter 1 point.
8. If your investments are balanced as the result of intentional plan, instead of by accident, give yourself 3 points.
9. Give yourself 1 point for each year you and your spouse made the maximum contribution to an IRA (since 1982).
10. If you pay yourself first by setting aside a designated portion of your earnings to savings and investments every month, give yourself 3 points.

TOTAL SCORE

How do you shape up?:

16 or above: You are fiscally fit.

12–15: Your fiscal fitness program needs some shaping up.

11 or less: You are financially out of shape.

SOURCE: National Association of the Self-Employed

needs like the kids' college educations and retirement? Maybe you've always wanted to retire early and want to set aside enough by a certain age so you can. Or maybe you've already retired, and you're interested in generating a steady supplemental income while doing something you enjoy from the comfort of your home office or shop.

A more common goal is a reasonable one—a home business that returns a middle-class living with provisions for retirement. It doesn't come without hard work and determination, but Americans are doing it all the time.

Provisions for Retirement

As the proprietor of your own home business, you will be responsible for devising your own retirement plan. As you assess whether or not starting a home business is for you, it makes sense to consider your expectations for retirement.

Are you looking forward to relaxing, buying a retirement home, and traveling extensively? What kind of annual expenditures will that require in today's dollars? How much more money will the same standard of living require after you calculate inflation (a conservative inflation rate would be 3 percent annually)? How much do you have set aside now to finance your retirement? What kind of return is it generating? How much in additional funds are you setting aside annually? If you continue saving at the same rate until the planned year of retirement, will you have accumulated enough to provide for your planned retirement lifestyle?

If you haven't saved enough, will you continue working through your retirement? Perhaps the home business is meant to be or become part of your retirement income. Or perhaps you will be looking to sell your business at retirement age and live off the proceeds.

Whatever your retirement plans, it's important to integrate them into your decision to start a home business. Make sure your expense projections include savings for retirement—failure to do so will likely guarantee that you'll need to continue working—and it's always easier if you can choose whether or not to work.

Counting on Social Security

Most financial advisors will tell you not to count on Social Security as your sole retirement income. Federal budget surpluses at the end of the twentieth century may give us more confidence that Social Security will exist in 20 or 30 years, but those born after 1959 won't be eligible for full benefits until they turn 67. In any case, it's wise to consider Social Security benefits as only part of your retirement plan.

Request a copy of your "Earnings and Benefit Estimate Statement" (Form SSA-7004) from the Social Security Administration. This will show your earnings history and how much you have paid in Social Security taxes. This figure will help determine what payments you can expect once you are eligible for Social Security.

Assessing Risk

No matter how well you analyze and prepare yourself, risk will be involved in starting up your business. The analysis you've done of your current finances, your projected personal needs, and the financial needs of your business is ultimately only a way to gauge the amount of risk. It's up to you to decide if you're comfortable with that level of risk.

Will starting your own home business put the ownership of your home at risk? If so, are you willing to accept that risk? How about others in your family—are they comfortable with the risk, or will it become a source of conflict in the future? It's always better to think through and discuss these issues, making sure everyone understands them before making a decision.

Consider, too, what you're giving up. Are you only a few years away from full pension at a well-paying job? You'd be giving up a lot to start your business now—you might be far better off exhibiting some patience and starting a retirement business once your pension kicks in. Conversely, if you're toiling away at a relatively low hourly wage with few benefits and feel that you could replace your current job virtually anytime, then there's little reason to hesitate as long as a home business fits the rest of your lifestyle and personality.

There is risk in everything we do, and you aren't likely to fulfill your dreams without taking some chances. So don't make an element of risk a convenient excuse for holding yourself back. Use common sense, and try to assess that risk realistically so that you can make sound business decisions.

Determining the Needs of Your Business

Once you have a clear and realistic idea of what your personal financial needs are, you next need to determine what it will take to start and operate your home business until it can generate the

revenue to support itself. The best way to do this is to create a business plan, which is discussed in chapter 7.

But as part of the decision-making process, it is helpful to have a ballpark idea of how much you need to help you evaluate whether or not a home business is right for you at this point in your life.

Capital Costs

Will you need to invest in any equipment to get your business up and running? For example, if you're hoping to open a beauty salon, will you need special chairs, sinks, and other equipment? If you're opening a car body shop, will you need tools? Will your work space require significant changes, such as ventilation, improved plumbing, upgraded electric, and dedicated parking spaces to accommodate the business? If so, estimate those costs. If you're unsure, find out. Call equipment vendors, check trade catalogs, or call in a contractor to estimate the renovations you'll need. You don't want to be surprised with significantly higher than estimated costs once you've made the leap to starting your home business.

Operating Capital

How much money will you need to cover operating costs during your start-up phase? Make a list of your operating expenses: payroll (you, or for employees), insurance (business and health), taxes, utilities (electric, telephone, water, Internet access), cost of goods (inventory for resale, supplies for making a product), transportation (cost of a vehicle, gas, maintenance), and anything else that comes to mind. Be honest, and estimate higher rather than lower. You don't want to invest a lot of time, effort, and money in a business only to fail because you didn't plan well enough for your needs.

Cash Reserve

You've estimated your foreseeable expenses, now estimate how much might be reasonable to cover unforeseeable costs? You might buy insurance to cover catastrophic problems (theft of all your equipment), but what if it takes you twice as long to build

The Get-Rich-Quick Syndrome

One of the most common small business errors is unrealistic revenue expectations. More plainly put, people often don't make as much money as they thought they would when they first planned the business.

Whether you're planning on surviving on the proceeds from day one or only hoping to generate enough to pay back a start-up loan, it's important to have a realistic sense of your cash flow, especially the revenue side. Sure, things may go far better than you expected, but if you plan for the best and experience the worst, you may find yourself in trouble.

One way business planners avoid this trap is to prepare three estimates of revenue and expenses. Put down your worst case, best case, and most likely scenarios. The real number will be in there somewhere.

the revenue base? What if you have to replace a vehicle? Having at least a modest cash reserve can lead to great peace of mind.

Financing Your Home Business

Once you've determined how much money you need, where are you going to get it? Maybe you have enough in personal savings. If so, great! All you need to do is decide whether you're comfortable risking that money on a home business.

More commonly, though, home business entrepreneurs either borrow or bootstrap.

Borrowing

It's rare that an entrepreneur with little more than a good idea and a willingness to work can walk into a traditional bank and get an unsecured business loan. Bankers usually don't take foolish risks. If yours is a start-up business, without a track record of revenue and a solid customer base, you shouldn't count on walking into the bank and getting money handed to you.

That said, your bank may be a source of funds. If your personal credit is good, you can still apply for personal loans, home equity loans, or perhaps a vehicle or equipment loan. But understand that the credit you're getting is based on you personally, in combination with certain collateral. If your business flops, you'll still owe the money.

Let's take an example. You're planning to open a catering business, and you know that among other things you'll need a vehicle that can accommodate prepared foods, equipment, etc. Your bank might not give you a general business loan, but it might, with your good credit history, be willing to give you a vehicle loan for the van you need. The van itself will be enough collateral. You can spend your other capital on other start-up costs and finance the vehicle.

For many Americans, a house is their single biggest asset. And if you've been paying off your mortgage for years or have it paid off, the reduced principle and increased value of your home can be a source of credit. Just as a bank would be willing to give you a home improvement loan based on the equity in your home, you can often borrow—essentially take a second mortgage (or first mortgage if you currently own your home outright)—against the value of that home. Since the loan is secured with collateral—your property—the interest rates are often attractive.

Again, while this is a common source of borrowed capital, make sure you understand the risks involved. If your business fails, will you still be able to make the payments on the house? Losing a business and a home makes the failure doubly traumatic—not just for you, but for the rest of your family as well. What will you do if the real estate market collapses, as it did in New England in the late 1980s? You could find the market value of your home well below the amount you owe on it. Will the bank then call the loan? And if so, can you deal with it?

Small Business Administration

The Small Business Administration, or SBA, is often looked to as a potential source of funding. In most cases, the SBA does not directly loan money—rather it works with banks and Small Business Investment Companies (SBICs) to guarantee a loan for a small business that might otherwise be unable to qualify for a traditional commercial bank loan. In addition, most SBA programs are geared toward helping finance the growth of ongoing businesses rather than small, home business start-ups.

The SBA does have a Microloan Program, which was developed to increase the availability of very small loans to prospective small business borrowers. Once again, the SBA doesn't lend the money directly—instead they make the money available to nonprofit intermediaries, who then can make loans to eligible borrowers. The average loan amount in the Microloan Program is $10,000, with amounts ranging from $100 up to $25,000.

Each of the nonprofit intermediary lending groups has its own loan requirements. Typically, these will be similar to what you might find at a bank—it will probably be easier to get a loan to purchase an asset that can stand as collateral, and your personal guarantee will still be required. (If your business goes under, you still owe the money!)

SBA Loans Online

The list of nonprofit lending groups working with the SBA's Microloan Program is also available on the SBA Web site: *www.sbaonline.sba.gov*.

Venture Capital

With the possible exception of a high-growth-potential Internet, computer software, or similar high-tech business, venture capitalists are not likely to be interested in investing in the average home business. They are willing to take risk, but they are typically looking for a high rate of return that would come from relatively fast and significant revenue growth.

Although established venture capital firms may not be interested in your home business, you may be able to find a patron who is willing to back you. Have you impressed a successful local businessperson who has money looking for a home? Get your business plan on paper, make an appointment, and go talk to him or her. The worst that can happen is that you'll get turned down. You might get an introduction to someone else who can help, an offer of help in some form other than cash, or at least a reference as you attempt to establish credit in the business community.

Family Members

A more likely source of borrowed capital is family members. Family members often enjoy helping out their own, and they probably know you and trust you better than anyone else. Is Great Aunt Jane willing to stake you in your new business? If so, you may be on your way.

Although borrowing from family is a time-honored source of start-up capital, think it through carefully. Can the family member making the offer to lend you money really afford it? What will happen to that relationship if your business fails and the money is lost? Businesses come and go, but family ties are uniquely important. Make sure the family member understands the risk and is comfortable with it.

Make sure, too, that you are comfortable borrowing from family. Will there be unspoken obligations as a result of this transaction? Will Great Aunt Jane expect you to visit every weekend to show your gratitude, and if so, are you willing to do it? Will she want regular updates about the health and status of the business? Will she question your judgment when she hears you bought a new car before paying her back? Money usually comes with strings attached.

There's nothing wrong with that, just go into any arrangement understanding explicitly what those strings mean and accept them.

When you do borrow from family, take it seriously. Draw up paperwork showing the amount lent, the interest rate, if any, and when it's to be paid back. Honor that commitment.

Credit Cards

We've all heard stories of entrepreneurs who started with nothing more than a revolving credit account from a credit card company. There are tales of energetic self-starters who applied for multiple credit cards and used the collective available credit to make their mark on the business world.

And, yes, credit cards can be extremely helpful when you're starting or operating a home business. But it's important to understand that there's a cost to all this easy credit. Interest rates, depending on the economic climate, range in the 12 percent to 21 percent range. At 21 percent, if you're not paying off your monthly balance due, you're paying a lot for the use of that money. High-interest loans can eat away profit margin in a big hurry, and if your business is in a delicate cash flow stage, those credit card payments can mean the difference between success and failure.

Given that caveat, it's not a bad idea to have credit cards available in case you need them. They can help out when it comes to cash flow management. If you need to borrow a small amount of money, say $1,000, for a short time, less than 30 days, in order to squeak by until a client pays his bill, credit cards are an easy option. Just as in our personal lives, they come in handy for emergencies—if your computer monitor goes dead in the middle of a job, you'll need a new one pronto, and the credit card might be the one thing that makes that possible.

Credit cards can also be a way of establishing a better credit for your home business in the long run. As soon as you register your business, credit card companies will besiege you with offers for business credit cards. Make no mistake—they are relying on your personal credit history, and as a sole proprietor they'll make sure you pay up even if the business has long gone under. But, managed well, using a credit card responsibly with your business is one more piece of evidence for a potential future lender to consider.

Consider credit cards a helpful tool, but be wary of misusing them.

Bootstrapping

Home-based entrepreneurs are famous for bootstrapping their way to success. In other words, they cut corners, start small, and continually reinvest in their business to foster growth, and find every creative way in the world to make their business work in the absence of a big pot of money to start. In that great American tradition, these entrepreneurs pull themselves up by their own bootstraps.

So how does bootstrapping work? The specifics depend on the business, so let's take a simple example.

A Case Study: Jim Dandy Landscaping

Jim was fresh out of tech school with a degree in landscaping. He tried working for another firm, but he just didn't get along with his boss. He was perceptive enough to recognize that, as a strong-willed person, he wasn't likely to be happy working for any boss. He wanted his own landscaping firm. But Jim had nothing, save for a small, high-mileage car and a healthy portfolio of student loans. How could he start a business of his own? He had little credit history, no savings, few tangible assets.

Then a friend told him about an elderly woman who needed someone to cut her lawn. He asked another friend to print up some business cards on the computer for "Jim Dandy Lawnscaping." Although he didn't even have a lawn mower, he took the cards and introduced himself to the woman in question. He pitched his services, and said, "Sometimes customers prefer that I use their equipment so that it's always adjusted correctly for their lawn and to prevent the potential spread of weeds. I'm happy to use your mower if you prefer." The woman agreed, and a deal was made.

Jim went far beyond the usual call of duty on the woman's lawn. He drew up a list of recommendations for bringing the lawn and garden up to its full potential, and quoted the woman a price for the additional work, which she then contracted. He gave her some extra Jim Dandy Lawnscape business cards and told her he'd give her a $10 discount for every new job she found for him among her friends.

For one of his new customers, he needed his own equipment. He visited a small engine repair shop (a home business) and made a deal to do some landscaping in exchange for a used lawn mower. He traded his car for a small truck so he could transport his equipment. He posted his business cards everywhere he could think of—town hall, local restaurants, garden centers, grocery stores. He made some simple photocopied flyers and dropped them off in the neighborhood. He offered every customer a discount for bringing new customers onboard. He did a free landscape design for a client in order to get the job of creating the design. It worked.

Then Jim put on his best shirt, took some business cards, and visited a local garden center. He convinced the owner to offer him 30 days credit on landscaping materials. With that, he could take on bigger jobs involving more landscaping than straight mowing. He applied for and received a six-month deferment of his student loan because he currently did not receive a paycheck. The local Sears store was offering credit cards to any local college grads—he applied, was accepted, and bought some new equipment using it. He was starting to get busy, so he hired a couple of junior high kids to help him with the lawn mowing, carefully showing them how it needed to be done and checking up on their work once it was finished.

By the end of the season, Jim Dandy Lawnscapes: Design & Maintenance had 56 customers. He had billed more than $14,000. Jim paid his bills and established credit. He was contemplating upgrading his truck. All starting from scratch.

Lots could have gone wrong for Jim during his start-up. But as a young college grad, Jim didn't have much to risk—he didn't have to worry about a mortgage payment or feeding a family. But given Jim's resourcefulness, he probably could have overcome those challenges as well. Jim is a classic bootstrapper—narrowing his business down to his most basic needs and then finding a way to get what he needed. Step by step, he built his business.

Basic Bootstrapping Techniques

The home business is ideal for bootstrapping. After all, you're not looking at additional rent, additional utilities may be minor, and you can use that old table in the garage for a desk to get started. While the ideal setup might call for a completely separate space for your business, with separate phone lines, e-mail address, and plenty of storage space, you very well may be able to get your business going without any cash outlays.

Following are some basic bootstrapping techniques.

Liquidating Assets

If the conventional sources of capital don't yield all that you need, you might consider liquidating one or more of your assets—which is a fancy way to suggest that you sell a car, motorcycle, coin collection or other collectible—or anything else you own, aren't overly attached to, and is worth some money. Many home-based businesses don't require a lot of start-up cash, so sacrificing a few toys may be the best way to raise the money you need. If you're having a hard time with the idea of giving up a hard-earned perk, think of it as an investment: with success, you can buy three more toys just like it in the future.

Bartering Services

Consider your talents and labor among your assets. If you don't have cash, you might be able to swap services with someone who has what you need—especially if he or she is in a similar situation. Don't forget to keep a record of such exchanges for tax purposes (many people are willing to barter but prefer to exchange checks—I'll give you $300 for your service if you give me $300 for my service).

No-Cost Promotion

As a bootstrapper, you'll want to leverage every available no-cost promotion of your business. Constantly ask for recommendations from your current customers. Call the local newspapers and find a story angle to get yourself in the paper (more on this in chapter 20). Depending on your business, go door-to-door if you have to.

Credit Cards

The cautions discussed previously in this chapter do apply, but bootstrappers love credit cards for short-term credit. But interest rates are too high to keep balances for the true bootstrapper. Money paid in interest could be used for something else!

Vendor Credit

Bootstrappers will use their personal reputation to establish credit where they can, and as their business grows, continue to establish additional credit with other vendors and suppliers. Pay your bills in a timely fashion, but use the terms other businesses are willing to offer. It's money you can put elsewhere to grow your business in the meantime.

Additional Revenue Sources

Though your dream may be to have a full-time home-based business doing nothing but party planning, as a bootstrapper you may find yourself looking for additional sources of cash. Part-time jobs, renting out a room in your house to a student—a bootstrapper will do anything legal in order to earn some extra cash to put into the home business.

Buying Used

The best bootstrappers always seem to come up with just the right bargain on used equipment. Auctions, liquidators, used office supply stores—someone has what you need at a better than brand-new price. But be careful of buying something at a bargain price if it isn't what you need. Your tools and equipment are what will help you be successful, and if the machinery doesn't work, the bargain wasn't worth it.

Be a Cash Flow Hawk

Bootstrappers are constantly watching their cash flow. They know exactly what they have to pay out and exactly what's due at any given time during the month. They are quick to collect their receivables on a timely basis, and make full use of any terms offered by others on payables due. It's all about staying solvent while making your available cash and credit work for you.

PART II

Starting Your Home Business

CHAPTER SIX

Steps to Starting Your Business

C ongratulations! You've made the fateful decision to start a home-based business. Now, what's next? Well, whether your business will be part-time or full-time, you'll need to take care of some basics. For example, will your business be a sole proprietorship (most likely), a corporation (a bit more complicated), or an LLC or S Corp? (We'll get to all that.) You'll also want to register the business name and open an account at the bank.

Choosing When

You know you want to start a home-based business, but when should your ready-set-go date be? Well, why not get started right away?

If you're planning to give up a regular job in order to start a home-based business, then your resignation date will be an important decision. Consider your personal financial situation carefully—work through the process of determining you and your family's own financial needs as well as the projected needs of the business as suggested in Chapter 5. You don't want to procrastinate, but the more you can get done in preparation for your business while you're still getting paid by someone else, the better.

Choosing the Form of Business Organization

Your home business will take one of three basic forms: a sole proprietorship, a partnership, or a corporation. Most home-based businesses will be sole proprietorships, some will be partnerships, and a few might be corporations.

Sole Proprietorship

This form of business is the most common, in part because it's the easiest. You are the owner, the only owner, of the business, and from a legal and tax perspective there's no difference between you and the business. The good news is that starting and operating a sole proprietorship is relatively simple. As the sole owner, you get

Giving Notice

In today's cutthroat corporate world, giving notice can sometimes be like announcing a death. If you currently work for a large company, even if you give a four-week notice, the policy may require your boss to ask you to pack up your desk and leave immediately. No warm and fuzzy good luck going away party from your coworkers. Just a walk to your work area, supervised collection of your personal effects, and a "thanks-for-nothing" walk to the door. The final pay-checks will be in the mail. It sounds cold, but many companies are deeply concerned about theft, sabotage, and potential harm, and to them a lame-duck employee is no longer a safe bet. Even a small, family business can take your resignation personally—especially if they realize you're about to start a competing business.

Of course it's not always this way. If you're planning on providing a product or service your current employer will want (perhaps "out-sourcing" your current job), they may be very willing to work with you over the course of several months, allowing you to gradually reduce your hours as you build your business. Or, your old boss may be the type of person who realizes that his company isn't in a position to offer you the challenge and potential of your own busi-ness, is sorry to see you go but takes pride in having helped you learn the business.

The point is that you need to consider what reaction your resigna-tion is likely to cause, and time it accordingly. And if you gave four weeks' notice and they escort you to the door, rejoice! After all, you now have paid time to focus on your business!

Ethical Considerations

For many home business entrepreneurs, the business they are planning is directly related to their current job. Will your new business be a competitor with your current employer?

Be sure you haven't signed a noncompete clause. Review all the paperwork you signed when you took the job, and make sure there isn't a clause prohibiting you from operating a directly competing business. Sometimes these clauses are difficult to enforce, but it's a good idea to know what you're up against. To hire a lawyer to fight it will be expensive. An alternative might be to take a job in a similar but not directly competing industry before you start your business.

If you're free and clear of signed noncompete clauses,

(continued on next page)

to make all the decisions and keep all the profits. And if you decide to shut down the business, it's relatively easy.

The bad news is that if your business closes involuntarily, all of your personal assets are on the line. Creditors are free to come after your house, car, speedboat, and coin collection when push comes to shove. And, as a self-employed person, you can't get unemployment insurance or workers' compensation.

Although this might be a frightening thought, for most home-based businesses it only makes sense. You are the business, your home is the address of the business. If you're borrowing money, you're likely to be using your largest asset (the home) as collateral. Trying to separate the two legally might be tricky anyway.

Partnership

When you combine forces with another person in business, you've created a partnership. A partnership is essentially a multi-party or dual proprietorship (and if all goes well, it won't turn into a " duel proprietorship"!). For many home-based businesses, a husband and wife will be the two partners in the business. Partners, as in a sole proprietorship, are self-employed.

A partnership is easy to organize and combines the talents and resources of more than one person. Where one might fail, two might succeed. With two or more people, the business can benefit from more time, money, and expertise.

However, partners still have unlimited liability—plus each partner may be held liable for all the debts of the business. Consequently, you could lose your assets based on a boneheaded mistake your partner makes. And though two heads are sometimes better than one, partnerships can often lead to conflict.

You can also create a limited partnership. In this setup, one partner (the general partner) must have unlimited liability. But others might have limited liability, in which they are only liable for as much as they've invested in the partnership. Essentially, a limited partner is an investor, while the general partner operates the business.

The key to a successful partnership is outlining the partnership agreement ahead of time. You and your partners should get down on paper who is going to invest what, who will decide what, who will do what work, decide how and when profits will be divided, and how you will buy each other out in the future. It's always easier to decide these matters when the partners are in a good frame of mind—things get ugly if the finger pointing is done as the business founders.

If you're considering a partnership—even with a family member— it would be wise to sit down with a lawyer once you have the basics of your partnership worked out.

Corporations

Corporations are legal entities separate from the owners. On the plus side, this means that shareholders have limited liability in the case of losses. However, forming a corporation is more complex and more expensive to create and maintain and won't be the choice for many home-based businesses. Corporations are taxed on their own income, and shareholders must pay tax again on their salaries and dividends. But if you foresee considerable growth, extensive outside investment, and lots of risk, forming a corporation might be worthwhile.

S Corporations

For home businesses, Chapter S Corporations might be the choice if incorporation is desired. Geared for small businesses, an S Corp doesn't pay tax on its income, but rather income and expenses are divided among the shareholders, who then report them on their own income tax returns. Unlike a partnership, liability is limited. In a way, S Corps provide the small businessperson with the best of both worlds.

However, there are stringent record-keeping and reporting standards for S Corps (which translates into bookkeeping expenses), so for most home-based businesses, an S Corp is likely to be unnecessary. Keep in mind that it's possible to convert a sole proprietorship or a partnership into an S Corp in the future.

Ethical Considerations

(continued from previous page)

you need to balance your own needs against any ethical considerations. It's not a good idea to sabotage your employer by stealing proprietary information to help you start your own business. And avoid approaching clients before you've left your job. And don't even think about taking copies of any files or other information.

Acting ethically toward your former boss is in your best interest. Every trade or industry is a small world unto itself, and if you get the reputation of being willing to cut corners on ethical behavior, you'll only be hurting your own business prospects for the future.

Limited Liability Companies

The Limited Liability Company, or LLC, is a more recent form of business not unlike the S Corporation. Now offered in all states, LLCs are designed to provide some limited liability while avoiding double taxation.

Choosing a Business Name

One important starting point is deciding on your business name. It's possible that the name you've spent months choosing is already in use by someone else. Have a second and third choice handy.

Think carefully about your business name. The name you will be "doing business as" (dba) should be straightforward enough to let prospective customers know what product or service you provide. Being clever can help customers remember your name, but that means little if they don't have a clue what you do. And what seems clever today may get old a year or so down the road.

For example, consider a business named PetsPeeve. Any idea what they do? Something with pets, one would assume. Dog grooming? Veterinary services? A kennel? Pet supplies? You'd have to call to find out. On the other hand, Pet Grooming by Linda isn't particularly snappy, but immediately lets the customer in on what shouldn't be a secret: Linda is a pet groomer and she's open for business! Another name, Shampoodles, combines wordplay with enough information to be helpful. Ditto DoggieDoos, though there may be some image problems to overcome.

Create an Image

A business name can also help create an image for the business. Are you Crusty Pete's Haircuts Express or Pierre's HairExcellence Beauty Salon? Consider how you want a potential customer to think of your business. Day care businesses are particularly good at coming up with names that evoke the lighthearted days of childhood, easing a guilty parent's conscience when they drop their firstborn off at Merri-time Child Care or Country Sunshine Day Care or Learn-a-Lot Kids Care.

Get a Lawyer!

If you think incorporation at any level is a viable choice for your home-based business, seek the advice of a qualified attorney. He or she will not only help you make the final decision, but can then steer you through the paperwork involved.

Many home and small businesspeople use their own name as part of the business name. This is appropriate, especially if you offer a service that is or will be closely tied to your personal reputation for quality work. Lawyers almost always use their name, as do accountants—they are trading on their good name. First names often suggest a smaller business: Brenda's Catering, Bob's Appliance Repair. Last names carry a more generic image of size: Sullivan Tire or Goodwin's Optical could be one-person shops or regional firms with multiple venues.

A combination of first or last names is also used, but carries the disadvantage of sounding odd or being unrecognizable. JimJen's Snowplowing may be a cute combo for a husband and wife home business, but it does little to help promote the business. If you want to combine names, try something simpler: Ever hear of Ben & Jerry's or Smith & Wesson? If you just stepped off the boat, you wouldn't know which sold ice cream and which manufactured guns, but at least you wouldn't be scratching your head trying to figure out what a "JimJen" is.

Remember—as a home business, you're not likely to have an annual multimillion-dollar advertising and promotion budget to help build a brand. So do yourself a favor and decide on a name that tells your story.

Your Logo

Another aspect to think about in naming your business is your logo. How will the business name look in print on business cards, letterhead, and advertising? Do you want a catchy or special design? You might consult with a graphic designer before you register the name (but wait until you know the name is available before you commission a logo or order up reams of letterhead!). Overly long names might cause problems: Mortimer Schladweiler's Keep-It-Safe-All-the-Time Locksmith Services may tell the right story, but you could find it cumbersome when you go to design a Yellow Pages ad.

Large corporations go to great expense to build the brand names of their companies and logos, their products, and the trade dress of those

Your Business Name

Elmwood Home Builders, Doggerville Pest Control—using the name of your town, street, or a feature of the surrounding landscape are popular ways to name a business.

Place names can be particularly advantageous in a small or medium-sized community where you might be the only business of that type and the population is large enough to serve as your entire market. If you need to sell your services to more than one town to survive, it might be better to use a more generic name.

Businesses often use a "power word" in the name to suggest how well they do the job. Precision Typing, Good Deal Antiques, Fast and Safe Movers, Momentum Marketing, Sparkle-Clean Maid Services are all names that convey a kind of service and a superior quality of service.

products, and for that reason they will also register those trademarks and go to great lengths to protect them. Consequently, you should be very careful not to knowingly violate an existing trademark. Whether it's Big Mac, Mr. Clean, Mickey Mouse, or Toys-R-Us, you want to avoid naming your business in a way that trades on those well-known trademarks. Even if your business name is in a gray enough area to make for a good debate over its legality, just forget it—the debate itself will be more expensive (paying your lawyers) than it's worth. You're better off spending that money building up your own brand.

Registering Your Business Name

The process of registering a business name will differ state by state, so check with your state or county government, Chamber of Commerce, or Small Business Development Center on which office handles the paperwork. Typically there will be a search for similar names before they'll let you register yours. (Sometimes you can call ahead to have them do a search for a name you've selected.)

Registering an assumed or fictitious name applies to sole proprietors. If you use a name for your business other than your legal personal name, you have to register it. Typically this is a simple process involving little more than a one-page form and an application fee. Some states require you to advertise a notice of your assumed name in the newspaper.

Even after you register a business name, it's possible that another business out of state or in a different industry will also register and use that same name. But the registration will give you some rights, especially in the face of a potential competitor using your business name or a similar one.

Check with the registration office to find out how long the name will be valid and whether the registration needs to be renewed at any point. You don't want to go to all the trouble to register a name, build the business, and then lose the name to someone else five years down the road because you forgot to renew it!

If your home business is a legal partnership, you'll likely need to file a partnership formation notice with your state. The formal name doesn't have to be the same as your trade name—just file a dba ("doing business as") form either with your state or your county court. The secretary of state's office can point you in the right direction. If you decide to incorporate, when you file for incorporation with the secretary of state's office, you'll automatically register the name in the state.

If you'll be operating nationally or internationally (with the Internet, this may be possible for some home-based businesses) and want to prevent another company using your name in another state or country, then you may want to consider getting a trademark. Getting a trademark can get complicated and requires research and expense, so you might be best off consulting with a law firm that specializes in intellectual property law.

Employer Identification Number

If you plan to hire any employees or if you choose a form of business other than a sole proprietorship, have a Keogh plan or need to withhold income tax, then you will need to contact the IRS to acquire an Employer Identification Number, or EIN. In the same way that you personally have a taxpayer identification number (your Social Security number), an EIN identifies your business for tax purposes.

If, on the other hand, you are a sole proprietorship without employees, you can simply use your Social Security number. Remember that as a sole proprietor you are not an employee of the business.

To file for an EIN, use Form SS-4 (available anywhere IRS forms are found—post offices, public libraries, online, or by contacting the IRS).

If you have more than one sole proprietorship, you must use the same EIN for each one. If you change your sole proprietorship to a partnership or corporation, you'll need to apply for a new EIN. If you buy someone else's business, you can't use the previous owner's EIN but must apply for a new one.

Double Identity

If the business name you simply have to have is currently registered to another business, it might be worth finding out if they are still using it. Sometimes people get as far as registering a business name but never actually open the business. The registering agency in your state will likely give you the contact information for whoever has "your" business name—then give them a call. Perhaps by reimbursing them for the cost of their business registration they'll be willing to give it up so you can register it yourself.

Be careful, though, in taking a "used" name. Reputation is everything. You don't want to take on the name only to find out that the previous holder went bankrupt and left dozens of vendors unpaid—especially if it's the same trade or industry.

Business Licenses

Certain kinds of businesses require not just registration of the business name, but licensing. Businesses or professions that usually require some level of licensing include accountants, auctioneers, chiropractors, lawyers, optometrists, architects and land surveyors, dentists, funeral directors, psychologists, veterinarians, electricians, plumbers, restaurants or food preparation services, insurance sales, day care providers, and financial planners.

Check with your state to find out if your kind of business needs to be licensed in your part of the country. Your place of business may need to be inspected as well, so leave plenty of time before your planned opening date to get the appropriate licensing in order.

Business Bank Accounts

Once you've registered your business name, you can head to the bank to open a business checking account. You could, of course, have done this previously, but since you'll probably want your business name on your checks, you don't want to order checks until you're certain of the name.

Banks offer a wide array of services, often at an equally wide array of fees. Most home businesses can get along fine with a conventional checking account. As a sole proprietor, the bank will consider you and the business the same financial entity anyway. It is also much cheaper than a so-called business account, which can involve not only a monthly charge but charges for each deposit as well as each deposit item, each check written, and so forth. Business checking accounts may have the advantage of some additional reporting and recordkeeping, but this probably won't be necessary for the typical home business. If, however, you are registered as a corporation, the bank may require you to use a business checking account.

Master of Your Domain

As long as you're registering your business name with the state, you might consider registering a related domain name for the Internet as well, even if you have no current plans to use it. A domain name appears between "www" and ".com" (or .net or .org) to make up the address of a Web site.

A Web address can be up to 26 characters long, including the ".com." Letters and numbers can be used in a Web address, as can hyphens (though not at the beginning or end). Although anyone can register a name using .com, .net, or .org, typically .com is used for businesses.

To register a domain name, you'll need to work with an accredited registrar. In the 1990s, Network Solutions (*www.networksolutions.com*) was the primary registrar with no competition and the cost of registration was flat—$70 for the first two years, and $35 per year after that. However, starting in 2000, numerous other companies were allowed to compete as accredited registrars, driving prices down.

For a list of accredited registrars, and reliable information about domain name registration, go to the Department of Commerce's InterNic Web site at internic.net.

It is often the case that the domain name that you think best matches your business is already taken. You can find out whether or not that is the case by doing a search (Network Solutions has a good search engine for this), and if "your" name is already registered, you can find out who it's registered to. If it's important to have that name, and it's registered but inactive, you may be able to contact the registrant and acquire it from them. More likely, however, you'll have to come up with another domain name.

You may find it easier to contact your Internet Service Provider (ISP—the company that provides your access to the Internet), as most ISPs offer domain name registration as part of their services. It may cost a few dollars more, but they can make sure the technical information is correct, and it's likely that they'll be involved in hosting your site anyway.

Do I Really Need a Separate Business Account?

When it comes time to do your taxes, you'll be glad you have a separate checking account for your home business. The IRS strongly recommends keeping all personal and business finances separate. This may be hard to do for the home business some-times, requiring painstaking record keeping—which will be absolutely necessary if you're called upon to justify your business deductions.

Besides, a separate business account will be seen as more professional to your vendors. A home business is sometimes not taken as seri-ously as a conventional busi-ness. So it behooves you to work a little bit harder to show that while you may

(continued on next page)

Picking a Bank

Begin by sitting down with the customer service representative at your current bank. Ask him or her about the various checking and savings accounts available. If your business involves holding money in escrow, ask about escrow accounts as well. As you make your choice, think about how many checks you're likely to write in a month's time and how many deposits you might have. Is there a limit on either? ATM cards, even for businesses, can be helpful for making deposits. (Night deposits are available, too.)

Using your current bank can save you time—one trip for per-sonal and business purposes. But be sure to comparison shop. You may have chosen your current bank when you had your paycheck direct-deposited—as a home businessperson, you are likely to be driving to the bank to make deposits on a daily or weekly basis. Another bank may be more convenient to your home or may offer a better deal for small business customers.

If you envision needing a business loan in the future, you may want to establish an account with the bank that seems most open to that possibility. Even in today's world of corporate banking giants, personal relationships can matter.

Credit Cards

If you are planning to open a retail business, then you'll want to consider accepting credit cards for purchases. Credit card compa-nies will tell you that credit card customers spend more per visit on average, and it's certainly a convenience for the customer.

But from a retailer's standpoint, it's not free, and you'll want to shop around for the best merchant account for your needs. Start with your bank—they likely work with a reputable credit card pro-cessing company, and you can always enlist the help of the bank if you ever have problems. You'll want to find out not only how much they charge, but which cards they can allow you to process and what the fees are for each.

Fees and percentages for merchant accounts will vary from company to company, however—best to do some shopping around.

If you sell via direct mail, phone and the Internet exclusively, expect to pay a higher percentage (3–4 percent) than for face-to-face sales in which you are able to process the customer's card in person and get a signature. In addition to a percentage of the sale, you may also be charged a fee per transaction, a monthly fee, and an application fee. Depending on your business and your volume, some companies may require you to buy or lease equipment, while others may be able to offer you a simple authorization-by-phone set-up with no equipment. Review your needs with a representative of the credit card processing company and shop around at various banks or online.

The Grand Opening

You've selected and registered your business name and opened a business checking account. You've begun research for your business plan. When should you open the doors?

If you've been running your home business as a hobby, then it's easy: start today! Making the transition from hobby to business is as easy as changing the way you do the paperwork. But if you're starting from scratch or trying to decide when to quit your regular job and make your home business a full-time occupation, the decision is more difficult. More than likely it will come down to money.

Most important, though, is being ready for customers. You don't want to open your doors, only to provide poor service because you're unprepared. This is especially true for anyone opening a retail business. If your craft shop has no crafts or the crafts are

Do I Really Need a Separate Business Account?

(continued from previous page)

operate out of your home, you do things in a professional way.

If you open your account early on in the process, it will be easier to track all those miscellaneous expenses that crop up during the start-up process. Every legitimate expense is an investment on your part, so tally them up! If you use a personal credit card for a business expense, pay that amount directly out of your business checking account when the bill comes.

Scheduling the Service Business Nightmare

If you provide a service and do it personally, scheduling your time can be a real challenge. It's easy to feel that if you don't take the job when it's offered, then you'll be left twiddling your thumbs, earning nothing. This is an especially easy trap to fall into when you're just starting out—your revenue figures are untested, and you want every job you can win.

But don't forget to think long term. If customers end up dissatisfied because you didn't show up when promised, took twice as long to do the job, or did less than your best work because you were so frazzled, you'll lose out in the long run. A better idea is to plan on ramping up your business over time so you can get a feel for how to schedule your time.

piled in the middle of the floor because your display shelves aren't ready, you won't be doing yourself any favors by inviting the public to view your mess.

Like so many things involved in running a home business, planning is the key. When would the ideal opening date be? Consider your sales cycle—is Christmas a key season for your business, bigger than any other time during the year? Can you be open in time for it? And if so, will you be able to handle a potential rush of business right from opening day? Could you be ready to open in August in order to have a couple of slow months before the Christmas onslaught begins?

Whatever date you choose for your opening day, back plan from then, making a schedule of everything that needs to be done beforehand. Do you need to manufacture a full inventory of items for resale? If so, how long will that take? Do you need to renovate part of your home to accommodate the business? Bring in phone lines? Buy a computer? Estimate the time it will take for each item on your to-do list. Give it a deadline. Put it on the master schedule. If it's critical, give yourself twice as much time as you think it will take.

Does your opening date still make sense? You don't want to procrastinate, but you do want to start out as prepared and ready as possible.

For more information on this topic, visit our Web site at businesstown.com

CHAPTER SEVEN

Creating a Business Plan

How Long Will It Take?

Many home businesspeople claim they just haven't found time to put together a business plan.

But for a home-based business in which the proprietor already knows something about prospective customers, a basic plan can be completed in just a few days.

If creating a plan seems like an overwhelming task, try breaking it down into basic elements and tackling it one piece at a time. Start with a projected expense budget. Start with one month, estimate the next month, take it out for 12 months, two years, then three years. Then create a projected revenue budget. Compare the two to compute your gross margin. Doesn't that make you curious about your cash flow month to month?

Many thousands of small businesses have been launched and run successfully without a business plan. Many businesses with extensive business plans have failed. Creating a business plan isn't required for success, nor does it guarantee success.

Yet that doesn't mean it's not a good idea to have a business plan. Most small business consultants strongly recommend creating a plan. Think of it as a road map for a long journey. Sure, you can just hop in the car and drive across the country without a map. With a general sense of direction, you have a good chance of getting where you're going. With a road map, however, you'll waste less time making wrong turns, won't have to stop and ask for directions, are less likely to run out of gas, and have a way to measure your progress during the trip.

The most common reason to create a business plan is the need for outside financing. Banks require a business plan if you're applying for a business loan. So do other small business loan organizations. But the most common reason isn't necessarily the best reason. A business plan will help you forecast revenues and expenses, track your progress, and analyze your business in order to make the best decisions. More than having a business plan in place, it's the process of creating the plan and referring to it later that's most valuable to home businesses.

A business plan typically includes a written overview of the business, with a description of the product or service it provides, the market it serves, the competition it faces, and the people involved in the business. It also shows financial projections going out three to five years, with revenue and expenses detailed monthly for at least one year. If your business is in operation already, your business plan would also include past financial documents such as income statements and balance sheets.

Sounds like a lot of work, doesn't it? Again, think of taking that trip using a road map. If you expect to drive from San Francisco to Miami in seven days, your chances of meeting your goal are greatly enhanced by spending time tracing your route from start to finish before you jump in the car. You'll predict how many miles you can go in a day, how many stops you'll need to make, and budget enough money for gas and food so you don't go broke before you

Business Plan Outline

- Title page
- Statement of Purpose
- Table of Contents
- Business Description, including:
  - Product or Service
  - Location and Competition
  - Management and Organization

- Market Analysis and Marketing Plan, including:
  - Description of the overall market
  - Target market of the business
  - Analysis of the competition
  - Customer needs and characteristics
  - Overall sales plan

- Financial Data, including:
  - Capital equipment needs or assets
  - Funding sources
  - Balance sheet
  - Break-even analysis
  - Cash flow projections (one year)
  - Income projections (three years)
  - Past financial history (balance sheets, income statements up to three years)

- Supporting Documents
  - Resumes of management and partners, letters of recommendation
  - Personal financial statements and cost-of-living budget
  - Relevant contracts and legal documents
  - Documentation of market research, if available

The depth of detail appropriate for your business plan depends on the level of risk, the complexity of the business, the nature of the competition, and the margin or room for error. If yours is a part-time service business without inventory in a strong market with few competitors, you can get away with the basics. If you're investing your life savings in a highly competitive business with razor-thin margins, you're going to want to plan every step carefully and constantly review your projections in order to make the critical decisions that will determine your success or failure.

get there. Sure, you may decide to take a detour or two along the way, or you might run into unexpected delays due to road construction. But you'll be better prepared by knowing exactly how far you are from your destination and have a better idea of how long it will still take to get there. Pre-trip planning—and pre-business planning—can make all the difference.

The Planning Process

But where should you start? You might consider starting with the section of your plan that is most familiar. Do you feel you have a clear understanding of your market? Then dig into the marketing plan right away—it will help you with your financial projections. Have you been operating your business for a while as a hobby and are hoping to expand it? Then you might start by tidying up your past financial statements and projecting income and expenses. Or, if you prefer to start things at the beginning, try writing the description of your business in a concise way.

Description of the Business

Gail Gutierrez always had a flair for creating beautiful gift baskets, which she often made up as Christmas and other holiday gifts for friends and relatives. On numerous occasions she helped out friends in need of a gift by creating baskets for them. With her youngest son recently graduated from high school and heading for college, Gail wanted to take on a new challenge. She decided to start a business using her gift basket talents. A friend suggested she begin by creating a business plan. Gail started her planning process by describing her home business:

Gail's Gift Baskets will create custom decorative gift baskets for resale to retail customers to give for Christmas, birthdays, thank-yous, and other special occasions. This full-time home-based business will serve customers living in the area around Gail's home and will focus

Drive thy business or it will drive thee.
—Benjamin Franklin

initially on individuals and then branch out to potential corporate and business customers.

The owner of this sole proprietorship will purchase the baskets and a variety of basket contents from wholesalers and create the gift baskets in a room dedicated to the purpose above her garage. Orders will be taken over the phone or in person, and customers may pick up the basket in person, pay to have the basket shipped directly via UPS or other commercial shipper, or pay to have it delivered locally by the proprietor.

There are currently no similar businesses within a 10-mile radius of the location. There is a retail florist and a retail herb and gift store, but neither of them offer gift baskets at this time, and the gift store does not deliver.

The 52-year-old owner, Gail Gutierrez, is the only worker and intends to build the business initially through networking among her many acquaintances in the area. There is a hospital eight miles from her home, and she envisions regular deliveries there. She anticipates significant increases in business during the Christmas season, Valentine's Day, and Mother's Day.

This statement tells the reader what kind of business it will be, gives us an overview of the market, the competition, as well as the primary customers.

Market Research

When Gail was still deciding whether or not to start a home business making gift baskets, she did some basic research to learn more about the market. She found out whether or not there was a similar business in the area by checking the Yellow Pages and doing a search on the Internet. She included florists, since they sell to the same target market. She also researched gift stores and then called or visited each one to see if they were selling gift baskets. One gift store did, but it did not deliver and was located 25 miles from Gail's planned home business. (Another gift store owner said that she did not have gift baskets, but was frequently asked about them, and wished she had time to create them. Gail made a note

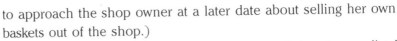

to approach the shop owner at a later date about selling her own baskets out of the shop.)

Gail next wanted to know how many potential customers lived or worked within a reasonable distance from her home. She checked with the county records office, which had local population figures by town and city. At the local public library, the reference librarian helped her look up the latest census data, where she found additional demographic data, such as average household income. The area within 10 miles of her house had above-average income, but was not extraordinarily wealthy. She could use this information later to help in pricing. She also discovered that a town just outside her 10-mile radius had a very high income level, and as a result she decided to include it in her geographic market.

Customer Needs and Characteristics

Although Gail had a feeling for what her customers would be like, she wanted to get as much information as she could. She created a simple questionnaire asking potential customers questions (see Customer Information box).

Gail then printed up copies of her questionnaire and gave two or three to each of her friends. She asked those friends to give the extras to people they knew within her geographic market. Within two weeks, Gail had 40 responses—not a scientific survey, but enough to give her a sense of the customer's needs.

After tallying the answers, she determined that most gift basket buyers were repeat customers buying two to three baskets a year, usually for female friends or coworkers, in the $26–$50 range, with a phone call—though she noted than six people reported buying gift baskets in the more than $100 category. About half were used to having the baskets delivered; the other half liked to pick them up.

Forecasting Sales

Armed with a more focused sense of the market, competition, and customers, Gail then tackled forecasting sales. She started by considering the best-case scenario: 10 baskets a day, five days a week, with an average price of $50. With gross sales

1. Have you ever given a gift basket to anyone for any reason? If not, why not?

   Not available   Too expensive   Never thought of it   Not appropriate

2. If so, how many times a year do you give gift baskets?

   1–2   3–5   More than 5

3. What occasions are most appropriate for gift baskets?

   Christmas   Valentine's Day   Mother's Day
   Birthday   Thank-you gift   Friend who's ill

4. To whom do you most often give gifts or gift baskets?

   Female relative   Male relative   Female friend   Male friend
   Female coworker or employee   Male coworker or employee

5. What items do you think are most appropriate to be included in gift baskets?

   Baked goods   Fresh fruit   Flowers   Magazines or books
   Nuts and candies   Herbs and spices   Small gifts

6. How much do you typically spend for a gift or gift basket?

   $5–$10 $11–$25 $26–$50 $51–$100   More than $100

7. Do you pick out the contents of the gift basket based on price? Contents? Aesthetics?

8. When you purchase a gift basket, do you want it to be delivered to the recipient?

   All the time   Some of the time   Never

9. If gift baskets were available in your area, would you purchase them as gifts?

10. In your opinion, what would be the best way to select a gift basket?

    Printed catalog   Telephone call   Retail display   Online catalog

of $500 a day, or $2,500 a week, she'd be looking at annual sales of $130,000.

Then she considered a worst-case scenario: if she were only able to sell two baskets a day, and the average price was $30, she'd gross $60 daily or $300 weekly, meaning annual sales might only be $15,600. Ouch!

But Gail felt confident she could do better than two baskets a day, so she estimated her most likely scenario as somewhere in between: five baskets a day at an average of $40, giving her weekly gross sales of $1,000 and annual sales of $52,000. She knew it would take time to build up her business to five baskets a day, but she was certain the business could be found.

Wanting to project her sales for three years, Gail estimated reaching her five baskets a day (25 per week) goal within 18 months, with projected annual growth of 10% afterward, so that by the end of her third year, she planned to be selling just under 29 baskets a week.

Cost of Goods

Gail's next step was to figure out what it would cost her to create the baskets. When she did them for friends, she usually bought the contents at retail outlets. This wouldn't be practical or economical for a home business. She began tracking down distributors and wholesalers for various items and found that by establishing accounts, with her projected volume of business and certain minimum order sizes, she could get a minimum of 30% discount, and sometimes as much as 50%. She factored in freight costs to get the items to her home.

Gail also talked to a few local craftspeople and bakery owners and arranged to get similar discounts on items she bought for resale.

Overall, she calculated that for the kind of basket she felt was worth $40, she would have to spend $20 on her Cost of Goods (COGS), including the basket itself, wrapping material, and ribbon. That gave her an average 50% gross margin on her average sale.

Operating Expenses

The next step was to figure out operating expenses. Gail's house included a walk-out basement that had been used as a family room when the kids were still at home, but since she and her husband were now empty-nesters they agreed that it would be a good place for her business—there was plenty of space for inventory storage, a separate entrance for customers who wanted to pick up their baskets in person, and an open area to create a good work space. Heat and electricity costs would not likely be much more than they had been. She figured on additional phone expenses of no more than $50 a month, since most of her calls would be local. She called her insurance agent and found that she could add business insurance (liability, plus coverage of her home when used for business) for a modest addition to her current homeowners policy. She'd have freight costs, of course, and figured those to be no more than 5% of her COGS.

A significant expense would be her vehicle. Initially, she planned to make all her deliveries herself and figured she could use her five-year-old minivan to get started. Based on her survey, half her customers would want delivery. Her market was the 10-mile radius around her house. If the average delivery was 10 miles round-trip and vehicle costs were, on average, 30 cents per mile, then she projected vehicle expenses of $3 per delivery, or 7.5% of her $40 average retail price per basket. She decided to charge $5 for delivery of baskets costing less than $40.

In order to reach her goal of 25 baskets per week within 18 months of start-up, Gail knew she'd have to advertise. She made some calls and found out the rates and readership of a variety of media—local newspapers, radio stations, direct mail coupons, Chamber of Commerce flyers. Although she planned to network among her friends for as much business as possible, she devised an advertising plan that included direct mail, Yellow Pages, plus advertising in the local newspaper prior to major holidays. Although she would list advertising as a fixed operating expense, she noted that based on what she wanted to do, advertising would cost about 10% of her gross sales in her start-up year and then about 6% in following years.

SBDCs

Small Business Development Centers (SBDCs) offer a wide range of assistance for entrepreneurs and are particularly helpful when it comes to creating a business plan. Many centers offer business-planning workshops or can refer you to a business-planning consultant who can help. They can help put you in touch with trade associations and point you toward information about your local market. As you begin your research, make sure you look up your local SBDC and find out what it has to offer.

Last-Minute Planning

I used to work at a book publisher specializing in small business titles. It seemed like every Friday afternoon we'd get several "gottahaveit" calls from desperate last-minute entrepreneurs.

We were a small business ourselves, and we often tried to do our best to make sure our customers got the information they wanted. They were buying a book on the phone, so we'd take the time to tell them what was covered in the book, and we often learned something about their business—or business-to-be.

(continued on next page)

Other administrative costs would include office supplies (letterhead, invoices, receipts, etc.), insurance, and legal and accounting expenses. Gail planned to do the bookkeeping for the business herself, but would hire an accountant to help her with filing her tax return.

Pro Forma Income Statement

Gail started adding up her figures to get an idea of her projected income. She made two tables:

REVENUES AND EXPENSES FOR AN AVERAGE MONTH OF SALES		
Sales of Baskets	$4,320	(108 baskets @ avg. $40)
Delivery Charges	$ 135	(108 x 25% x $5)
Total Sales	**$4,455**	
Cost of Materials	$2,160	(Avg. 50% of Sales)
Freight	$108	(Avg. 5% of COGS)
Delivery Costs	$323	(Avg. 7.5% of Sales)
Total Cost of Goods Sold	$2,591	
Gross Margin	$1,864	(42% of Sales)

OPERATING EXPENSES	
Advertising	$260
Utilities	$50
Office Supplies	$25
Insurance	$75
Accounting	$25
Depreciation	$200
Misc.	$150
Total Operating Exp.	$785
Net Profit (Loss) Before Taxes	$944

Projecting Income

Gail was assuming it would take her 18 months to build her business up to the level of selling 25 baskets a week, or approximately 108 per month. Gail then did her best to estimate sales in the first 17 months of business. She found it easiest to estimate the units sold (number of baskets), then multiply those by her projected average price per basket ($40).

She knew that if she added six baskets to her sales each month, after 18 months she'd reach her goal of 108. But she also knew that her business was far more likely to start slowly, then gain momentum. She also hoped that her advertising plan would affect sales, as would key holidays like Valentine's Day, Mother's Day, Secretary's Day, and of course, Christmas. To forecast income over the first five years of her business, she assumed her revenue would grow by 10 percent annually and her expenses would grow 5 percent.

When Gail finished the income projections for the first 24 months, she was a little disappointed with the resulting figures, but she also felt they were conservatively realistic:

Break-Even Analysis

Gail was curious to understand how much she would have to sell in order to break even. Having estimated her gross margin at 40%, Gail knew that she could calculate her break-even point using the following formula: Break-even Sales = Fixed Costs ÷ Gross Margin. With fixed costs (those that wouldn't change regardless of sales) at an estimated $9,300, and a gross margin of 40%, she calculated that her annual break-even revenue would be $23,250 ($9300/.40=$23,250). That meant she would need to generate $1,937.50 per month to break even, or sell 48 baskets at an average of $40 per basket.

Cash Flow

Gail knew she would not reach her break-even point right away. In fact, according to her income projections, she wouldn't reach that point until November, 11 months after she started her business. She wondered how much cash she would need to be able to pay the bills until then.

Last-Minute Planning

(*continued from previous page*)

I always got a chuckle out of the "gottahaveits." They'd ask if we had a book on business plans. We did, more than one. Could we overnight it to them? We could, of course, if it was really necessary. Oh it was, they'd say. They had to have a business plan done that weekend, in time for an appointment with the bank on Monday.

Well, we sold them books, and no doubt some of those last-minute planners have gone on to great success. But a business plan is a valuable tool, and the process of creating it is invaluable as you make decisions about your business. Rushing it without good research or creating it only as an exercise for the bank is almost a waste of time.

GAIL'S INCOME PROJECTIONS YEAR 1

	JAN.	FEB.	MARCH	APRIL	MAY	JUNE	JULY	AUG.	SEPT.	OCT.	NOV.	DEC.	TOTAL
Sales													
Baskets	80	400	320	480	1,000	600	800	1,000	1,400	1,800	2,200	3,000	13,080
Delivery Charges	5	15	10	15	35	20	25	35	50	60	70	100	440
Total Sales	85	415	330	495	1,035	620	825	1,035	1,450	1,860	2,270	3,100	13,520
Cost of Materials	40	200	160	240	500	300	400	500	700	900	1,100	1,500	6,540
Freight	2	10	8	12	25	15	20	25	35	45	55	75	327
Delivery Costs	6	30	24	36	75	45	60	75	105	135	165	225	981
Total Cost of Goods Sold	48	240	192	288	600	360	480	600	840	1,080	1,320	1,800	7,848
Gross Margin	32	160	128	192	400	240	320	400	560	720	880	1,200	5,232
Operating Expenses													
Advertising	500	50	50	1,000	50	50	50	50	50	100	500	250	2,700
Utilities	50	50	50	50	50	50	50	50	50	50	50	50	600
Office Supplies	25	25	25	25	25	25	25	25	25	25	25	25	300
Insurance	75	75	75	75	75	75	75	75	75	75	75	75	900
Accounting				600									600
Depreciation	200	200	200	200	200	200	200	200	200	200	200	200	2,400
Misc.	150	150	150	150	150	150	150	150	150	150	150	150	1,800
Total Operating Expenses	1,000	550	550	2,100	550	550	550	550	550	600	1,000	750	9,300
Net Profit (Loss) Before Taxes	-968	-390	-422	-1,908	-150	-310	-230	-150	10	120	-120	450	-4,068

GAIL'S INCOME PROJECTIONS YEARS 3–5

	JAN.	FEB.	MARCH	APRIL	MAY	JUNE	JULY	AUG.	SEPT.	OCT.	NOV.	DEC.	TOTAL	YEAR 3	YEAR 4	YEAR 5
Sales																
Baskets	2,600	4,000	3,000	4,000	5,000	4,320	4,400	3,600	4,320	4,640	4,640	5,000	49,520	54,500	59,950	65,945
Delivery Charges	80	125	100	125	150	135	140	115	135	145	145	150	1,545	1,700	1,875	2,060
Total Sales	2,680	4,125	3,100	4,125	5,150	4,455	4,540	3,715	4,455	4,785	4,785	5,150	51,065	56,200	61,825	68,005
Cost of Materials	1,300	2,000	1,500	2,000	2,500	2,160	2,200	1,800	2,160	2,320	2,320	2,500	24,760	27,250	29,975	32,973
Freight	65	100	75	100	125	108	110	90	108	116	116	125	1,238	1,363	1,499	1,649
Delivery Costs	195	300	225	300	375	324	330	270	324	348	348	375	3,714	4,088	4,496	4,946
Total Cost of																
Goods Sold	1,560	2,400	1,800	2,400	3,000	2,592	2,640	2,160	2,592	2,784	2,784	3,000	29,712	32,700	35,970	39,567
Gross Margin	1,040	1,600	1,200	1,600	2,000	1,728	1,760	1,440	1,728	1,856	1,856	2,000	19,808	21,800	23,980	26,378
Operating Expenses																
Advertising	500	50	50	1,000	50	50	50	50	50	100	500	250	2,700	2,835	2,977	3,126
Utilities	50	50	50	50	50	50	50	50	50	50	50	50	600	630	662	695
Office Supplies	25	25	25	25	25	25	25	25	25	25	25	25	300	315	331	347
Insurance	75	75	75	75	75	75	75	75	75	75	75	75	900	945	992	1,042
Accounting				600									600	630	662	695
Depreciation	200	200	200	200	200	200	200	200	200	200	200	200	2,400	2,520	2,646	2,778
Misc.	150	150	150	150	150	150	150	150	150	150	150	150	1,800	1,890	1,985	2,084
Total Operating																
Expenses	1,000	550	550	2,100	550	550	550	550	550	600	1,000	750	9,300	9,765	10,253	10,766
Net Profit (Loss)																
Before Taxes	40	1,050	650	-500	1,450	1,178	1,210	890	1,178	1,256	856	1,250	10,508	12,035	13,727	15,612

Gail's Cash Flow

YEAR: _____

SUMMARY	JAN	FEB	MAR	APR	MAY	JUN	JUL	AUG	SEP	OCT	NOV	DEC	TOTALS
Opening Balance	3,000	2,262	2,112	1,925	257	367	302	322	432	717	1,122	1,297	3,000
Total Receipts	85	415	330	495	1,035	620	825	1,035	1,450	1,860	2,270	3,100	13,520
Total Disbursements	823	565	517	2,163	925	685	805	925	1,165	1,455	2,095	2,325	14,448
Total Cash Flow	-738	-150	-187	-1,668	110	-65	20	110	285	405	175	775	-928
Ending Balance	2,262	2,112	1,925	257	367	302	322	432	717	1,122	1,297	2,072	2,072
RECEIPTS													
Cash Revenues	85	415	330	495	1,035	620	825	1,035	1,450	1,860	2,270	3,100	13,520
Receivables													
Loans													
Other													
DISBURSEMENTS													
Wages/Salaries/Benefits													
Material	48	240	192	288	600	360	480	600	840	1,080	1,320	1,800	7,848
Merchandise													
Equipment/Vehicles, Bought													
Equipment/Vehicles, Leased													
Advertising	500	50	50	1,000	50	50	50	50	50	100	500	250	2,700
Supplies													
Services				600									600
Maintenance/Repairs													
Shipping/Postage/Delivery													
Travel Expenses													
Rent/Mortgage													
Insurance	75	75	75	75	75	75	75	75	75	75	75	75	900
Telephone													
Utilities	50	50	50	50	50	50	50	50	50	50	50	50	600
Taxes													
Loan Payments													
Other:	150	150	150	150	150	150	150	150	150	150	150	150	1,800
Other:													

Note: You can change any Income or Expenditure category.

Reviewed by: _____

She planned to start with $3,000 in working capital, and based on her cash flow projections, it looked as if that would cover her for the start-up year. She knew that she had some wiggle room— she planned on starting out with $2,000 in materials inventory, and though she wanted to maintain that inventory level at all times, she knew she could survive with slightly less at any given time. What she wanted to avoid, however, was having no working capital (cash) and no inventory—without materials or the money to buy them, she couldn't make baskets. Consequently, she planned to monitor her cash flow situation closely.

Gail did not plan to take any money out of the business in its first year, and in fact if her projections turned out to be accurate, she would lose money in the first year. In year two she would need to remember that her net profits were pretax and that she'd have to pay not only income tax but self-employment tax.

Capital Needs

Gail planned to acquire additional shelving, worktables, a new computer, an additional phone line, a fax machine, and additional lighting for the walk-out basement. She costed out a sign for in front of the house. Eventually she'd want a shrink-wrap machine, but felt she could wait until the business was on its feet before she made that capital investment. Overall, she estimated she would need to invest $5,000 in start-up costs, which she would take from personal savings.

Gail's overall investment in the business would include $10,000 cash ($5,000 in capital expenses, $2,000 inventory, $3,000 working capital) plus the depreciation of her car, which she would use for the business. Looking to the future, she knew she'd need to invest in a vehicle for the business in a few years.

What Are Gail's Chances?

Gail's business plan could be inaccurate in any number of ways. Her projected average price could be off. The cost of deliveries might be low. In fact, given that Gail has little sales history to go on, it's likely that one or more of Gail's projections is off target.

Pro Forma or Just an Amateur?

Business jargon can be confusing at times. "Income statement" is easy enough to figure out without a degree in accounting, but what the heck is *pro forma*? Think of this term as the same as "projected"—a projected cash flow statement would be the same as a pro forma cash flow statement, meaning a statement that predicts cash flow in the future based on assumptions you're making today. For definitions of other business terms, see the glossary at the end of this book.

However, as she tracks her actual revenues and expenses, she'll be able to compare that reality with her expectations. She'll quickly see where her projections are off and can react accordingly. She might adjust expenses (increase or decrease advertising, for example) or adjust revenues. She might learn that she can be more profitable by selling fewer but more expensive baskets and adjust her marketing focus appropriately. She might begin selling some baskets wholesale to other retailers to create another revenue stream.

Even though you want to be as accurate as possible, the point of a business plan is to help you focus on your business, understand as much as possible about that business, and come away with a road map to help you on your business journey.

Sample Business Plan: Brakes 'n' More

Brakes 'n' More started as a part-time home business, expanded to full-time, and, at the time this business plan was written, wanted to expand further to include a second location, buy more equipment to speed turnaround and improve profit margins, and hire an employee. As you can see in the plan, they were proposing to borrow $180,000, collateralized with $252,335 in property and equipment. Although the cash flow of the business was not particularly strong, the owners were supplementing their home business income with a full-time job and baby-sitting.

The following sections represent the actual business plan used by Brakes 'n' More (the name of the owners and the business as well as the location have been changed to protect privacy).

Table of Contents

- Marketing Analysis and Promotional Plan
  - Description of the overall market
  - Target market, customer characteristics
  - Analysis of the competition
  - Marketing initiatives
- Financial Data
  - First quarter income statement
  - Pro forma cash flow statement
  - Capital assets
  - Loan fund dispersal
- Supporting Documents
  - Resumes of owners
  - SBA Form 912
  - Personal financial statement
  - Income tax returns for three years
  - Real estate paperwork

Statement of Purpose

Brakes 'n' More, a partnership established in 1984, is a home-based automotive repair business specializing in brake work, located in Farmdale, Illinois. The company wants to borrow $180,000 to expand the business by purchasing new equipment, inventory, make improvements to the existing property, hire an employee, and purchase another location.

We will be better able to serve our customers with more timely and cost-effective jobs. With the purchase of $15,000 in equipment, we will be able to do our own machine work rather than contracting it out. Each piece of equipment will give us more profit on a job. Using $1,000 the current shop will have a better appearance with some finishing touches. Allowing $10,000 to have the driveway and parking area at our home business location will make it more appealing and easier to maintain. Having $10,000 inventory on hand will allow us to be able to do jobs on demand and sell parts to customers, speeding up turnaround and improving customer satisfaction. Working capital would be put in part toward additional advertising, including a new sign at the proposed additional location.

Expenses As Percentages

Part of the process of creating a business plan is playing the "what if" game. What if I doubled unit sales? What if I doubled the price of my product or service? As you estimate the impact of these changes on your bottom line, it's easier to express your variable expenses (those that go up or down depending on sales) as a percentage. That way, if your sales go up, you can easily figure (or have your computer spreadsheet program figure) the new cost of a variable expense.

Pricing Your Services

Pricing your products or services appropriately can be a tricky science, especially when you're just starting up and need all the business you can get. Sometimes it's difficult to ask potential customers for what you think you're worth, especially on an hourly basis.

The market will likely define the broad limits of your pricing strategy. If you're a carpenter in an area where there's plenty of competition at $25 an hour, it might be a challenge to price yourself at $75 an hour for the same kind of work. Sure, quality counts, but Americans have proven themselves to be price-conscious shoppers.

(continued on next page)

The purchase of an additional property ($115,000) will give us visibility on a high-traffic route where we can display our used cars for sale, as well as store and sell new parts. We will also advertise our car repair business at this location and do some repairs. The four-bedroom house and mobile home lot on the new property will be rented for additional income of $1,000 per month.

We also plan to hire a part-time mechanic. Working capital is needed for wages and insurance.

Description of Business

Brakes 'n' More offers automotive repair and service including brakes, exhaust, shocks, struts, steering, oil changes, state inspections, tire sales and repair, automotive cleaning (interior and exterior), new parts sales and used car sales.

Company History

In 1982 we started by doing our own car repairs and maintenance. People in the family needed work done on their cars, so we did it for them. Our friends were impressed with our work and started asking for help and repair work on their vehicles. By word of mouth we started getting more and more customers. Our customers have been very satisfied and are very happy to see a decent car repair business in the area. We have since put a sign by the road and started advertising. We are also now an inspection station and a used car dealer.

We found it necessary to expand the business. We began with a one-bay garage and a two-car carport, and expanded it into a four-bay garage with over 1,200 square feet. We have purchased several pieces of equipment and a variety of tools. The equipment and tool purchases were made by cash. The expansion of the building was done by borrowing money from two banks, and some cash. Both loans will be paid in full by the end of this year.

Location

Our current operation is located on Rt. 122 in Farmdale, which has a population of approximately 10,000. There are several other car repair businesses in the area, but they are either too busy to take on new customers or suffer from a poor reputation.

Management and Organization

The business is a partnership, owned by Terry and Leigh Ann Lehrer, who are husband and wife. Terry continues to work at a full-time job as a transportation manager for a large company in a nearby town. Leigh Ann Lehrer is the manager, and her duties include:

Make estimates and set up appointments
Price out, order, and pick up parts
Car auctions
Detail cars
Some mechanical work
Work with vendors
Buy and sell cars
Inspect cars
Supplies and Inventory

Terry Lehrer is the assistant manager, and his duties include:

Mechanical work
Buy and sell cars
Make estimates
Inspect cars

Ellen Lattimer is the bookkeeper, a part-time employee of the business. Her duties include:

Keep books
Balance accounts
Organize records
Work with accountant

Market Analysis and Marketing Plan

Description of the Overall Market

The current location is on a state highway with 6,000 cars driving by daily. We currently attract customers from a five-town area, including Farmdale, Middleburg, Uniontown, Burnsville, and

Pricing Your Services

(continued from previous page)

However, it's easy to sell yourself short. You must cover your operating expenses and make a profit in order to survive. By pricing your services too low, you can create the impression that what you offer just isn't worth much. After all, a $10 haircut is just a haircut, but a $40 hairstyling is something special.

As you determine your prices, first figure out how much you need to charge to reach your goals. Then check the industry averages and the pricing of the local competition. The right pricing will be close to or a compromise among those numbers.

Orlington. Purchasing an additional property on Rt. 14 will give us visibility to over 14,000 cars a day. We plan on advertising the car repair business there as well as selling used cars and new parts. Currently there is a successful business located on this property.

Target Market, Customer Characteristics

Our market niche is brake repair and undercarriage work. Not only are brakes a safety and inspection point, but most people want them to function properly. Ten percent of cars need brake repair of some sort each year. The average brake job is $150. Getting just 10% of the drive-by traffic of 14,000 cars daily (1,400 x $150) equals a market of $210,000 in annual brake repairs alone.

We target those people who are looking for affordable car repair and sales, who are concerned about customer service and are happy to find someone who really cares. We target senior citizens by giving them an additional 10% off their repair orders.

We have built a strong customer base, including some contractors. We also just added a large customer, Kwiki Express, located in a nearby town. They spend $75,000–$100,000 in repairs annually. We will begin this account in June.

Analysis of the Competition

Gilly's Auto Repair—Has established clientele, busy, hard to make appointments with. Doesn't normally have room for any new clients.

Bill's Garage—Has established clientele, busy, hard to make appointments with. Has a large customer base and doesn't have much time for the regular customer.

Elwin's—Starting up again. People hesitant to go there for repairs. Not a very good reputation.

Napa Auto Parts—Only parts store in the area. People need another place to have a choice. Marshall's Auto Parts are usually better quality for better prices.

Rt. 14 Auto Sales—Will attract business to our car sales, because people like to shop around. We would be only two miles north of them, therefore people are likely to come and compare cars.

G&G Fabricating—The larger part of their volume is trucks and large vehicles. They have decent prices and they have a good location. They also have a large variety of services.

Gulf gas station—They have a two-bay garage and do simple repairs. Seems to be a small operation.

Marketing Initiatives

Detailed sign by side of road

Specials sign by side of road

Advertisements of brands of tires and parts

Magnetic signs on car used for business

Lettering with detail information on truck used for business

Advertising in *Town Crier* and *Lilac Estate* newsletters

Color ad in Burnsville area Yellow Pages

Money mailer coupon ad with five specials

Discounts of 10% to senior citizens

Choice of cash, check, or charge (MC/Visa)

Customer referrals (word of mouth)

Financial Data

The financial reports that follow reflect the current status of the business.

BRAKES 'N' MORE FIRST QUARTER INCOME STATEMENT
(JAN., FEB., AND MAR. 2000)

	Income	Expense		Income	Expense
Labor	$2,633.57		Loan	$1,000.00	$4,584.82
Parts	$3,767.89		Interest	$ 4.67	$146.83
Tools		$563.35	Building Addition		$1,070.20
Fluids	$ 106.01	$280.54	Car Sales	$2,630.00	$2,630.00
Welding Labor	$ 10.00		Inspection Station	$ 460.00	$ 127.50
Subcontracting	$ 103.00	$ 39.95	Towing		$ 45.00
Supply		$129.57	Misc.		$5.00
Office Supply		$112.71	Car Cleaning	$115.73	
Oil Disposal	$ 26.50		Tire Mount Balance	$ 24.00	
Oil Filter Disposal	$ 12.00		Fees and Dues		$140.00
Anti-Freeze Disposal	$ 8.00		Paid Help		$28.00
Tire Disposal	$ 2.00		Investments	$4,420.20	
Advertisement	$ 41.00	$171.00	Discounts	$ (116.31)	
Utilities		$180.16	Cash & Opening Balance	$ 622.52	$91.00
Rental of Bay	$ 347.50		Charges		$69.81
Rental of Car	$ 75.00				
Insurance		$829.00	**Total**	$16,293.28	$14,792.88
			End-of-month balance	$1,500.40	

CAPITAL ASSETS FOR BRAKES 'N' MORE

Real Estate

Current premises of the business, a 4.02 acre lot valued at $160,000 with an outstanding mortgage of $87,000	$73,000

Equipment

Gemini 9,000 lb. lift, model GPO9A S/N 3-19-06829	$2,600
FMC computer wheel balancer, model 58001, S/N 1495	$1,800
PRO 4000 60 gal. 5 hp air compressor	$ 390
Century Powermate 100 welder	$ 360
Delta drill press	$ 180
Cutting torches	$ 130
Campbell Hausfeld air compressor	$ 200
Toro snowthrower	$ 675
Trolley	$ 200
Misc. tools	$12,000

Furniture & Fixtures

Computer system w/ software & printers	$3,600
Furnishings	$1,700
Office Supplies	$ 300

Inventory

Parts & liquids	$1,000
Cars: Mercury Lynx, Ford Escort (2)	$4,000

TOTAL ASSETS	$102,335

LOAN FUND DISPERSAL FOR BRAKES 'N' MORE

Real estate (added location)	$115,000
Improvements to added location	$ 5,000
Equipment	$ 15,000
Current shop improvements	$1,000
Paving for current shop	$10,000
Parts inventory, including tires	$10,000
Used car inventory	$10,000
Working capital	$14,000
TOTAL	$180,000

NEW ASSETS TO SERVE AS COLLATERAL FOR BRAKES 'N' MORE

Real Estate (new property on Rt. 14)	$115,000
Equipment (Brake lathe, multipurpose lift, brake bleeder, tire changer, strut compressor, machine press, accessories for each)	$ 15,000
Inventory	
Used cars for resale	$ 10,000
New parts for resale	$ 10,000
TOTAL	$150,000

Supporting Documents

Included with this plan (but not shown here) were the resumes of the two partners, their income tax returns for the previous three years, personal financial statements, and a list of five credit references for the business. Also included was an insurance quote for the proposed new part-time employee and paperwork relative to the proposed purchase of the additional location.

The business plan, though simple, was successful: the loan was approved. The business continues to thrive today, though not entirely as the owners envisioned. Finding qualified employees proved difficult. The additional location turned out to be more trouble than it was worth, and they sold it. The parts supply business did not materialize as they had hoped—a large mass-merchandiser set up shop a few miles away. However, the core business activities—car repair and used car sales—has grown steadily. The owners have continued to invest in up-to-date equipment in order to service late-model cars.

For more information on this topic, visit our Web site at businesstown.com

CHAPTER EIGHT

Setting Up Your Home Business Office

Budget Stretching for Style

Don't be afraid to spend money on things you really care about and skimp elsewhere. Perhaps you've always wanted an antique library table as a desk, an object that is beautiful, valuable, and on which you can really spread out. Consider your budget, and see if you can squeeze in the desk by being more frugal in other areas, such as using simple, assemble-yourself bookshelves instead of antique ones. It's only temporary until you can afford to fill in the rest of your wish list. Remember, you'll be spending a lot of time in this office, and no one is setting the rules but you!

How much of your home will you need to turn over to your home business? The space needs of a home-based business vary widely according to the type of business you are starting. If you plan to run an automotive repair business, you'll need to focus your efforts on the shop space that will accommodate the vehicles and your tools before worrying about office space. On the other hand, if you are running a financial planning service out of your home, your office space is a key part of your business and you will need to give it careful attention. However, any business, from auto repair to cake decorating to freelance writing, will require some level of desk-type office space from which you make phone calls, create invoices, and do your day-to-day bookkeeping.

Determining Your Needs

The most important part of determining your needs is to know your chosen business as well as you can before setting up shop. Are you a retail business? Will customers or clients be visiting often? Will more than one customer or client be coming at once? What kind of storage will you need? How frequently will you need access to that storage?

The Non-Office-Based Business

Drive through any rural area of the country, and you will see homes with outbuildings decorated with vintage automotive-related advertising signs announcing "Ed's Body Shop" or "Country Joe's Automotive Repair, Please Honk." A business like automotive repair has very specific space requirements, and rural areas where outbuildings are common and neighbors at a distance are conducive to home-based auto repair success. If automotive repair is your chosen home-based business and you can find room for your office right within the repair shop, so much the better. Then when Mr. Johnson comes in wanting some maintenance work on his Ford truck, you don't have to run to the house to get access to the files showing all the previous work you've done on that truck for Mr. Johnson.

Edna Faulkner posted a hand-painted sign on the big oak tree in front of her house that simply said "Cake Decorating" with her phone number. For Edna's successful business, she spent most of her time near an oven. But any business, including cake decorating, whose main function doesn't require you to sit at a desk still needs a certain amount of office work.

Other non-office-based businesses include those that take you out on the road, particularly sales. These businesses also require a fundamental amount of space in which to do record keeping, client calls, and follow-up work.

Basically, any home-based business is going to need to have at least minimal office space. Let's get into the basic options.

The Corner-of-the-Living-Room Office

If your business is one that is conducted mostly in a specific space, then your office needs can be easily met. Edna the cake decorator equipped the side porch of her home with a refrigerated showcase and storage area for her cakes. She found a lovely white painted writing desk at an antique shop and set it just to the right of the front entrance. The desktop's day-to-day function was to display a scrapbook of her past creations. But when she needed the desk for bookkeeping, she could easily move the scrapbook and have the whole desktop to spread out on.

Your family heirloom rolltop desk that already sits in the corner of the living room can work just fine, although it may not hold that indispensable contemporary office tool, a computer. If you don't already have a desk tucked away in the kitchen alcove, the living room or dining room, or other multifunction area of the house, take a good survey and pick a spot to put a desk.

When you've decided on an office space and have cleared away the stack of old *National Geographic*s or the bags of clothing you've been meaning to take to the Salvation Army, be sure to measure it before you head out shopping for the desk you will put there. This may seem like a no-brainer, but if you have limited space to consider for an office and shop for hours for just the right desk in the right style, you sure don't want to bring it home and find out you'd

Family Matters

If setting up an office in a common area of your home, don't forget to enlist the opinions and advice of other family members who will be using the space. This will save a lot of arguments and changes later on.

either have to bump out a wall or shave off a couple inches of your new desk to make it fit.

Since the desk will be part of the decor of the room you are putting it in, and you and perhaps your family members will be in that room doing other things, you may want to hunt down a desk that fits the style of the room and will be pleasing to the eye. In other words, because your home business doesn't require you to use the desk to any great extent, you certainly could get away with a functional used metal desk. But is that what you want to look at every time you walk into the living room?

A couple Saturday mornings at yard sales could easily provide a reasonably priced desk. If yard sales aren't your idea of fun, check the Yellow Pages or the newspaper for places that sell used office equipment. Or you could get a simple unfinished pine desk and paint it to match the rest of the room.

Voila! you have an office space.

Stocking the Desk-Sized Office

If your office is in the corner of the living room, you will probably want to have a desk that has enough drawer space to tuck most everything away. You don't want Susie to come home from soccer practice, grab the schoolbooks she left on your desk, and in her rush to get upstairs and study, she accidentally grabs a stack of invoices too, and then, discovering this, returns them to the desk, but one invoice has slipped into the back of her biology book, which she may or may not discover at the end of the school year . . . Well, you get the drift.

A rolltop desk is a way to cover everything up without having to move it somewhere else, but drawer space is your best bet to get things out of general view. You'll also want to have a place to tuck away a small stock of office supplies, so that your pens don't disappear like chocolate chip cookies left on the kitchen counter. Chances are you'll have stationery and office forms that you'll want to keep neat and professional looking by keeping them flat in a drawer.

Free Up Desk Space

You won't need those little framed pictures of your family or pets anymore. They'll be right there at "the office" with you!

The Office-Centered Business

Many home-based businesses require much more office work than a few minutes at the end of the day. Bookkeeping, accounting, freelance writing, editorial services, graphic design, legal services, are but a few office-centered businesses.

Ideally, for a business where your office plays such an important role, you will have an extra room in your home—with a door you can close—that you can transform into a separate space dedicated solely to your business.

This is ideal for a variety of reasons:

- It is the best way to separate your business life from your personal life, which is one of the biggest challenges for home-based entrepreneurs.
- A distinct definition of work space and personal space can have a positive psychological effect on your productivity.
- A closed door is better protection against Johnny accidentally spilling chocolate milk all over your invoices.
- Your family won't have to listen to all your business phone conversations.
- Conversely, your clients won't have to hear *My Three Sons* reruns playing on the television in the background.

If you don't have a separate room that could readily be taken over for your office, you need to get a little more creative. You will be amazed at where you can carve out a defined office space. Do some detective work around the house looking for areas that could give up a few square yards to convert to private office space without requiring a huge renovation budget.

Basements often hide useable space. You will need to be extra mindful of dampness or flooding problems. But with a little basic carpentry to make a partition, some damp-proofing paint on the walls, and a couple hundred dollars' worth of professional electrical work, you might be able to find yourself a nice work space.

Similarly, walk-up attics can offer potential office space. Where dampness is a problem facing the basement, heat is the concern in

A Room of Your Own

A separate room with a door that shuts is the ideal home office space. This allows you to better define that fine line between your personal life and your work life, which is perhaps the biggest challenge for home-based business owners. Not only can you shut the door and walk away at the end of the day, but you can better shut off those after-hours work calls that, if you hear the phone ring, you are tempted to answer. The "out of sight, out of mind" adage certainly applies here.

Your House—from the Customer's Point of View

Will customers or clients need to regularly visit your home-based business? If so, a huge concern is liability insurance. Those rickety front steps that you've been putting up with for three years—now's the time to repair them! Before hanging out your shingle, you might consider having a friend or family member role-play as a customer. Have your friend point out anything that strikes her as dangerous—from potentially dangerous things like the dog toy obstacle course in the hallway to small inconveniences like there is nowhere to hang their raincoat. Be sure to read Chapter 12 carefully, and be sure to get professional advice on insurance coverage. (Don't forget your insurance agent, who will probably want to visit as well.)

the attic. Maybe this can be cured with a whole-house fan or a window air conditioner.

Is there one end of your garage that, with a couple simple renovations—a partition, a self-contained heating unit, and a carpet remnant—could make a cozy office space?

Do you really need that little room upstairs that the ironing board and a sewing machine occupy 24 hours a day and that you use for a total of two hours the entire year?

If you carve out one of these almost-ideal office locations, consider setting aside a little nest egg marked specifically for a renovation to create a more workable office space, especially if your business will grow with any speed. Perhaps $5,000 could make the peak of the two-car garage into a perfect spot from which to conduct business. Perhaps you have an outbuilding that could be transformed. Do the best you can for now, but plan your upgrade. (But be sure to check zoning before you get too attached to your plan, and certainly before you incur any expenses on it.) The most successful business owners, home-based or not, decide how much they can make do with for the time being and plan for changes at certain stages of financial success.

Setting Up Your Office

The most important consideration in setting up your home business space, office or retail, is whether or not customers and/or clients will be coming to your home. If all your work is done via phone, mail, fax, or computer, then your options are much simpler. But if people are coming to your home office, the things you need to consider become a bit more complicated. We'll discuss the self-contained office first, then provide some specific considerations for the office situation that needs to greet clients.

The One-Person Office

Before you begin to buy or borrow anything to put in your office-to-be, consider the empty space:

The walls. If the walls need painting, now's the time. Frank was planning to set up his marketing consulting office in an extra room in his old colonial house. The room had wallpaper that had been there when they bought the place. The wallpaper was in good enough condition and the room was not used for anything more than storage, so he and his wife had concentrated on other projects for the five years they'd lived there. Yet once the room was empty of all the junk stored in it, the wallpaper not only looked kind of yellowed, but its pattern of pink roses was just all wrong for a business atmosphere for Frank. When he really thought about how much time he was going to be spending in that room, he decided it needed to be painted a color that was soothing and productive for him. Of course, doing the painting yourself will be kinder to your budget. But whether you choose to do it yourself or hire a contractor, the key is to do this kind of project now, while the room is empty and you haven't settled your business into it.

The floor. Is the room cold in the winter? Would a nice room-sized wool rug help? Perhaps you'd rather section the room off into work areas using large throw rugs. Carpet stores often have remnants, which will help the budget, and there are even stores devoted entirely to remnants. Corporate offices have industrial-strength carpets to cope with the traffic. If you go for a room-sized rug, you may want to splurge on a well-made carpet that will hold up to everyday use. Then you won't have to clear the room every few years to change the carpet.

Wiring and lighting. To choose lighting, watch the movement of light during the days and place lights accordingly. Don't forget to consider the room during nondaylight hours—as an entrepreneur working from home, you'll surely sometimes be in your office before dawn and after dusk. If you want track lighting or ceiling lights wired ask your electrician, but at this early stage you may want to have floor and/or table lamps that you can move around as you get a better sense of your space. Plan to have an electrician install grounded

Getting in the Zone

Every town or city has zoning laws that either must be followed or must be challenged with an application for a variance for your specific circumstance. Know these zoning laws before you get your heart set on your business arrangement. And don't assume just because the guy up the street did something it's legal. It's not worth the expense and bad publicity to be unaware of or ignore zoning laws.

outlets and a few phone jacks for your computer modem, fax machine, and phone.

Once you have the walls and floors taken care of, it's time to move in the furniture. We'll consider the basics next—desk, desk chair, file cabinets, bookshelves. Depending on the work you do, you may need a few other items—a worktable that's kept mostly bare so you can spread out projects, perhaps a separate side table for the fax machine. If you have the budget and space, a few "extras" such as a comfortable reading chair and a stereo of some kind would be nice. Then we'll get to the important and expensive electronic equipment and some of the services you'll need.

The Basics

Desks. Whatever you choose for a desk, be sure it is computer-friendly. You can opt for a simple pressboard work surface bought inexpensively at an office store. These come with holes in the backboard for the many connection cords to slip through, as well as keyboard holders and monitor shelves. Computer tables also come in higher-end models—you can be quite stylish while still being computer-conscious. You can purchase your desk at a furniture store, which may well have many matching accessories like file cabinets and desk risers that you can add to the set as you can afford them. Or, if you are planning well in advance, you can go all out and have a desk custom-made to suit your exact specifications. Remember, if your business is an office-based one, you will be spending a lot of time with this piece of furniture.

Chairs. You will need a comfortable office chair, perhaps one that matches your computer table or desk. Office supply stores keep many on hand—sit in them all, and slide them up to one of the display desks. Buy a high-quality chair—your chair affects your posture and your back, and if you are uncomfortable you will be less productive besides risking your health. Be sure the seat fits, both from back to front and from seat to floor.

Bookshelves. Almost no matter what your business is, you'll need at least one bookshelf in your office, if for nothing more than the raft of manuals that come with the electronic equipment you purchase. Maybe you have a few professional books you like to

---

This Is Not Your Same Old Life

If you have left the commuter world to become an entrepreneur with a home-based business, why not make sure you do some things you couldn't do when you worked for someone else? Perhaps your former employer had a policy that no one could put bird feeders outside his or her office window. Well, no one's stopping you now but yourself!

Feng Shui for Your Office

Feng Shui (pronounced "fung shway") is commonly defined for the Western world as the Chinese art of placement, usually of home furniture, and is based on energy flows throughout rooms and buildings. But Feng Shui is used in offices as well—in fact, in the Far East, before large office buildings are sited and built, a Feng Shui practitioner is consulted to advise on location and orientation.

If this kind of advice interests you, you might want to consult a book or two to get some advice on picking a place for your office and/or arranging the furniture. For instance:

- Placing a desk so that your back is to the entrance to your office is undesirable.
- The "moneymaking" direction is Northeast, so if you want your business to have the best chance to be profitable, locate your office in this wealth area of the house.
- If your house or office doesn't allow you to follow this advice, remember that part of Feng Shui practice is to use moveable items that can redirect energy—mirrors, candles, prisms—to redirect energy flow from negative to positive.

Even if you don't follow the practice to the letter, Feng Shui is a great way to gain some direction in setting up your home office. If a couple mirrors and the direction of your desk might help your business be successful, why not?

Chair Ergonomics

If you're going to do a lot of deskwork in your home business, busting your budget a little is worth it to get the right office chair. Try out chairs at an office furniture/supply store before you buy, and pay close attention to these features:

- Height: The seat should be from 8 to 10 inches from the underside of your work surface. Your feet should fall flat on the floor.
- Chair Back: Should be adjustable vertically, so that the curved section cradles the lower back.
- Seat: Depth should be from your knees to the base of your spine—this aids leg circulation.
- Armrests: Needed to support the arms and shoulders, but should not impede the ability to push close to your desk or worktable. If you do a lot of computer work in your business, armrests will be in your way.

have on hand. And you need a nice spot to stack that weekly trade journal. If you are, for instance, in the book publishing or writing business, you will definitely need more than one bookshelf. Bookshelves range from the most basic pressboard styles for around $50 to those that are more like pieces of furniture, which can run a couple hundred dollars, to custom-made bookshelves or even built-in shelves for a lot more. Build in only if floor space is extremely limited—once the bookshelves are there, your room can be set up basically one way and that's it!

File cabinets. Are you a tax accountant who will be building up client files and adding to them every year? If so, you may want to start off with a fairly substantial file cabinet. Consider what kind of documents you will be storing and choose either legal or letter size. A regular desk typically comes with at least one file drawer, which is great for those active files that you need within easy reach of your phone or computer, but you will still most likely need at least one "dead storage" file cabinet.

Handy Items

Worktable. If you do a lot of projects that require spreading out, you can always use the dining room table. But if the projects need to be spread out over a few days, your family may tire of eating off their laps in the living room. If you have the space, a good worktable that's kept clear most of the time or is easily cleared is extremely useful.

Other tables. Once you've read the equipment section and decided what you need, be sure you have someplace to put that equipment. You won't want noisy printers or fax machines on your desktop right near the phone. Faxes and printers also need space to accommodate paper bins, so think positioning through carefully. An end table with a riser offers a bit of space to store a spare ream of paper or two, leaves surface free to hold your coffee cup should you place it next to your reading chair (see below), and doesn't take up much floor space.

Comfort Items

Reading chair. After you've spent hours at your desk working on your computer, a little change of scenery is always nice. An easy chair where you can comfortably read a magazine or two or review a manuscript or printed report can be a nice addition to your office. A recliner might not be the best choice—or maybe it is, if you'd like to put your feet up and take a quick catnap midafternoon!

Stereo. Some people like to have music or the news or talk shows on in the background while they work. What used to be a bone of contention at the office is now yours for the choosing! You can buy a decent "boom box" with CD player, tape player, and radio for well under $100. Choose one with a remote control. If you place the radio across the room so it isn't right in your ear, you'll have to play it loudly enough to hear, which may be too loud when you are on the phone. A remote control allows you to shut it off when you answer the phone and turn it back on when you're done without having to jump out of your chair each time.

General Services

Trash

A simple consideration, but what kind of trash does your home business generate? Is it within the range of your town's trash service limitations? Do you pay-by-the-bag for trash service in your town? If so, be sure to budget in the extra costs that your business will create. Is your trash considered "hazardous waste"? If you are running an automotive repair shop, you need to get an answer to that question—certainly waste oil needs specific considerations. Ask your waste management service, or start with your town or city office if you don't know the service's name.

Cleaning

Chances are you won't hire a cleaning service for your one-room home office. Just don't forget that now you are responsible for the cleanliness of your office—no one comes around during off-hours and makes your office magically clean the next morning! If

Extra Supplies

Don't get caught short on office supplies. Be sure to always have extra printer ink cartridges or laser toner on hand, as well as a good supply of paper, and other things that aren't as easy to substitute; it's usually easy to use a large rubber band instead of a binder clip, but if you are out of computer printer ink, there's really no other item that will do the job. Of course, don't go in the other direction by over-stocking supplies (and over-spending), which is easy to do in these days of office supply warehouses. You don't need enough paper clips to last for thirty years. And some things, like computer and photocopy paper, have a real possibility of getting damaged with too much moisture or other factors to make it unusable.

Design for Good Health

- Buy the best desk chair you can afford. You will sit in it for long periods of time and it is key to your physical well-being.
- If you paint or install new carpets in your office, be sure to air out the room for at least a couple days before you begin to work in it. The fumes from fresh paint—even water-based latex paints—and carpet glue and synthetic fibers are not healthy to breathe.
- Place your computer without windows behind it, to reduce screen glare. And perhaps spend the $20 for a glare screen for your monitor. Your eyes will thank you for it.
- Carpal tunnel syndrome and tendonitis are common ailments of the computer generation—use padded wrist rests for your keyboard and your mouse pad.

you have clients that come into your home office, you'll definitely want to make sure it's always tidy.

Mail

Despite the proliferation of e-mail and the convenience of the phone, you'll surely need to mail things—how much depends on your type of business. Is your current mail receptacle sufficient for the volume of incoming mail you'll be getting? Will it all fit through the slot in the door? Will the carrier need a separate bag just for you? Is your rural mailbox the largest size, so packages don't have to be hung from the latch and get wet? If your volume of mail is large, you should consider getting a post office box. Post offices are conveniently located and, what the heck, it may be nice to be forced to get out of the house once a day!

As for outgoing mail, the United States Postal Service is far from the only mailing service you'll use. Even though the USPS provides all the services you will need for mailing, you will definitely find yourself using UPS, FedEx, Airborne, DHL, you name it. Set up accounts with the ones you use the most—this makes it much more convenient to use the service. (Not to mention helping to stretch the cash flow. If you don't have a FedEx account, they will accept a credit card number on the airbill.) If a FedEx drop-box is not convenient to your home, many of them will do pickups the day they are called. Find a covered spot for these delivery services to pick up and drop off your packages if you are not home.

When Clients Come to Your Office

We've covered the various services, furniture, and equipment you might need for your basic home office setup. Businesses that require lots of visits from lots of customers are rarely home-based—most of these businesses will need some sort of storefront, in-town visibility to be successful. But if your business will require that clients occasionally visit your home office, there are a few other things to consider.

Zoning. Always check zoning laws on everything you do with your home office—before you do it. Don't hang out a shingle for your home-based business and sit back to wait for customers only to find that your town's zoning prohibits home businesses that require customers to visit.

Parking. Does your driveway allow enough space for a visitor to park? Are other family members going to be frustrated by constantly being blocked in? Look for a way to carve out a space especially for customer parking, and then put up a sign to direct customers to it specifically. Is the only parking you have on the street? Will customers—or your neighbors—get frustrated because they can never find a parking space? Consider these things before you set your heart on a specific kind of business—the zoning code in your community may require a minimum number of parking spaces.

Entrance. Preferably, you will have a separate entrance for a business that requires customer visits. Make sure the entrance is clearly marked. Make the entrance attractive and inviting; show your customers that you are expecting them and you care about their initial impression. Flowering shrubs near the entrance or a small garden and brick walkway, a welcome sign, and a modest-sized wreath on the door will do the trick.

The Office. How much of your home will your customer have to walk through to get to your office? Will he or she need to walk by a sinkful of dishes or pile of dirty laundry? This can be a bit of a turnoff. Keep your pets confined—not only are they a huge liability, but customers are not there to see your pets, and believe it or not many people do not like dogs. And dogs aren't the only problem—lots of people are allergic to cats.

Once the customer gets to your office, is it neat and tidy? Is there a place for him to put his coat? A solid, comfortable, clean chair to sit in? A place to spread out any materials that you both need to look at?

The upshot is, if your business requires a customer to come to you, you need to consider that scenario in every decision you make about your home office.

Well, that's it. You're up and running—efficiently, comfortably, perhaps even a little stylishly. Now, get to work!

Who's Going to Clean?

If you keep your office simple enough, cleaning shouldn't be a big problem. Just don't forget that your office isn't vacuumed and trash emptied every morning when you begin work, as it may have been at your last job. It's either up to you to clean, or up to you to hire a service to do it for you. Perhaps you have a housekeeper or cleaning service for the rest of your home—be sure to check if that person or the service will add your home office to its agenda, and budget it in as a monthly expense. And plan to work somewhere else while the cleaning folks are doing their job—there's little chance they will be doing it overnight as they do in corporate offices.

CHAPTER NINE

Home Office Technology

Home business entrepreneurs are often called upon to do two, three, or more things at once. As a sole proprietor, you'll need to field calls from customers, receive shipments, and keep up with your bookkeeping, all while doing work that generates income. Technology can help, and most home-based businesses will need at least two pieces of electronic equipment: a telephone and a computer. How complex your setup will be beyond that has a lot to do with the kind of business you are starting. How complex you get with the two essentials is up to you.

Telephone

While your home phone might suffice at start-up, you'll quickly see the need for a second line dedicated to your business (see "Services" at the end of this chapter). And though you can buy a neon pink phone with quarter-sized numbers that light up in the dark for $9.95, it's not likely to be sturdy or sophisticated enough for even the smallest home business. However, you don't have to spend too much more to get a perfectly efficient phone with quite a few bells and whistles (and beeps!).

Most quality phones come with ring volume control. Better yet, find a model that allows you the option of shutting the ringer off. Unless your home office is completely and utterly separate from your personal space or you absolutely can't hear the phone ring outside your office walls, be assured you will want this feature. If you can hear that phone ringing during off-hours, you will think about potential lost sales or a client who thinks you are not dedicated enough because you aren't sitting at your desk to answer at 9:30 Saturday night. When you are done for the day, turn the ringer down or off and forget about the business for a few hours.

If there are numbers you will call regularly, memory storage for those numbers is almost a must-have feature—read the manual and use this speed-dial feature. It is a timesaver and saves your own memory for other things.

Many phones now come with Caller ID, which can be handy if you're trying to concentrate on a job and want to screen your calls.

The name of the caller and his/her number will flash on a tiny LCD screen. Caller ID requires signing up for the service with your local phone company and will cost $5 to $10 a month.

If your business relies enough on the phone to make you think you might need two business lines in the near future, two-line phones are readily available within a reasonable price range. While you are in the phone-buying mood, pick up some good accessories like extra long cords for both the receiver and the cord that plugs into the phone jack.

You may want to consider a cordless telephone. That way if you need to be in another area of the house—say you are using the dining room table to spread out on or you are working on the back deck on a sunny summer day (these things are possible when you work for yourself!), you can have your cordless phone with you and not miss any calls or not have to run up and down the stairs to catch the phone when it rings. It's also helpful if while on the phone you need to go to another room of the house to check inventory, or answer the door when the UPS delivery truck pulls into the driveway.

Cordless phones cost anywhere from $20 to $500—be sure to invest in a cordless phone of reasonable quality so that your voice comes through clearly and without interference. There are key differences in the technology used. Analog phones are inexpensive, but have the shortest range and are easy to listen in on. Digital or Digital Spread Spectrum (DSS) phones cost more, but provide greater range and more security from eavesdropping.

Toys vs. Tools

Technology offers a dazzling array of tools. But don't get caught up in buying electronic toys just because they're cool—instead equip yourself with the tools you need to communicate professionally in today's business world.

Some cordless phones will have a keypad on the base as well as on the handset. This can be useful if you regularly key in orders or check availability of inventory from vendors—you can key in the numbers while listening for the prompts. A speakerphone feature on the handset will be equally as useful.

If you're willing to invest closer to $400, Siemens manufactures a two-line cordless phone system that allows you to purchase as many handsets as you want or need. You can assign extension numbers, transfer calls from one extension to the other, and have separate voice-mail boxes, all without having to rewire your home-based office.

Is a cell phone necessary? Clearly, if you spend a lot of time in your car, a cell phone is probably a must. If your business takes you on the road making lots of sales calls, it is helpful to be able to call from the road to confirm or reschedule appointments or check directions. And if you are in your car a lot a cell phone can be a safety tool as well if you get stuck on the road. Likewise, if you spend a lot of time in your car, you may be able to get a little work done during an untimely traffic jam or while waiting to pick up the kids from soccer practice.

One last phone item to consider: If you are on the phone a lot or need to look for things in a file drawer or on the computer while talking with clients, a headset can save you a lot of neck cramps. Quality hands-free phones can be a significant added expense—anywhere between $100 and $200 at the moment—but they are well loved by those who have splurged for them.

Answering Machines

For not much more than $50, your phone will come equipped with a perfectly serviceable answering machine. In fact, this is almost standard in most business-type phones. You'll want to make sure recording quality is up to par—once you've recorded your message, call yourself from another line and test the message for sound quality and that it does what the manual says it does.

Whether your answering machine is built in or is a separate unit, you have a variety of features to consider. You'll want to make sure your answering machine can hold enough messages (you may not want to have to restrict callers to 15 seconds, for example, or be limited only to record a few messages before the machine is full) for your needs. In addition, some answering machines allow you to set up multiple voice-mail boxes, which would be useful if you're using one phone line for home and business.

Computers

Ah, the computer. A tool that even 20 years ago would not be part of the inventory of a home-based business is now practically solely responsible for the boom in home businesses. This incredible machine has made it possible to make the smallest of businesses operate in the most sophisticated of ways.

Just like every other key business tool, it is important to assess how you will use a computer. Here are some things to think about:

- Will your computer serve as not much more than a revved-up typewriter used for generating letters? Or will you need to work with graphics or spreadsheets?
- Does your business rely on the building of a large, complex mailing list?
- Will you use your computer for accounting, bookkeeping, tax calculations, and a multitude of other functions?
- Will you want to be able to perform tasks with windows open to several different files and programs at one time?
- How much experience do you have with computers? If little, are you willing to learn?

Most uses of a computer rely more on software choices than the hardware itself—the big thing is to make sure your chosen hardware has enough short-term and long-term memory capacity to run the software you need to do the things you want to do on your computer. You'll need to consider how fast it can perform multiple functions if you will need it for that level of work.

Most computers these days, even the models that might previously have been designated as "student computers," come with extraordinary amounts of memory. It's easy to get overwhelmed with the technical jargon, and state-of-the art specifications change so quickly that it's sometimes hard to keep up, but for general use, you can buy almost any of the latest models and be all set for three to four years.

Laptops

Desktop computers are most common, but laptop computers are desirable for their portability. Typically you'll pay considerably more for comparable specifications. And though laptop screens are much improved, they are still inferior to a desktop monitor. Some computer manufacturers offer docking stations that make it possible to use your laptop with a standard monitor and keyboard when you're at home. These options will depend on your budget.

Mouse Hunt

A mouse is a mouse is a mouse, right? Not when it comes to a mouse with a "double click" button! Although double clicks may be going the way of the dinosaur, many functions on a computer still require two clicks on the mouse button. So companies like LogiTech have come up with a mouse that has a third button that double clicks with just one touch of the button. This may seem frivolous and irrelevant—until you use one. Not something that will be high on the list of a tight budget, but if you want to do something nice for yourself, spring for the $40 mouse with a double-click feature.

Computer Basics

Dominating the business market are the PCs or "Wintel" (Windows + Intel) machines—computers made by manufacturers such as IBM, Hewlett Packard, Dell, Compaq, Gateway, Sony, and others using microchips from Intel or AMD and using Microsoft Windows as an operating system. Also available are Apple computers, which have held sway in the educational and graphic arts markets. Apple's newest generation of computers is fast, price competitive, and stylish. Both do amazing and comparable things. Because Wintel computers are more prevalent in business, software tends to be more varied and less expensive for them.

A computer is made up of three key pieces: the central processing unit, or CPU; the monitor; and the keyboard.

The CPU is the brains of the operation. Typically, the newer the computer the faster it will run, determined for the most part by the kind of chip it contains. Chip makers like Intel continually upgrade—from the 486 chip to the Pentium, to the Pentium II, Celeron, Pentium III, and so on. Software makers continually add features that take advantage of the faster chips. The CPU also contains a hard drive, on which software and files are stored. The bigger the hard drive, the more files you can save. The CPU will also have a certain amount of RAM memory—the more you have, the bigger the programs you can run on your computer. You can usually add RAM (expand it) to a CPU. If 64MB of RAM is standard for an off-the-shelf computer today, you can bet that 96 or 128MB will be standard soon. And so forth.

Within the CPU will likely be one or two removable disk drives—a floppy disk drive (or Zip disk drive, which holds more information) and a CD-ROM drive. The CD-ROM drive is standard these days for many software packages.

The CPU will also usually include a fax modem, which allows you to connect by phone line to an Internet service provider (ISP) as well as send and receive faxes. The fax feature can be very useful if you are faxing documents that you create on the computer (letters, invoices, etc.). But if you're sending and receiving paper documents, a stand-alone fax machine is usually more convenient.

The monitor is the viewing screen, and virtually all monitors are color these days—a lot more fun when using the Internet! Buy as large a monitor as you can—a 17″ screen is helpful, though not absolutely necessary for most business applications. If you looked at a monitor from just five years ago, you would probably find the monitor screen too small.

Most computers still come with a standard keyboard. However, sales of ergonomically designed keyboards are on the rise and are readily available in most computer outlets. People who use them like them, but again this is a personal choice. Keyboards also now come with an array of specialty buttons for one-touch Internet access, volume control for the speakers, and many other possibilities. These are often determined by the particular brand of computer you purchase.

Computer Accessories

You will absolutely need a printer. The capacity to print color is worthwhile and almost standard these days in inkjet printers. These are perfectly serviceable and much faster than the old dot matrix tractor-fed models (the kind for which you need the paper with holes on the side). If you will be printing a considerable amount— long documents such as book manuscripts—it may be worth springing for a laser printer. They are expensive, but they are fast and offer high-quality output. Printer speed is discussed in pages-per-minute (ppm) and obviously the higher the number the faster the printer.

Will you be doing a lot of graphics work or maybe a newsletter? A scanner—a device that acts something like a photo-copier, only instead of getting a paper copy of the image you place on the glass, it is transformed to digital form (from which you can print out a paper copy)—will be useful. And a scanner can do double work as a simple photocopier! Prices are going down and features are changing all the time, but plan to spend around $150 on a simple but serviceable model. Be sure it is compatible with your computer and software—a salesperson can help you.

Digital Cameras

The price and quality of digital cameras has improved for consumers and they're now a viable alternative, especially for posting images on a Web site. If your business will frequently require digitized photos (real estate agents, for example, need photos of houses and interiors), a digital camera may be more useful to you than a scanner, since you won't have to have the photos developed.

Zip drives allow you to store large amounts of information without taking up space on your hard drive, and the Zip disks are removable and portable so you can give huge files to someone else to output if necessary. They are also a handy way to back up critical information—your mailing list, sales, or accounting information.

While CD-ROM drives are standard in computers these days, you can get external (not built-in) CD-ROM drives that also allow you to record, or "write," information on them. These are called read-write CD-ROMs and can store considerably more information than a Zip drive, for example.

Computer Supplies

Buy computer cables that are extra long. That way you can place your computer almost anywhere in your office without having to be stuck near an electrical outlet. Since your computer and your phone will probably be an integral part of your desk setup, a long printer cable will allow you to place your printer well away from your computer and, therefore, your phone. Even the best printers are a bit noisy to have a phone conversation around.

Be sure to read the manual to learn what ink and paper you need for your computer, and keep a ready supply on hand. You don't want to run out of either just as a potential customer is waiting for a written price quote.

Buying the Computer

Consumer computer sales are highly competitive. You can buy at a retail outlet, direct mail, or online. You can buy a standard package or have a computer built to your specifications. You can buy added tech support, extended warranties, etc., etc. It's easy to get confused.

But here's the good news: computers aren't that expensive. You can walk into a national chain electronics store, plunk down $750 to $1,500, and bring home a computer that should be viable for at least three years. Even if you come to the conclusion six months down the road that you would have preferred a different model, you haven't lost a lot. And though you might have been able to save $100 by shopping around some more, the truth is that in six

Free Software

The highly competitive computer and software market makes for good deals sometimes. Sun Microsystems makes Star Office, a suite of programs similar to Microsoft Office, available free. You can simply download it off the Internet and off you go, saving as much as $400 to $500 for the cost of rival programs. Many other "freeware" and low-priced "shareware" programs are available on the Web. Use the Web search engines to find them.

months your computer will be worth hundreds of dollars less anyway.

Since things change so quickly when it comes to buying a computer, it helps to do some research. Check the consumer magazines, but also talk with friends who have computers. Ask them:

- What do they do with their computer and what software do they use to do it?
- What feature(s) do they use the most and couldn't live without?
- What feature(s) do they wish their computer had?
- What is their opinion of the technical support of the brand they bought?
- Where did they buy their computer?

When you are ready to buy, visit numerous locations where computers are sold and carefully compare prices. Plan to spend some time with the salespeople and get your questions answered. If you are a complete neophyte to the computer world, offer to treat a techno-literate friend to lunch if he or she will spend most of the day with you talking the computer talk with the salespeople.

Software

Software is what allows you to do things on your computer. There is word processing software, graphics software, accounting software, spreadsheet software, and on and on—the amount of software available is mind-boggling. However, your computer will likely come with a basic software package (or "suite" of word processing, spreadsheet, and other software), and its suitability for your needs is something to consider as you price computers. For instance, some hardware manufacturers affiliated with Microsoft offer the Microsoft Works or Microsoft Office package, while others preload with the Lotus Smart Suite. This "bundled" software provides the basics, enabling you to go home with your new computer, plug it in, and type a letter—or maybe much more, depending on the package. Your computer might also come preloaded with Quicken, Microsoft Money, or other personal financial software in the mix.

Software

Not only are there myriad software choices available for small businesses, but there are different versions of the same software. *Microsoft Office* comes in several configurations, depending on the sophistication of your needs. So does QuickBooks, a popular and useful small business accounting software package. When you're making your choices, think "small business" and you'll likely steer yourself in the right direction.

Most of these are fine programs; if you ask around for recommendations you will get as many conflicting opinions as there are programs. It boils down to personal preference. If you've used one or the other predominately in your previous work life, then you may lean toward that program because of its familiarity. But be careful of locking yourself into a specific hardware package because it comes with the software package you want—you can buy the software package separately and install it on your chosen computer for a relatively small cost.

Photocopier

A photocopier can be a convenient item to have in your home office, especially if you need to do a lot of short copying projects during the course of a day. But if you have access to a good photocopy shop you might want to postpone this purchase. A good quality photocopier is fairly high on the price scale—as much as $1,000—and even the best models are notorious for needing regular maintenance and repairs. For one or two pages, you can use the copier function on your fax machine or even your scanner. For documents you are producing from your computer, you can make extra copies when you print it out.

Fax Machine

Even in these e-mail-laden days, and even though you will likely have a fax modem in your computer, a stand-alone fax machine comes in handy. Transmission is immediate and you'll probably use it quite often. Most midlevel fax machines (in the $200 range) have the ability to make crude photocopies, but you won't want to rely on this copy feature for more than one- or two-page documents, as the quality isn't as good as a photocopier.

Keep On Negotiating!

When you first sign up for a new or second phone line, you'll quickly be deluged by calls from rival long-distance providers with offers and incentives to switch. While it's tempting to make your decision and then stick with it, it just might pay to renegotiate your long-distance service plan every so often. After establishing service for six months, call a few other providers and see if you can do better. There are so many competing plans—even individual providers have multiple plans and offers—that it pays to ask for something better. As long as the long-distance market stays competitive, you're likely to find a better deal.

Buy a machine that has a decent amount of paper capacity—200 sheets seems average. Be sure the model you choose has a good supply of memory so that if the paper runs out, it will store incoming faxes and print them when you restock the paper tray. And, like the speed-dial feature of your phone, you will want to be able to program in some frequently used fax numbers on your fax machine.

Phone and Internet Services

Phone

What the phone system can do these days is amazing. It is worthwhile to spend some time talking with your local phone company to assess the services they offer and what you may need for your home business. But be careful, they'll try to sell you whatever service they can and you may incur monthly charges for things you don't use. Phone bills tend to be so complex these days that you might not be able to tell what you're paying for.

Though it might be tempting to save money by using the phone number you already have, you should definitely consider getting a separate line to be used exclusively for your business. The cost is not outrageous, it's more convenient, allows you to separate your home and business lives, and—most important—makes it easier for your customers. Factor in dial-up Internet use and one additional line is the least you'll want to consider.

Based on your business, assess the types of calls you'll be making. Will they be mostly local? If so, don't buy all sorts of monthly fee-based long-distance call packages—you'll be spending money on a service you don't use. If most of your calls will be long distance, will they be in-state or national? Most phone services offer in-state packages in which you get a certain number of hours of calling time each month for a set price.

Many phone services are quite helpful to a small business and are worth the added monthly charges. Any one or more of the following services could make life easier for you.

Package Deals

Are you convinced that you can't run your home business without being constantly in touch? Need not just a few extra phone lines, but a cell phone, beeper, unlimited Internet access, and more? Review with your phone company what services they provide—they may come up with a package deal. Or your cell phone provider may be able to provide beeper service as well. Don't let yourself be sold on something you don't need, but if you've decided you need it, let providers know so you can work to get the best deal.

Shop Around

Maxine, who runs a small publishing business, was thrilled when she got a few international clients, but she was less thrilled when she saw her phone bills. So she shopped around for long-distance providers and found a better company with an international calling plan that cut her monthly bill almost in half.

- **Call Waiting.** When you're talking on the phone, call waiting will beep you when there is an incoming call. You can choose to ignore the beep, which is difficult, or you can press the receiver button to put your current call on hold and answer the other call; you can use your receiver button to toggle back and forth between calls depending on what you decide. If you have only one line, call waiting is a significant business tool, but it can be annoying to your customer. Consider other options, such as having a second line, forwarding your call to another phone that has an answering machine, or getting the phone service's voice-mail system instead.

- **Call Forwarding.** This feature reroutes an incoming call to another line if you are on the line that the call comes in on. You can use this to forward an incoming call to your home phone when your business line is busy—which may be particularly helpful if you use your business line for the Internet. But be aware that you may not be making the best business impression if this means that your five-year-old may answer the call. You can also use call forwarding to a cell phone if you are on the road a lot, or to another line in another location if you, for instance, spend every Tuesday working from your elderly mother's home. This feature can usually be turned on and off at will, and the line you forward to is selected on an as-needed basis. There is, of course, a monthly charge whether you use it or not.

- **Additional Lines.** A second or even third line could be necessary if you have more than one person working from your home office. You may want to have a number that you don't hand out to other people. You can use that line strictly for outgoing calls to keep the number that is on your business card free for incoming calls.

- **Distinctive Ring.** If you decide to have a fax machine, distinctive ring is almost a necessity. This feature is cheap, around $3 a month, and allows you to have a separate dedicated phone number to hand out as your fax number. Then when a fax comes in, the ring will allow you to distinguish

it from a voice call. This has three distinct advantages: 1) people won't have to call you first to tell you they are sending you a fax, which many times defeats the purpose of the fax; 2) you won't answer the phone only to hear the screech of an incoming fax in your ear; 3) distinctive ring with a separate fax number avoids interference with your answering machine.

- **Voice-Mail.** If your phone company offers voice-mail in your area, it is very much worth considering. It is the best way not to miss calls, and you can leave a message you record yourself. Some businesses may benefit from an actual answering service, but there's nothing more annoying than to have a person answer the phone and give your long explanation of why you're calling, only to hear, "I'm sorry, but this is only Ms. So-and-So's answering service." The last thing you want to do is irritate your customer from the first moment of contact!

Internet

If your business requires you to have a computer, you will want to be able to access the Internet. This is done through an Internet Service Provider, or ISP, which offer various access options, and will likely offer more in the future. Most common is dial-up access, so it's important when you choose an ISP to make sure it can be accessed with a local or toll-free phone number. Internet providers have sprung up in small towns where the big national providers—such as America Online (AOL)—don't always offer local calling access.

There is a monthly charge for Internet service, whether you are with AOL or a local provider. Don't add to it with a long-distance ISP number. The long-distance charge ticks along the entire time you are online just as if you were simply talking to Aunt Mary halfway across the country.

Find out from the ISP you're considering the speed of the service—is it only 28K, 56K, or V.90? There's no point spending the money on a fast modem if your ISP isn't yet offering service to match.

Does My Computer Come with Internet Access?

Most over-the-counter computers will come with one or more software packages installed from AOL, Compuserve, or one of a host of other Internet Service Providers. With a click of your mouse you can dial in, sign up, and be on your way. While this is convenient, it's not always the cheapest or best service. And you're certainly not required to use one of the pre-installed ISPs. Check your local options, and find what will be best for your needs.

Providers like AOL offer bells and whistles that the local providers don't, but this is a case where you should measure the services compared to what you need and will use. What good are bells and whistles if you never ring them?

Local providers often also offer Web site development as part of the package, a good thing if you plan to have a Web site for your business. Again, ask friends what they like and don't like about their Internet provider.

When you pick an ISP, you will set up an account. The larger providers will automatically charge a credit card; local providers often send a bill electronically via e-mail. You'll have a choice from several plans—from $10 a month or so for limited use, to $20 or more a month for unlimited use, to more for hosting Web sites.

Your ISP will supply you with an Internet browser and connection software, which will have to be installed on your computer (unless it's already there). Then it's just a matter of connecting and you're on the Net!

Consider Cable

Many cable television companies also offer Internet access via the coaxial cable already connected to your home. Given that it is relatively fast, won't tie up a phone line, and may be inexpensive, it's worth checking with the cable company about availability in your area.

For more information on this topic, visit our Web site at businesstown.com

CHAPTER TEN

Buying a Business

When it comes to owning and operating a home business, the thoughts that come to mind often don't include buying a business. It somehow seems more like an option for storefront or other kinds of small retail or service businesses.

But in many ways, a home-based business is like any other small business. A service or product is provided to customers in exchange for payment. A home-based business will need a reputation (goodwill), a customer base, and possibly, inventory. Sometimes it's easier, faster, or more economical to buy those necessary aspects of a business rather than building them from scratch.

Why Buy a Business?

There are four good reasons to consider buying a business to operate out of your home: location, time, money, and competition or market share. If an ongoing business has an ideal location, can save you time, save you money, eliminate competition or provide market share, it may be worth paying for.

Location

Does your home-based retail business require specific zoning? Many zoning ordinances prohibit or limit retail operations in residential zones. If you are determined to operate a home-based retail business, you may have to consider moving. And as long as you're moving, you may find a good location that has not only the right building, housing, road access, parking, and so forth, but also has just the kind of business you want to run. If the owner is selling, and the price and other considerations are right, buying the entire business may be advantageous.

Let's say you've always wanted to run a kennel for dogs, cats, and other pets. You enjoy animals, it's a business that appeals to your stay-at-home personality, and you already know of many potential customers who know you and would trust you with their family pets while on vacation. But your current home isn't set up for a kennel, and

you're convinced that the neighbors would object strongly to the variances you would need to establish such a business there. You start looking around for a better property and find one: an established kennel not far away whose owners are ready to retire to Florida. If the location is perfect (remember, zoning variances go with the property, not the owners, so an established kennel is likely grandfathered), the kennel has a good reputation and a good customer base, it may be worth buying not only the property but all of the assets of the business.

Time and Money

No matter what kind of home business you want to start, it will take you some time to establish the business and create a customer base. If an established business of the same type exists with 250 loyal customers, for example, how long might it take you to reach that same level? One year? Five years? And during that time when your business is growing, will you be profitable? If not, how much will you have to invest to stay in business? Would it cost more or less to buy the already established business? Buying a business might yield a profitable operation virtually overnight for no more investment than might be required of a start-up.

Competition or Market Share

American business is based on the concept of competition. If you can beat the other businessperson's quality, customer service, or price, you can earn your share of available customers. But sometimes a competing business is so well established, and the size of the market so fixed, that there may not be room for more than one business providing a specific product or service. For example, if you have your heart set on running an automotive detailing home business, the area you live in is small, and there are already two automotive detailers who've been in business for years, then you'll be facing some stiff competition attempting to start a third in the same area. But you might find it possible to buy out one of the two existing businesses. If the price, among other things, is right, then buying might be the best choice.

Is It Fair to Look and Run?

There are plenty of stories of businesspeople who express an interest in a business, make an offer that is accepted, look through the books of the business for sale, then back away and start their own competing business.

Sound unfair? It's certainly not ethical, and if it could be proven that the prospective buyer never had any intention of buying the business but only wanted to sneak a peak at their future competitor's books, it would probably be actionable.

With a home-based business, your reputation is everything. Your long-term interests are best served by always conducting business in an ethical manner.

What You Can Buy

In an ideal world, once you plunk down an agreed-upon price for an ongoing business, you start running the business the next day and enjoy the profits, which will be high enough to pay off the price you paid in a reasonable time. Of course, it's rarely that easy.

You can buy everything involved in a business or only parts of it, assuming that the seller is agreeable to your proposal. Often business buyers will purchase only the assets of a business, not the accounts payable and receivable.

Real Estate

For some home-based businesses, you may be buying a home that includes a business. A country store, auto repair shop, or kennel might include buildings and a location that are specifically geared toward the business.

Equipment and Inventory

Along with real estate—or separate from it—you may be buying certain capital equipment involved in the business. Freezers and display cases, or hydraulic lifts and tools, cash registers, and so on might be included in the purchase price of a business.

Inventory—parts, items purchased for resale but not yet sold, and supplies—may also be part of the purchase price.

Goodwill

One of the most difficult things to put a price on is the goodwill associated with a business. If the dog kennel you're contemplating purchase of has been established for years, is well regarded by pet owners everywhere, has established good credit among vendors, and generally has an excellent reputation for cleanliness, reliability, and fine service, then that business has built up considerable goodwill over the years. That reputation is worth something. After all, how long would it take you to build that same reputation as a start-up?

Does the Business Include the House?

Although you may be buying a home business, you don't have to buy the home that houses it. In fact, many businesses are sold independent of the real estate that houses them.

Let's consider an example. Say you're handy with a computer, you've recently taken a number of graphic design and layout courses at the local college, and you're ready to start your own home-based newsletter business. In the midst of your market research, you learn that there's another, similar business, DesignWrite, operated by someone with similar skills who lives only a few miles away. DesignWrite has been in business for five years, and the owner/operator has dozens of regular clients and billings of $50,000 annually. It's exactly the kind of business you hope to build yourself over the next few years.

As you continue your research, you learn from one of DesignWrite's current customers that the owner is growing tired of the business. You contact the owner, and after negotiation, make an offer that's accepted. After due diligence, you are the proud new owner of the DesignWrite name, the client list along with ongoing contracts, the business phone number, the computer equipment, computer files of past newsletters, and so forth.

Since most customers never visited DesignWrite in person, and the business doesn't require any special facilities, it can be easily moved to your home. With a change of address form at the post office and arrangements through the phone company, all incoming communication will be forwarded to your address—and you're all set!

A Few Things to Watch For

Before you clean out your bank account to buy a small business, you'll want to do a thorough review of everything involved in that business—known as performing "due diligence." You'll want an accountant familiar with this kind of business to review the books, you'll want to inspect all inventory and capital equipment that is part of the sale, and you'll want to get a sense of customer loyalty.

Hidden Debts

If the purchase price includes inventory or equipment, is it all paid for? Make sure that liens are listed and bills are paid (or outstanding balance due is noted) as you finalize the purchase price. You don't want to pay $1,000 for existing pet supplies only to find out too late that the previous owner of the business never paid for them.

Overstated Earnings

You'll want your accountant to verify income statements, expenses, etc., to make sure that the previous owner is really generating the revenue and profits that are on the books. Even large, publicly traded corporations have been caught booking sales that haven't yet occurred in order to make the bottom line look good to prospective investors or buyers.

A craft business, for example, might have any number of items out on consignment, in which other retailers have agreed to take inventory and pay for it only when the product sells. If the business owner enters those figures as sales rather than inventory on consignment, a new owner might get a nasty surprise when he or she tries to collect receivables from those retail outlets, which will simply return the inventory.

Receivables

Business purchases often do not include receivables. When you buy a business, it's hard to know exactly what the previous owner said or didn't say to a customer regarding payment. When, as the new owner, you try to collect an outstanding balance, you might hear that "Joe promised me he'd give me a discount because the last shipment was no good," or "I paid that in cash to Joe, didn't he tell you?" Given that these are now your customers, you've left yourself in a touchy situation—you don't know what was said or not said, who's telling the truth, and you want to maintain an ongoing, profitable relationship with the customer.

That said, there is inevitably some confusion as a new owner takes over, and it's helpful to minimize that confusion for the customers. If you don't take on receivables, you're essentially asking longtime customers to open a new account with you, the new owner. This might be just the interruption the customer needs to look around for a new supplier of your product or service.

In the end, if during due diligence you determine that there are considerable oddities regarding the receivables and some questions about customer loyalty, you might decide to back off.

Financing the Purchase

Financing the purchase of an ongoing business may be easier than financing a start-up. Where banks will be leery of lending money to someone with little more than a pro forma income statement and a gleam in his eye, an established business with a proven track record of revenues and profits may well be worth the risk for a loan officer. You, as the prospective buyer (or your accountant) and the bank will want to examine the books closely to make sure the business can carry the debt of the purchase.

For example, a small home-based business might be for sale for $50,000. You have $10,000 in cash, but you need to finance the balance of the purchase price. It's a service business with no inventory—for the past three years the owner has netted $30,000 after expenses and before taxes. The bank is willing to lend you

Get a Noncompete Clause

Most business sales include a noncompete clause, in which the previous owner is not permitted to operate a similar business within the same market for a period of time—usually several years. You don't want to buy a business, only to have the previous owner turn around and open up a new shop catering to the same customers. A noncompete will help protect you from this possibility.

Get Help!

There are many hazards to watch out for in buying a business. The best advice if you're seriously considering buying a business is to get a lawyer who specializes in business acquisitions. You'll also need an accountant to examine the books of the business during due diligence.

Ask other businesspeople who've bought or sold businesses for recommendations. The local Chamber of Commerce or Small Business Development Center (SBDC) can also usually point you in the direction of established pros familiar with business acquisitions.

Although legal and financial experts cost money—and it's especially hard to think about paying them if you end up backing away from the potential business purchase—they are your insurance. Don't skimp on professional advice when it comes to buying a business.

the $40,000, unsecured, on a five-year note at 10%. That means your monthly loan payments will be around $850, or $10,200 annually, leaving a net of just under $20,000 before taxes. If you have personal expenses of more than $20,000, no other source of income, and don't believe you can increase the revenues of the business, your business may not be able to carry the debt load for that five-year period.

Another way to consider financing the purchase of the business is to have the owner hold the note and for all or part of the purchase price to depend on the financial performance of the business. After an initial down payment, if the business does well, reaches certain goals, then the seller gets a percentage of the profits. If it doesn't do as well, the payment is less.

For more information on this topic, visit our Web site at businesstown.com

CHAPTER ELEVEN

Legal Issues

The Corporate Veil

One reason that some entrepreneurs incorporate is to minimize their liability in case something goes wrong. By incorporating, you create a separate business entity from yourself, and as a stockholder your risk could be limited to the amount you have invested in the corporation.

Yet, it doesn't always work that way, and there are cases in which the courts have "pierced the corporate veil" and held individuals liable for things the corporation has done or let happen. This could happen, for example, if you—a corporate officer— personally provided a product or service, such as building a jungle gym for children. If the jungle gym

(continued on next page)

When it comes to legal issues, it's what you don't know that will probably hurt you. Consequently, there are various times during your home business venture when you would be wise to consult a lawyer before proceeding.

Which is not to say that you *must* use lawyers. Most common legal agreements are available as generic forms or as part of a software package. As long as you don't run up against a particularly difficult situation, you may never need more professional legal advice.

Then again, it would be a shame to find yourself in a legal bind that could have been easily avoided had you consulted a knowledgeable lawyer. It's a good bet that the upfront cost of consulting a lawyer will be far less than hiring one to extricate you from a legal conflict after the fact.

Think of a lawyer as a tool you can use to minimize your risk in business. Are you comfortable risking your entire business on your own knowledge of contracts, liability, real estate, taxes, and estate planning? If so, then you may never cross the threshold of a law office (which is not to say you won't end up in court!). More likely, you are comfortable with some risk (registering a sole proprietorship on your own), but recognize the wisdom of getting help when things get more complicated (taking on a partner in your business or hiring employees).

When You Need a Lawyer

Consider consulting a lawyer when you first set up your business. Sole proprietorships, the most common type of home-based business, are simple enough to register and start. But bringing a firm or lawyer onboard right from the beginning can help steer you straight and have a clear understanding of your business as the legal issues grow more complex.

Certainly if you're starting a corporation, professional legal advice is a good idea. A lawyer with experience can guide you through the process, avoiding pitfalls that may haunt you later on.

If you're starting a partnership, a lawyer is almost a must. Most partnerships dissolve at some point—sometimes amicably, often in

conflict. Partners should create a partnership agreement that includes an exit strategy, detailing the when and how each partner can bow out of the business or buy out the other. For that, you and your partner should consult a lawyer, and iron out any disagreements ahead of time. In fact, your lawyer may recommend creating a corporation, with you and your partner officers of that corporation, to help shield you from liability stemming from actions of your partner.

If you are considering one of the work-at-home franchises offered by any number of companies across the country, have your own lawyer review all the contracts and paperwork. Be prepared to listen to your lawyer and step away from the franchise agreement if he or she suggests that the terms are too stringent.

Contracts

In business, you are likely to enter into any number of verbal and written contracts. Many home businesses operate on little more than handshake agreements between client and service provider—and that might be fine in a lot of instances. However, your lawyer can help you identify those times when a written contract is preferred and can help you make sure that the contract protects and serves your interests.

Intellectual Property Protection

Will you be applying for patents or copyrights? Will you be creating a product and then selling to others the right to use that product while you maintain ownership of it (such as software, writing, or graphic arts)? Will you be hiring independent contractors to provide your intellectual property as "work-for-hire"? You'd be wise to have a lawyer with experience in intellectual property review your contracts.

Equipment Leasing

Will you be taking on a long-term lease of equipment to be used in your business? Automobiles, trucks, construction equipment, computers, and food preparation equipment are often leased instead of

The Corporate Veil

(continued from previous page)

broke due to gross negligence on your part and caused serious injury, the corporation may not protect you.

In many cases, business owners fail to administrate the corporation properly, thus opening themselves to liability. If the owner treats the business like a sole proprietorship, the courts will treat it as a sole proprietorship, regardless of its legal structure.

In order to avoid these problems, work with a lawyer familiar with the establishment and administration of a corporation.

purchased. You'll want to consult your lawyer to make sure that the lease agreements have enough flexibility and protection for you and your business. A tax lawyer or consultant can help you work out whether a purchase or lease is better for your business financially.

Buying or Selling a Business

If you plan to sell your business or if you're contemplating buying an existing home-based business, find a lawyer who works frequently in this area. Buying or selling a business can get complicated, especially if there's a conflict or misunderstanding between buyer and seller—you'll want to have your lawyer at your side from the beginning.

Real Estate

Do you have a tricky zoning situation to deal with in order to work from your home? A lawyer can help you sort through the zoning code and apply for a variance if necessary. Is there a complication regarding multiple owners of your home? If you're starting a business in a house owned by yourself, two sisters, and an aunt, what are your rights and responsibilities? A lawyer can help you avoid future conflict with your relatives.

Think of it this way: if you were buying or leasing a location for your business, you'd probably consult a lawyer. Legal considerations are no less important just because your business is in your home.

Taxes

Your law firm may have a tax specialist, lawyer, or accountant who can help you structure your business to minimize your taxes. The more taxes you pay, the more reason to get all the help you can. And, of course, if you run afoul of the IRS, your lawyer can help negotiate with them to come to a reasonable settlement.

Estate Planning

Will your business survive you? Will a daughter, son, or spouse take it on after you retire or pass away? If the business has value beyond your own involvement in it, you'll want to consult a lawyer

to organize the transition. What if you end up getting a divorce? What happens to the business? Prepare for the worst.

Collections and Bankruptcy

Does a major client owe you a lot of money? You might turn it over to a collection agency, or you might use the persuasive power of your attorney to help collect what you're owed. You also may face being a creditor in a business that is going or has gone bankrupt. Your lawyer can help you attempt to get at the front of the line when the assets are divided up.

Or, in a worst-case scenario, you may find yourself facing bankruptcy. A good lawyer might be able to keep you out of bankruptcy court by negotiating with your creditors. But if you do end up filing for bankruptcy, you'll want to find a legal specialist to help you keep what you can.

Filing a Suit

Taking action against another business or individual is expensive and time-consuming—certainly it will distract you from focusing on your core business. But there may come a time when you find it necessary to take a client or vendor to court to solve a conflict. In an ideal world, your lawyer will help you create contracts that will keep you out of court—but there can be times when that just isn't possible.

Picking a Lawyer

If you're going to spend money on legal advice, make sure you get the best advice you can afford. Law, like so many professions, has become highly specialized. It's unlikely you'll find one lawyer who can handle every possible legal need you might have. But you might find a law firm with a well-rounded group of attorneys who can help you in most instances.

Try to work with a firm that has experience representing others in your field. If you work with horses, you'll want someone who knows the liability issues. If you fix cars, you'll want someone who has expe-

Fees

Lawyers may charge a flat fee for a particular service (creating a will, filing for bankruptcy, etc.), and they may charge hourly for other matters. Ask what the hourly rate is. Expenses—such as long-distance phone calls, faxes, etc.—may be extra.

Most home businesses will not need to pay an attorney a monthly retainer, but will pay on an as-needed basis. In other cases, an attorney may take a case on a contingency basis, in which he or she keeps a percentage of the eventual settlement. If your business suffered greatly due to the improper action of a vendor, for example, you may be able to sue for damages and have an attorney take the case on contingency.

rience with other auto-related businesses and is perhaps familiar with regulations for proper disposal of chemicals and waste oil.

As a home-based business, you aren't likely to be a large client. Consequently, you may find it difficult to get the attention you want or need at a large, prestigious firm. On the other hand, having a large firm on your side can sometime intimidate the competition should you find yourself in a legal conflict. If your home business involves significant risk (building and selling wooden play equipment for children, installing underground fuel tanks), you'll want as much legal horsepower as you can afford.

More likely you'll find a small or medium-sized firm with reasonable business experience that is willing to call in help when a specialist is needed. Or it might be a one-lawyer shop that can handle most of your garden-variety needs but knows when to call in the cavalry for special situations. Above all, you want someone you trust—someone whose advice you'll listen to. You want someone who will advise you and then let you make your own decision.

Ask other small businesspeople you know for recommendations. Ask the Chamber of Commerce. Ask your accountant, if you have one. Perhaps you have a personal lawyer who has a partner or knows someone else who specializes in business law.

Don't be afraid to interview several potential lawyers. When you sit down with your prospective lawyer, ask about his or her experience with business issues in general and your field in particular. How would this lawyer handle issues he or she had little or no experience with?

Clarify the fee structure. If you call to ask a simple question, for example, are you billed a minimum 15 minutes? Is there a flat fee for an initial consultation on a given legal matter? Ask for a ballpark estimate on a relatively simple matter—reading over a sample contract, for example—and compare it to quotes from other lawyers you speak with.

How big is the firm? What are the specialties of other lawyers in the firm? There are no dumb questions, and if the attorney makes you feel stupid for asking a question, find someone else. You want to work with someone who respects your desire to understand how things work.

Working with a Lawyer

A good lawyer-client relationship works because both parties take responsibility for making it work. You should be able to have your phone calls returned and not be surprised by any invoices sent your way, get good information, be kept up to date on ongoing matters, and get good advice from your lawyer. In exchange, you should be prepared to give straightforward information, pay your bills, and respect your attorney's time.

Here are some guidelines that will help you get value for your money in legal representation:

- Be honest. A lawyer can only help you if you tell the truth, even when you realize you may have done something the wrong way.
- Be early. Better to bring a legal issue to your lawyer's attention as soon as possible. It's better and cheaper to pay the lawyer to help you create a good contract as opposed to getting you out of a bad contract that you signed in ignorance.
- Be thrifty but not cheap. Good lawyers will help you save money on legal fees, but be willing to pay them what they're worth for the work they do.
- Be organized. If you have your paperwork and records in order, it will save time (and money).
- Do work yourself. You may be able to create an agreement or contract for your lawyer to review, rather than having him or her do it from scratch. The more work you do, especially in routine matters, the less you'll likely owe your lawyer.
- Work with the paralegal. A paralegal's hourly rate is less than a lawyer's. If the matter is routine, don't insist on sitting down with your lawyer; work with his or her paralegal.

Juris Prudent

It's what you don't know that could hurt you when it comes to the law. You may not need professional legal advice to set up your sole proprietorship and handle routine business operations, but you would be wise to find a lawyer you're comfortable with before you need one. When questions arise, be willing to pay for legal advice early on—it may save your business.

CHAPTER TWELVE

Taxes and the Home Business

The IRS Online

The IRS produces thousands of documents geared to helping you understand what to record, what to deduct, and what to pay. Most of these are now available on the Internet as well as in print. The online versions are to a certain extent searchable, which means that if you have a specific question, it might be easier to access the documents or specific answer by calling up *www.irs.ustreas.gov*. Printed versions of forms and publications can be acquired by calling 800-829-3676 (800-TAX-FORM).

Operating your own home business may help you escape an aggravating commute, time-wasting corporate meetings, and frustrating office politics, but you can't escape taxes. In fact, as a sole proprietor running your own business, you have more responsibility than ever for proper record keeping, accounting, filing of tax returns, and—yes, it hurts—payment of an assortment of taxes.

If you are currently an employee of a business, then you probably have income taxes (federal, state, and perhaps city) withheld from your regular paycheck, as well as your Social Security and Medicare (FICA). Your employer is required to pay FICA as well on your behalf, plus unemployment taxes (FUTA). These are reported on a W-2 form the employer gives you.

As a self-employed person (sole proprietor or partnership) you are not an employee. You will pay income tax on your net profit, and you will have to pay self-employment tax to cover Social Security and Medicare. What is sometimes a shocker for the first-time self-employed is that you must pay about 15.3% on your earnings (12.4% of up to $65,400 for Social Security and 2.9% of all net profit for Medicare). This is double what you might be used to as an employee, since as a sole proprietor you're now paying the employer's share of Social Security as well as your own.

There are other potential taxes as well, of course. Collecting and paying sales tax is necessary for many businesses. Rooms and meals tax are sometimes required. New Hampshire has, for example, a business profits tax. The wonderful news about our country's many levels of government is that they all want revenue. Check with your local governments about specifics. Though state and local taxes vary, they generally use your federal tax return to determine your income (or loss) for a given tax year.

Working with the IRS

The easiest way to stay out of tax trouble is to do things the way the IRS suggests. Granted, the Internal Revenue Service is a large bureaucracy, and it's not uncommon to get different answers for the same question when you contact them. Certainly it can be a challenge to puzzle through all the various instructions for each form you need to file.

However, there are employees of the IRS whose job it is to help you get it right. The IRS routinely presents small business tax workshops for current and prospective small business owners as part of the Small Business Tax Education Program (STEP). These are free sessions in which the basics of small business taxation are discussed, with plenty of time for specific questions. Even if you plan on working with an accountant, these workshops can be helpful to understand how the IRS approaches issues like business expenses.

Among the many documents put out by the IRS is the *Tax Guide for Small Business* (Publication 334). This is for those who file Schedule C or Schedule C-EZ. As a home business sole proprietor, you will pick one of those two schedules to attach to your Form 1040. This tax guide takes you step-by-step through determining your tax year, accounting method, how to figure cost of goods sold and gross profit, business expenses, and even a sample small business tax return.

Another helpful document put out by the IRS is the *Small Business Tax Workshop Workbook* (Publication 1066). Used in the above-mentioned tax workshops, this booklet is a workbook—it takes the reader through various examples and case studies relevant to small business taxes, providing helpful examples of what the sometimes confusing IRS instructions really mean.

Federal Taxes

As a sole proprietor, you pay income tax on your net profits. In simple terms, you add up your revenue, subtract all your expenses, and pay a tax on what's left over. Of course, you still may have personal deductions, such as mortgage interest, that are listed on Schedule A.

You'll still be filing an individual tax return via Form 1040. However, as a sole proprietor you'll be filing Schedule C or Schedule C-EZ: Profit or Loss from Business. In doing so, you'll have to state your accounting method, show your gross receipts, cost of goods, and figure your gross income, then itemize and subtract your business expenses. Your income may be cash, checks, and charges from individuals, or you may be working as an independent contractor for other businesses, who then issue you a Form 1099-MISC at the end of the year.

Be Prepared

If your home business is relatively simple and you're used to filing your own tax returns, then you won't have too much difficulty following the directions for Schedule C or C-EZ. This is especially true if you're a good record keeper.

But if you find the tax return instructions bewildering, don't hesitate to hire a tax preparer. These professionals know the rules—and indeed many run home businesses themselves—and if you're organized in your record keeping, they may be able to save you money by identifying deductions you didn't consider. And remember, the cost of tax preparation is tax deductible.

AM I AN INDEPENDENT CONTRACTOR?

Relatively strict IRS guidelines determine who is an employee and who is an independent contractor. As a home-based businessperson doing work for other businesses on a contract basis, you presumably are an independent contractor. But the following should be true about the relationship between you and your client:

	Yes	No
I determine how, when, or where to do the work.		
I determine what to charge for the work.		
I determine what tools or equipment to use.		
I determine what assistants to hire to help with the work.		
I determine where to purchase supplies.		
I have significant investment in my business.		
I am not reimbursed for all my business expenses.		
I have an opportunity to make money or lose money in the venture.		
I do not receive employee benefits from my clients.		

And herein lies the challenge for home-based businesses: defining and tracking those expenses tied to the business while staying within IRS guidelines.

Estimated Tax

As a self-employed person, no employer is withholding money from your paycheck in anticipation of taxes due the following April 15. Consequently, you may have to make estimated tax payments on

your own. (See IRS Publication 505: *Estimated Tax Payments*, for more specifics.)

In general, if you expect to owe at least $1,000 in federal taxes (including income tax and self-employment tax), you'll need to make estimated tax payments. These payments are due quarterly, on April 15, June 15, September 15, and January 15. Form 1040-ES includes an Estimated Tax Worksheet to use to figure out how much tax you're likely to owe and includes payment vouchers for the quarterly payments. You must pay one-fourth of the estimated amount due each quarter. Failure to pay your estimated tax could lead to a penalty.

Estimated taxes may seem challenging the first year, since you're just not sure what your profits are likely to be. And, of course, money paid in estimated taxes to the IRS isn't earning interest or helping you with your cash flow. But you should try to estimate as accurately as possible—you don't want to end up unprepared for a huge tax bill that you can't pay when April 15 rolls around.

Business Income

In general, all the money you receive from your business is considered income. Most will be in the form of cash, check, or charges. But if you trade or barter services with someone, you must consider the fair market value of that service as income as well.

For a home-based service business, this is relatively straightforward. You perform a service and charge for it. Your receipts are your business income.

Of course, many businesses make or buy goods for resale and will deduct the cost of goods sold from gross income to determine gross profit. In order to do so, however, the IRS requires you to track your inventory of goods. Inventory would include merchandise, raw materials, work in progress, finished products, and any supplies that physically become part of the item for sale (packaging, for example). You must be able to identify and value your inventory items and be able to know the

Tax Software

While a generic tax software program isn't a replacement for specific tax advice from a qualified tax preparer, several good software packages are available that will help you file your taxes. These programs are relatively inexpensive ($15–$50), include every IRS form you might require, often include additional online support, and are designed to work with your accounting software, such as QuickBooks or Microsoft Excel. Programs such as Kiplinger TaxCut and TurboTax also streamline electronic filing, should you prefer to file your tax return via modem. Federal and state versions are available.

The programs can usually be used either by a question and answer format or you can go directly to the forms and fill in the blanks, as you would on paper.

value of that inventory at the beginning of each tax year. And, if you do maintain inventories, the IRS requires you to use the accrual method of accounting.

Business Expenses

Schedule C makes it clear what are considered business expenses in most cases. The list will echo your own record keeping. Advertising, bad debt, commissions, insurance, repairs and maintenance, utilities—all expenses directly related to the business—get subtracted from your income revenue.

For home-based businesses, these expenses are slightly more complicated since the place of business and various capital assets used in the business are often used for personal as well as business purposes. Not only do you use some percentage of your home for the business, you use a percentage of heat, electricity, perhaps even telephone expenses for both. You are likely to use your vehicle for both personal and business reasons.

When calculating business expenses and the percentage used for personal versus business use, try to be reasonable. In most cases, the IRS will be reasonable too. They understand, for example, that you might stop for a gallon of milk on the way home from a business appointment. But they are likely to demand an explanation if you write off the entire cost of a family trip to Disney World on the premise that you stopped in to say hello to a business acquaintance for an hour. They accept that you may need a subscription to a trade publication, but they don't expect you to deduct the cost of your local general circulation newspaper as a business expense.

Business Use of the Home

A lot has been written about the "home office deduction." It's been considered a trigger for potential IRA audits, and recent changes in the tax code clarify what you can and cannot deduct.

Most home-based businesses will not have a problem with taking a deduction for business use of the home because they usually meet the key requirements:

- The relevant part of the home is used *exclusively* and *regularly* for the business.
- The home is the principal place of business.
- The home is where you meet or deal with customers or clients in the normal course of business.

According to the IRS, a "home" can mean a house, apartment, condo, and, in certain situations, even a boat. It also means other buildings on your property, like a barn, detached garage, or greenhouse.

For an expense to be deductible, it must be related to the business. Some expenses may be indirectly related to the business and are therefore partially deductible. For example:

- If you paint the office of your home business, you can deduct that expense in full.
- If you repair the roof on your house in which you have an office for your home business, you may only deduct an appropriate percentage of the expense.

You can use a couple different formulas to determine the percentage of your home that is used for business. One is the area method. Take the area of your home used for business and divide it by the total area of your home. If your home is 1,000 square feet and your home business is in one room measuring 10′ x 10′ (100 square feet), then the business-use percentage is 100 divided by 1,000, or 10%.

You can also use the "number of rooms" method. If the rooms in your house are all about the same size, divide the number used for business by the total number of rooms. For example, if you live in an eight-room house and use two rooms exclusively for a home business, your business-use percentage is 2 ÷ 8, or 25%.

These percentages are then used to calculate how much of your indirect expenses, such as utilities, real estate taxes, mortgage interest, insurance premiums, and depreciation, can be deducted as business expenses.

As you can see, having a space dedicated exclusively to your home business is a big advantage when it comes to figuring your expenses at tax time. And if the IRS cares to check up on you, it's easy to show them how you calculated the business use of your home. Use Form 8829: Expenses for Business Use of Your Home, to calculate your deduction.

Gross Income Limit

Your ability to deduct expenses related to the business use of your home is limited by your gross income. In general, you can't create or increase a net loss by deducting depreciation, for example. But you can carry forward those deductions to another tax year. This may not be an issue for a full-time home-based business, but may pop up for a hobby or part-time business. See *Business Use of Your Home* (IRS Publication 587) for more specifics.

Depreciation

Some business assets lose value over time. Computers and vehicles are common examples, but any machinery or other property used in the business that lasts more than a year will depreciate. Inventory for resale is not depreciable, but copyrights and patents are. In general, the IRS makes it possible to deduct depreciation over a determined life of the asset, though you are not necessarily required to do so. There are some assets, like computers, that can be deducted as direct expenses in the year of purchase. This might be an advantage if you had a particularly good revenue year, for example.

Self-Employment Tax

As noted previously, not only do you pay income tax on your net profits, but you also must pay self-employment tax. You'll figure your self-employment tax using Schedule SE, and generally if you make more than $400 you have to pay the tax. There is a short form and a long form, though most will be able to use the short form. If you have more than one business (and thus more than one Schedule C or C-EZ) you add up all your self-employment profits and fill out one Schedule SE.

Record Keeping

Filing a tax return is rarely a pleasant activity, but it can be made immeasurably easier if you maintain good records. For the most part, the IRS takes your word that the financial figures you report are accurate. But they reserve the right to make you prove it. Good records do exactly that.

First and foremost, separate your business finances from your personal finances. Set up a separate checking account; don't pay personal expenses with it.

Keep copies of original documents such as invoices, bills and receipts, all of which should show the date, dollar amount, and description of the transaction. If there is a transaction without a receipt, make a record of it yourself.

Because you may want to depreciate certain assets, keep particularly good records of what the IRS calls "listed property." This includes vehicles, computers, video and stereo equipment, and cell phones. Make sure to keep receipts for all expenditures (purchase, repair, upgrades) related to them. If you use them for both business and personal reasons, keep a log in which you note the date, business purpose, and amount of business use of each item. This is particularly important for business use of your personal car or truck.

There are two ways to figure your vehicle expenses. You can use the standard mileage deduction of 31.5 cents per mile (for business-use mileage only, of course), or you can tally up actual expenses. Actual expenses allowed include gas and oil, insurance, repairs, tires, and lease payments. You can then deduct the business-use percentage of those actual costs.

Those Precious Receipts!

Keep all your receipts for travel, transportation, entertainment, and gift expenses, and use a log to record the business purpose of the expense. If you wait six months to sort through a huge stack of receipts, it's easy to forget what they're for. You can deduct up to $25 per person for each business gift and 50 percent of meals and entertainment.

PERIOD OF LIMITATIONS	
IN THE FOLLOWING SITUATIONS,	THE PERIOD OF LIMITATIONS IS:
1. You owe additional tax and situations (2), (3), and (4) below do not apply to you.	3 years
2. You do not report income that you should report, and it is more than 25% of the gross income shown on your return.	6 years
3. You file a fraudulent income tax return.	No limit
4. You do not file a return.	No limit
5. You file a claim for credit or refund after you file your return.*	Later of: 3 years or years after tax is paid
6. Your claim is due to a bad debt deduction.	7 years
7. Your claim is due to a loss from worthless securities.	7 years

*Individuals file a claim for credit or refund on Form 1040X.

Do You Have to Make Money?

You won't be alone if at the end of the year, upon tallying up your revenue and your expenses, you find yourself using the proverbial red ink to calculate your Net Operating Loss, or NOL. While we all want to be successful, an NOL has some advantages.

An NOL can be carried forward or back to other tax years. For example, if your first year as a home-based business ends in a loss, you can use that NOL to offset profits in future years or go back three years and use it to offset past income.

But what if you just keep on losing money? Will the IRS buy the idea that you can stay in business, even though you show an NOL every year?

No, they won't. In general, if you make a profit three years out of every five, you're OK. Otherwise, it comes down to your motives. The IRS will look at how you run your business, whether

you are working at it full-time and living off it, and whether or not you make obvious attempts to improve its profitability.

Taxes and Partnerships

Partnerships are similar to sole proprietorships when it comes to taxes—the business itself doesn't pay taxes, only the partners pay taxes on the net profits from the business. However, you will need to fill out Form 1065, which reports the income or loss of the partnership. Each partner's share of that income or loss is then reported to him or her on Schedule K-1. In general, a partnership agreement will determine how the distributions are to be divided among the partners. If there is no agreement, then it is determined by the interest each partner holds in the business.

It is then up to each partner to file his or her own 1040 and Schedule E. Each partner may have to pay estimated tax, and partners are usually limited in deducting losses to their interest in the business. (In other words, if the partnership is 50-50, then one partner can't take on 100 percent of the loss.) Except in the case of a limited partner, partners must also pay self-employment tax. For more specifics, see IRS Publication 541, *Partnerships*.

Taxes and Corporations

As described in Chapter 6, corporations are taxed differently than sole proprietorships or partnerships. Corporations exist as taxable entities in and of themselves. If you've set your business up as a corporation, you'll be looking at taxes from a very different viewpoint—the corporation will pay corporate income taxes on net profits via Form 1120, the corporate equivalent of an individual's Form 1040. Corporate tax rates range from 15 percent to 35 percent.

Corporations also differ from sole proprietorships and partnerships in that they pay the employers share of Social Security and Medicare.

How Long Do I Have to Keep My Records?

Normally, the IRS does not review tax returns after three years' time. Keep records relating to returns a minimum of three years and perhaps as long as seven years if you have claims from bad debt. You must keep employment records for four years and should keep any records relating to business assets for as long as you own the asset—and for at least three years after you dispose of it taxwise. For more specifics on tax record keeping, get a copy of Publication 583, *Starting a Business and Keeping Records*.

Of course, if you pay yourself as an employee of the corporation, you'll also have to file a Form 1040 and pay income tax on your salary. This double taxation is part of the reason small businesses stay away from incorporation.

- *S Corporations.* The S Corp (described in Chapter 6) provides some relief from double taxation, and functions in some ways like a partnership. Instead of the corporation being taxed on its net profits, those profits go to the shareholders, who then pay tax on the income. As with a partnership, Schedule K-1 goes to each shareholder, who then fills out his or her own individual return.
- *Limited Liability Companies.* LLCs can differ from state to state, but in general they work like partnerships, filing Form 1065 with a Schedule K-1 going to each owner.

Collecting and Reporting Sales Tax

Those home-based businesses that are selling merchandise will likely be required to pay a sales tax to the state. That sales tax is in turn collected from the customer at the time of sale.

It will be up to you, however, to keep a record and report taxable sales. Once you apply for the requisite resale tax number in your state, the state department of revenue will be looking for your report. Typically, it will be due quarterly.

If you travel out of state to consumer shows, you may be required to collect and pay sales tax on those sales to the host state. Check with the Department of Revenue in the state where you plan to do business.

Taxes and Employees

If your home business is hiring employees, then it must be growing—so we'll think of it as a good sign. But with employees comes plenty of paperwork, including tax obligations.

Withholding FIT

First off, as the employer you are responsible for withholding an appropriate portion of the employee's wages for income taxes. When you hire a new employee, he or she fills out a Form W-4 that claims the number of withholding allowances. You don't usually have to send the W-4 to the IRS. To determine the appropriate amount of federal income tax to withhold, you can use either the tables in IRS Publication 15, Circular E or a percentage basis, as described in Circular E.

Withholding FICA

As an employer, you must withhold Social Security and Medicare taxes from your employee's paycheck. Social Security is 6.2% up to $65,400, and Medicare is 1.45% of all wages.

Form 941

You must report employee compensation and taxes withheld, as well as your employer's share of FICA, on Form 941: Employer's Quarterly Federal Tax Return.

FUTA Tax

This is unemployment tax, and as an employer you must pay 6.2% of your employee's first $7,000 in earnings. Your state will also have unemployment tax, and the feds will give you credit for the state payment. The FUTA tax return is filed once a year on Form 940, or 940-EZ, and is due January 31 after the end of the reporting year.

Tax Deposits

If your total quarterly employment taxes are less than $500, then you don't need to deposit taxes using Form 8109: Federal Tax Deposit Coupon. (The IRS will automatically send you a supply of these forms when you apply for your Employer Identification Number (EIN) using Form SS-4.) Otherwise, assuming that your withholding taxes are less than $50,000 for the year, you'll need to deposit withheld taxes monthly, no later than the fifteenth of the following month.

Put Your Paperwork to Work for You!

Many who run small businesses often complain that our various levels of government stifle entrepreneurship by making it too difficult and too costly to do business given all the various taxes that must be paid and the paperwork that accompanies them. That may be true. But keeping good records and maintaining appropriate financials is a part of any well-run business—you use that information for more than just filing tax returns. Set up your system well, hire an accountant and/or tax preparer, and just consider paperwork a cost of doing business.

Forms W-2 and W-3

As if you didn't already have enough forms to worry about, you also need to complete Form W-2, which summarizes an employee's income and withholding for one year. Employees must receive their copy of the W-2 by January 31 of the following year. Then, you'll attach a copy of all your employees' W-2s to Form W-3 and send it to the Social Security Administration.

Taxes and Independent Contractors

Independent contractors are not employees; they work for themselves, performing services for you while not under your direct control. An independent contractor should provide you with a Social Security number (SSN) or employer identification number. Ask the independent contractor to sign a Form W-9 before beginning work.

If you pay one independent contractor more than $600, you must file Form 1099-MISC, which identifies the type of payment, the amount, who made the payment, who received it and the taxpayer identification number (SSN or EIN) of the recipient. The 1099-MISC goes to the IRS as well as to the independent contractor.

For more information on this topic, visit our Web site at businesstown.com

CHAPTER THIRTEEN

Insurance

When you bring a business into your home, your insurance requirements change. The nature of your liability changes. More strangers (customers) may be coming to your home (business) than ever before. Accidents happen. Some people might be quicker to sue a business than they would a private individual.

If you're of an entrepreneurial mind-set, you're comfortable with risk. This might make you consider keeping your insurance coverage at a minimum. But it's one thing to take a risk based on your belief in your own abilities as a businessperson, and quite another to bet on the unknown actions of others. You're trying to protect yourself against events that are beyond your control. While "going bare"—without insurance—might be a financial necessity in some kinds of businesses, in general you'll be wiser to take some basic precautions.

While there are many different kinds of business-related insurance (we'll get to that), there are several ways you can approach buying the insurance you need. Depending on the size and nature of your home business, you may be able to simply add endorsements to your current homeowners policy to cover your business assets and provide some basic liability insurance. For example, if you have little or no inventory and clients rarely visit you at your home office, upgrading your current homeowners policy may be all you need.

Insurance companies are also offering home-based business policies that include property and liability coverage as well as business interruption insurance, limited coverage for loss of valuable papers and records, accounts receivable, and off-site use of equipment. Small business owners policies are also available that offer broader coverage than a home-based business policy.

Finally, you may find that your needs are better met by buying coverage a la carte, picking and choosing specific policies to meet specific insurance needs for your business.

Property and Liability Insurance

You can, of course, buy insurance against almost anything, for a price. For businesses, and more specifically home-based businesses, you're going to be most concerned with property insurance and casualty (liability) insurance. You may want commercial auto insurance, too. Business interruption insurance and umbrella liability insurance may also be in order. If you have employees, you will need workers' compensation insurance. As part of your overall personal plan, you are also likely to consider health insurance, disability insurance, and life insurance.

Property Insurance

If you own your home, you almost certainly have some kind of property insurance. This protects your home, including the buildings and most of its contents, in case of fire and smoke damage, wind, possibly earthquake or flood, as well as burglary and vandalism.

Your current homeowners policy may provide you with some level of coverage for the loss or damage of property used in a home business. But it's more likely that that coverage is limited, that you'll want to increase it to cover the full replacement cost of equipment used in your business, as well as the cost of any improvements you've made specifically for the business.

If your business is located in a separate building on your home property, make sure that you have enough coverage to replace that building. You may want to make sure that any signage you have is covered. How about inventory?

Discuss the options with your insurance agent. Depending on your policy and the insurer, you may find that a few endorsements will cover your business assets. Or you may discover that based on your other insurance needs, a home business or small business policy is the better way to go.

Casualty (Liability) Insurance

This covers you against claims made by others against you for injuries or damages that happen on the premises or as a result of work you do or a product you sell. These claims might be for

The Claim Is in the Details

Insurance companies love steady customers, and reputable insurance carriers are happy to pay a claim if it is legitimate. But they also know that some customers are sometimes tempted to file fraudulent claims, so they make a point of investigating to find out what happened when claims are filed. If you're going to buy insurance, make sure to disclose fully the nature of your business. If you don't, then you're just wasting your money. You don't want to be denied compensation because you failed to mention the kiln you would be using to fire pottery in order to save a buck or two on your premium.

The Best Deal

Although you'll no doubt approach your current insurance agent regarding insurance for your home-based business, be sure to shop around as well. The insurance company you originally selected for homeowners insurance may not offer the best policies or rates for home business coverage, for example, so you may want to consider switching all of your coverage. If you know someone who is in the same kind of business, ask him about his agent—it's always helpful to work with someone who is already familiar with the specifics of your industry. Check with the trade association for your kind of business to see if it offers insurance. Or simply call some insurance companies or agents—once you get a few quotes, you'll have a much better sense of what the going rate is for the insurance you need.

property damage (a customer's car is damaged while on your property), personal injury (a customer slips and falls while on your property), product-related injury (a customer is punctured by a nail from the birdhouse you built and sold her).

Once again, your homeowners policy includes some liability insurance. But it likely does not include coverage for liability claims made as a result of business you conduct on your property, and you will need to have a business liability policy.

Business Interruption Insurance

As part of your business insurance package, you may want to consider insuring your economic losses should something happen to close down the business. Your property insurance may cover rebuilding in case of fire, but what about the income you're losing while you rebuild? If the business insurance policy you're considering does not include this, ask your insurer how much it would cost to add it—it may be a small price to pay for the survival of your business in case of future catastrophe.

Related to this is overhead insurance. While disability insurance and or business interruption insurance may cover income, overhead insurance covers rent, salaries, utilities, insurance premiums, and interest payments related to the business in the case of sickness or accident.

Umbrella Liability Insurance

This is added coverage against catastrophic losses or claims. In today's "sue first, ask questions later" world, you could well be facing a liability claim in the millions. An umbrella policy will upgrade your basic auto, homeowners, or business insurance policies to cover such situations.

Industry-Specific Insurance

Some home-based businesses may have special needs—lawyers and doctors, even beauticians may need specific professional liability insurance (malpractice insurance). Horse training or boarding facilities often require specific insurance coverage. Check with the trade organization associated with your business for special insurance needs.

Auto Insurance

Auto insurance includes both property coverage (damage to or theft of your vehicle) and liability coverage (claims against you related to the use of your vehicle). A certain amount of business use of your vehicle may be covered under your current policy. But if your home business will be making extensive use of your car, truck, or van, you will want to discuss your policy and its limits with your insurance carrier. There may be state-mandated minimums of liability coverage for commercial use. Your needs may change considerably if the vehicle is registered in the business's name. Make sure you'll be covered if you have employees who use the vehicle. And if you have employees who use their own vehicles for your business (not commuting, but delivery, for example), you may need to add non-owned auto insurance—coverage for you and your employee while she is driving her own vehicle.

Personal Insurance

In addition to the insurance for your business activities, you may want to revisit your personal insurance needs in light of starting a home-based business. How will you handle health insurance if you're no longer employed elsewhere? What happens if you become disabled? Your previous employer may have offered a life insurance policy as a benefit—should you consider taking out life insurance now that you're on your own?

Health Insurance

As health costs have become more expensive, health insurance has become a huge issue for everyone—individuals, small businesses, large corporations, and, yes, home-based businesses. Many people consider the cost of health insurance as a barrier to starting their own business.

Renters' Insurance

Just because you don't own your home doesn't mean you can't insure what's in it. Renters' insurance will cover your personal possessions. You may also be able to get endorsements to your existing renters' insurance to cover business property and limited business liability coverage. Endorsements typically are limited to businesses that have less than $5,000 in revenue.

And it can be prohibitive. If your current employer pays a substantial portion of your health insurance premium as part of your benefits package, it's not hard to suffer sticker shock when it comes to pricing similar coverage as a sole proprietor—especially if you have a large family with significant health problems.

But for most health coverage is available. When you first start your home business, you may find it cost effective to take advantage of the so-called COBRA coverage your previous employer must offer. Essentially, you have the right to continue with the coverage provided by your employer plan at your current cost for up to 18 months.

Another possibility is adding yourself to a spouse's policy if he or she is continuing to work outside the home. You can also simply go and buy health insurance as an individual from a carrier in your area. This could be traditional health insurance or coverage by a health maintenance organization (HMO).

You can also check rates of policies offered by trade organizations or organizations created to cater to the self-employed. The National Association of the Self-Employed, for example, offers health insurance through MEGA Life and Health Insurance.

However, it may be more economical to sign up your business for a group policy. Even if the business has no employees and covers only you as a sole proprietor, you can still qualify for a group plan.

Disability Insurance

Many financial planners recommend disability insurance, especially for younger wage-earners or businesspeople. After all, at 35 or 40 years old, you're more likely to be disabled than you are to die. If you're disabled to the extent that you can't earn a living, you not only can't provide for your family, but you are likely to be a financial burden as well. Disability insurance is meant to cover you should this happen.

Catastrophic Health Insurance

One way to save money on your overall health costs is "catastrophic" health coverage. Instead of buying insurance that includes coverage for your routine costs, you will pay for regular checkups and medicines out of your pocket. Protect yourself by getting coverage that kicks in in the case of hospitalization or at a certain deductible—say $5,000. That way, you won't be financially ruined by a significant injury or health condition, and you can manage your routine costs on your own.

Life Insurance

If you pass away, are you leaving your family with financial problems as well as grief? Life insurance is meant to provide income to those you leave behind as well as pay estate taxes and funeral expenses.

For the home businessperson, especially those in a partnership, life insurance has another role. If, for example, you are partners with a nonfamily member, his spouse may inherit the partnership share of the business when he dies. But you may not be in a position to buy her out. In order to avoid this situation, partners may agree to take out life insurance policies naming each other beneficiaries, with the proceeds to be used specifically for the buyout of the business.

You also might want to consider life insurance for any key individual involved in the business whose death might jeopardize the business.

Workers' Compensation

If you have an employee, part-time or full-time, you must purchase workers' compensation insurance. This is true regardless of whether you are a sole proprietor, partnership, or corporation. Workers' comp covers employees who are injured in the course of doing their job.

If you are organized as a corporation, then you and any other corporate officers are employees and must provide workers' compensation. Even if you are not taking a salary from the corporation (and thus would not receive income if you were hurt on the job), your medical costs for any job-related injuries would be covered.

As a sole proprietor or partnership, you are not an employee yourself and therefore, if you have no employees, you are neither required nor able to get workers' compensation.

Planning for the Worst

As part of your insurance coverage, you should have some sort of disaster recovery plan. If a fire does burn down your home-based

Adjusting the Deductible

With most types of insurance, there is a set deductible, which is the amount you must pay before the insurance company begins kicking in their share. An auto insurance deductible might be $250, or $500, or $1,000 or more. The higher the deductible, the less the premium will cost. The point of insurance is to guard against catastrophic losses. Will having to pay the first $1,000 to replace your $30,000 car put you out of business? Probably not. But if you're sued for $1 million and you only have $500,000 in liability coverage, you could lose not just your business but your home.

If you need to save money, raise the deductible rather than lowering the upper limits of your liability coverage.

Minimize the Damage

Just handing over the pre-miums for your insurance coverage is not enough. As a business owner, you need to take all reasonable pre-cautions for the protection of yourself, your business, and your customers. Is there a dead branch over-hanging the driveway where clients will park? Cut it down now before it falls and causes a problem. Is the wiring in the old garage where you've located your business a little shaky, especially since you have a space heater going half the winter? Call the electrician today and have it fixed.

business, what's your first step? Will you even have the phone number of your insurance agent at hand? Do any clients or vendors need to be notified? If your roof leaks, exposing valuable inventory to water damage, what are your local storage alternatives?

And remember, although insurance may cover the dollar cost of losing a computer or the financial impact of losing valuable data like mailing lists, you would be wise to go one step further. Consider renting a safe deposit box or other secure off-site place to save copies of key documents, backups of key electronic data, as well as a copy of your disaster recovery plan. You don't have to replicate your entire file cabinet or computer hard drive, just identify the info that you'd really be lost without.

If you can imagine the worst-case scenario ahead of time and consider your options, the better off you will be if disasters actually occur. If you have employees, make them part of the planning so they know their roles and can be as helpful as possible.

For more information on this topic, visit our Web site at businesstown.com

PART III

Running Your Home Business

CHAPTER FOURTEEN

Daily Operations

Whether you're turning your hobby into a business, operating part-time, or planning a full-time home-based business, you'll be best served by taking it seriously. The way you run your business on a day-to-day basis will greatly affect how your customers perceive the business.

Although you're the boss, it's your customers who will make this venture work for you. So it's not unreasonable to consider what your customer will think as you make decisions about how to present your business.

For example, if you walked into a chiropractor's office for the first time and found it dirty and unkempt, would you be comfortable as a patient? Probably not. Even if the doctor were one of the best, you'd likely be wary of his or her inability to maintain minimum standards of cleanliness. If an accountant never seemed to be able to find the right file and frequently had to ask you two or three times for the same information, you'd be justified in questioning his abilities—though he might be brilliant with the numbers. How you maintain and organize your office, answer the phone, compose letters and interact with customers speaks volumes to those customers, so it's important to come across as professionally as possible.

Meeting Customers' Needs

As you consider the best way to run your business day-to-day, start by considering the needs of your customers. What time of day will they be able to interact with you? Will keeping your business open only on weekends work for them? The answer, of course, depends on the nature of your business.

Are you a contractor, a plumber, or electrician? You'll likely need to interact with other workers on many projects, which means daytime work. Do you do business across the country? You may need to make yourself available at different hours because of the time difference. Are you a genealogist, helping people track down their ancestors? You may find that the evening hours are best for

Track Your Busy Hours

Small retailers can quickly run themselves ragged trying to keep their shops open as many hours as possible in order to catch every possible customer. This can also be a particular problem for the home-based retailer, who customers come to learn is always at home, and therefore, they assume, "always open."

To avoid turning into a 24-hour-a-day operation, keep track of when most of your business takes place. As a craft retailer in a tourist area, for example, you may find that 80 percent of your business takes place on Fridays, Saturdays, and Sundays from 11:00 A.M. to 5:00 P.M. Conversely, you may discover that although you do get some traffic on Mondays and Tuesdays, particularly those looky-loos who love to smile and say "I'll be back," actual sales figures on those days are inconsequential. Let the results of your tracking make you feel OK about closing up shop when the business isn't there. Yes, you may lose a sale or two. But you'll be fresher, more creative, and in a better frame of mind when the doors are open.

Finally, don't feel badly about being closed when the sign says CLOSED. Sure, you're going to get some people knocking on the door anyway, but unless you're convinced they're going to seriously lighten their wallets, ask them to return during the posted operating hours. And if it happens too often, then you might be closing at the wrong time and need to adjust your hours. If a potentially good customer says he or she just isn't available during your opening hours, offer to make an appointment.

Fun Is Important, Too!

Being serious about your home business doesn't mean you have to be humorless or hopelessly conventional. One of the great joys of running your own home-based business is that you can decide how to present yourself to the public. And that doesn't have to mean suit-and-tie formality.

How far you can go depends in part on the nature of your business.

Most important is presenting yourself as an organized, reliable businessperson who knows his or her job and takes pride in doing it well. If you can easily establish credibility, then casual dress, silly slogans, and a sense of humor about your business are welcome.

sitting clients down and getting them to focus on telling what they already know about their family.

Also, what about your suppliers? If your business involves receiving perishable shipments (a florist, for example), you'll need to be available during regular business hours to take deliveries. Or if you must regularly pick up parts or suppliers at a retailer, you'll need to adjust your schedule to meet those needs.

The point is simply that although you may be on your own, your work schedule will be influenced by others. Take your customers into consideration.

Be Predictable

You won't be able to satisfy every customer's whim, but try to establish some predictability. Customers who want or need your product or service will adjust their schedules if they know you'll usually be available for them. But if you tell a customer that you're "usually around Tuesday mornings," and then you're absent the next three Tuesdays, frustration and poor word-of-mouth will quickly set in.

Ideally, you'll want to set regular hours of operation. This will help organize your business, let customers know when they can contact you or stop by, and establish some needed boundaries between your home business and your home life. While some people thrive on being "on call" all the time, most of us do better with personal time and space away from the business world. This can be important for your family as well—children may come to resent you placing business needs ahead of their needs too often.

If regular hours aren't possible, pick some times that you will always be in the office or reachable by phone. Let people know what those times are. And then be reliable. This is particularly important for part-time businesses, hobby businesses, or businesses in which opening hours are nontraditional (in the evening, for example). People need to know when it's easy and appropriate to contact you. By establishing those times and sticking to them, you'll be rewarded with appreciative repeat customers who rave about your business to others.

Face-to-Face Communications

Most successful home businesspersons are comfortable being on their own. In fact, they may relish it. But in most home businesses, at some point you'll need to interact directly with customers, vendors, and others. Remember that as a solo entrepreneur you are the image of your business. It's fine to shuffle around in your slippers and a T-shirt decorated with yesterday's dinner if you know no one is going to stop by. But for face-to-face business transactions, it's important to present yourself in a neat, well-groomed manner that will build trust with your customers.

Granted, for some home businesses dirt is part of the job. A furnace duct cleaner isn't going to want to show up at a customer's home in white shirt and tie. But you can do a dirty job and still look presentable. Jeans and a workshirt can be fine—it just helps if your clothes fit well, you take time to tuck in your shirt, and comb your hair. "Dress for success" is a cliché that has meaning for the home-based businessperson.

When you meet with customers or potential customers, try to project confidence and self-assurance. If customers sense that you know what you're doing, they'll have more confidence in you and feel better about spending money with you. Look them in the eye; smile. Shake hands when you meet. Be personable, listen to what they have to say. Respect their opinions, be appreciative of their time. If they get to be regular customers, it's appropriate to take a personal interest in their family— but don't pry, and avoid being a gossip.

Phone Manners

One of the quickest ways to be taken seriously as a business is to develop a telephone manner in keeping with the nature of your business. Try to answer the phone in a way that will immediately

Keep a Lid on It

People will tell you the most amazing things. Traditionally, the barbershop or the beauty parlor, two businesses that can work well out of the home, are centers for gossip. Whatever business you're in, some of your customers will come to trust you and may reveal some interesting details about themselves or pass on some juicy tidbits about a neighbor. But as a businessperson, you can't afford to get a reputation as someone who can't keep a secret. You're better off keeping a zipped lip— you'll keep more customers that way.

More Than Dial Tone on the Phone

You'd check the mirror to see how you look before an important face-to-face meeting, right? Well, you might want to consider doing the same thing with your phone manner. Your voice holds the success of your business in the balance when you're doing business over the phone. OK, that might be overstating it a bit, but your vocal inflections when answering the phone and talking with customers conveys a lot of your meaning.

To help cultivate a telephone voice that will foster good customer relations, ask a friend whose judgment you trust to give you feedback about your phone voice. When you try this exercise, pretend you don't know the

(continued on next page)

let the caller know he's reached the correct number. While a big "Halloo!" is friendly enough, potential customers shouldn't have to ask "Is this Big Bill's Bicycle Repair?" It's fine to shorten the full name of your business ("Bill's Bicycle") to save time, but it's important to make your potential customer feel like she's called just the right place. Adding a simple "Can I help you?" in a friendly, confident tone invites the customer to tell you what she needs.

One of the great challenges of some home businesses is dealing with phone inquiries promptly without unduly interrupting your ongoing work. A typical home business is a sole proprietorship—with an emphasis on the sole—and often there aren't other employees available (especially in the start-up phase) to act as receptionist while you focus on the task at hand. Whether you're a car repair mechanic or craftsperson, it can be frustrating trying to finish a job with the phone ringing off the hook.

Consequently, it's a good idea to come up with a compromise that will allow you to work when you need to work but won't make you too unavailable to your customers. One way to minimize the interruption is to use a cordless phone, which gives you the flexibility of answering the phone from anywhere on the property. If you choose this option, invest in a good one. Not only do some models give you a range of up to 2,000 feet, but it's important to have a clear signal to communicate easily with callers.

But cordless phones still require answering, which is an interruption. Another solution is to treat telephone calls as many people today treat e-mail. Let incoming calls be answered by an answering machine or voice-mail, and then check for messages regularly and make appropriate callbacks. This technique has a double advantage in that you can plan to sit down and make all your callbacks in one or more sessions during the day. The downside, of course, is that you may not reach customers when you call them back, setting up a frustrating game of phone tag that doesn't benefit you or them. It's a compromise.

A disadvantage of letting the answering machine pick up most incoming calls is that some cus-

tomers want a response quickly, which they are used to getting from other businesses. One way to mitigate their frustration is to be extremely reliable in calling people back. Regular customers will quickly learn that they can count on you to get back to them in a timely fashion, even when the answering machine is on.

One of the reasons that many of us start home-based businesses is that we want to be free to set our own schedules. Night owls may do their best work long after traditional business hours; others may rise early in order to spend the day with children. If you train your customers to be comfortable with your answering machine—and you're religious about calling them back—you can feel free to leave the home office behind without worrying too much about missing a potential customer or sale.

Correspondence

Business letters are a wonderful thing for the home-based business. Why? Because you are at no disadvantage when competing with your corporate counterparts. By investing in quality letterhead, your outgoing letters and invoices can have the look and feel of a multinational corporation.

Letterhead

Quality letterhead doesn't necessarily mean that you should immediately go to a print shop and order up a dozen reams of expensive three-color letterhead with matching envelopes. You can retain your budget during the start-up stage by creating letterhead on your home computer with one of the office suite programs. Even with an inexpensive color printer, relatively high-quality logos can be printed out easily along with the letter you're writing. Small quantities of correspondence-quality paper are available with matching envelopes. If you're going to spend some of your capital, consider hiring a graphic artist to help you create a logo and help you make typeface choices for your correspondence.

More Than Dial Tone on the Phone

(continued from previous page)

person calling. Have him make a typical call—perhaps at an unexpected time—and ask you typical questions. End the call and call the friend back. Ask the friend to tell you about your voice on the phone—is it friendly? Do you sound pleased to hear from the caller? Do you sound as if you're welcoming their business? Are you polite, but not overly chatty? Do you listen? When you speak, are you clear?

These may seem like obvious elements of good phone manner, but a quick survey of many businesses, small and large, will show that all too often they are lacking. You can make your business a better one by making sure your phone approach is appropriate.

The Greeting

As you try to build your home business from a hobby or part-time operation into a growing, thriving full-time concern, there will be occasions when you might want to appear as big as you will be tomorrow rather than as small as you are today. If you answer the phone with a simple "'Yo-dee-ho, Buddy here," it conveys a small-time operator. Maybe that's perfect for you.

On the other hand, a more professional greeting like "Lawn Care Associates, may I help you?" not only conveys responsible attitude, but doesn't let on as to whether the company has a fleet of high-end Toros or it's just you, the dog, and a broken-down Murray. Who knows, the caller may be from a large company, looking for an annual contract worth thousands! A professional response on the phone could make the difference in getting that contract.

Business Letters

Well-written letters make all the difference. Even if letter writing is not your forte, you can find help. If you're comfortable with a computer keyboard, many of the word processing programs—especially the small business editions—include numerous templates for most typical business letter applications. Chances are you can edit one of those to suit your needs. By using spelling and grammar-checking tools within the word processing software, you can generate letters without stepping on too many grammatical land mines.

If letter writing is just not something you prefer to do, consider hiring someone else to do it or hiring someone to help you create standard letters that will suit most of your needs. Chances are someone in your area—perhaps a resume writing service—would be happy to help you out for a reasonable fee.

Important, though, is making every attempt to ensure that your correspondence is neat and professional. A poorly written, hand-scrawled note can be quaint but can put you at a disadvantage in certain situations.

E-Mail Etiquette

With the explosion of the Internet in the 1990s, e-mail has become a common way for businesses to correspond. In fact, for many home-based businesses, e-mail is almost required in order to compete. However, be cautious about how you use e-mail in your business.

When you send e-mail, you should consider it as carrying the same weight as a formal letter. If you quote a customer a price, make a service promise, or extend credit, the recipient will hold you to your word and will consider the e-mail a written offer or contract.

On the other hand, when you receive a quote for services or products via e-mail, you should ask for written confirmation. E-mails, strictly speaking, aren't signed, and the company you're dealing with shouldn't have a problem confirming a deal on paper.

Similarly, if you're trying to collect an outstanding debt or make a vendor aware of a problem in a timely fashion, there's no substitute for sending a letter that requires the recipient's signature. If

Family Phone Manners

Family members can be a great help with a home-based business, but they can turn potential customers away, too. If you are running a home business that puts other members of your family, especially children, in the position of answering the phone for you on occasion, make sure you have a quick training session on how to answer the phone, speak to customers, and take a proper message.

Customers feel their needs are important, and if a twelve-year-old in a hurry to play with friends answers the phone with a motor-mouthed "He's-not-here-right-now-I-don't-know-when-he'll-be-back-can-you-call-again-later?" it leaves the customer with little confidence that you care about those needs. Tell kids and others to either let the answering machine pick up the incoming call or answer professionally. "Lawn Care Associates. I'm sorry, Mr. Weedwonder isn't in right now, but if you'll leave your name and number, I'll make sure that he calls you as soon as possible." If callers push for more information, have the family phone answerer simply say that "Mr. Weedwonder would be the best person to ask. Is there a good time for him to call you back?"

Make sure that the area near the phone is uncluttered and that a message pad and pen or pencil is on hand. A preprinted message pad, with spaces for name, phone number, and reason for calling is helpful for family members who might otherwise forget to get all the pertinent information.

Dedicated Lines

Here are some good reasons to consider adding another phone line dedicated to your business.

- You can answer the phone appropriately. Rather than a simple "hello," as is customary for a home phone, you can always answer a dedicated line with your business name.

- You can have a separate answering machine (or voice-mail) with a business-related outgoing message.

- Your business line won't be tied up with personal calls. This can be especially important if you have others in your household (teenagers, for example) who use the phone frequently.

- It's easier to identify your business telephone expenses.

- You can arrange for automatic call forwarding from your business line to your home line so that you won't miss a call because of a busy signal. (Voice-mail service can also help you with this.)

- You can use your home line for Internet service during business hours without fear of missing incoming calls from customers.

you're trying to build a paper trail for possible future legal action, e-mails may help, but you're better off with just that—a paper trail.

Those caveats pointed out, e-mail is a terrific tool. For one monthly fee you can seek information, negotiate prices, check on the status of shipments, send reminders and negotiate prices around the world without running up phone bills.

How often should you check your e-mail? Well, you might consider this version of the Golden Rule: Use your e-mail with others as you would have others use e-mail with you. Like phone calls, e-mails are relatively instantaneous. But that doesn't mean you can always expect a reply within hours. Many people only check their e-mail once a day. But if you're using e-mail regularly for business, you'd be wise to check it at least two or three times daily. If you get in the habit of doing so at the same time each day, your customers will pick up on this and send you messages in anticipation of a response.

For all forms of correspondence, consider an informal hierarchy: important communications with legal implications should go by mail in all cases, daily back-and-forth communication that isn't deadline sensitive can go by e-mail, and matters that need an answer right away or involve some delicate personal discussion are better by phone.

Organization

One of the keys to working and running your business efficiently is staying organized. This doesn't come naturally for many of us. But when it comes to a home business, it's critical.

Home businesses can be particularly challenging in this regard. After all, you're sharing your office or professional work space with all the elements of a home—which is one reason home-based businesspeople are advised to separate their office as much as possible. Home businesses are often in tight quarters, requiring creativity when it comes to storage.

In running your business, it's important that you maintain accurate, up-to-date records, file correspondence so that you can find it

Beepers and Cells

For some businesses, beepers and cell phones are critical tools. For example, plumbers, electricians, heating repair technicians, and veterinarians are bound to get emergency calls. In fact, you may want to make your ability to respond in an emergency part of your sales pitch.

If you have a business that requires emergency calls, make sure that it's easy for your customers to get a hold of you. Regular customers should have the emergency number to call directly. Otherwise, instruct your family members on how to get in touch with you if an emergency call comes in to the home-based office while you're elsewhere. Or use technology to ensure that emergency calls get forwarded to you—a call to your local telephone company will help you know the various ways you can set up a system.

A Vote for the Note

In the fast-paced, technology-dominated business world, our society has lost a certain amount of character with the disappearance of the handwritten note. While formal business letters, printed out or typed, are appropriate in most situations requiring correspondence, the old-fashioned handwritten note can provide a much needed personal touch. Thank-you notes and quick apologies for small mistakes, for example, can carry more meaning if you take the time to write them out by hand. A quick personal note on a Post-It™ attached to other correspondence can help build a relationship with a customer. Don't hesitate to use a handwritten note when you sense it's appropriate.

when you need it, and keep your area neat and clean. The best reason to do so is for yourself—it will save time and make it easier to work, and certainly will help when it comes time to do your taxes. But if you can't motivate yourself to stay organized, then do it for your customers. Those who do business with you don't want to waste time while you search around for a product catalog or copy of an invoice. Customers want to feel confident that you are in control of your business and can help them with their needs. Confidential files need to stay confidential. Business records need to be current. Computer data should be backed up regularly.

Like so many other elements of a home-based business, it may help to try to determine your needs. Will you need a file for every customer? How many customers will you have? How much file space will you need as a result? Do you have to stock inventory for resale, or parts and supplies for making your product? If you determine your space needs ahead of time and plan for them, it will be easier to stay organized.

If dealing with customers often keeps you hopping, consider setting aside a time each week that is dedicated to keeping up with filing, cleaning, and organizing. Perhaps you'll decide to go into your home office early each Thursday and spend an hour getting your files up to date. Whatever your schedule, it will be easier to stay on top of it if you organize it regularly. The once-every-six-months pile-removal method isn't recommended.

If neatness is not your strong suit, consider hiring an outside cleaning service. Knowing that someone will be showing up once a week or twice a month to vacuum and dust may be the motivation you need to keep those piles under control.

Plenty of profit-making home businesses out there manage to survive without adhering to any of the advice in this chapter. However, business is more competitive than ever, and you want to do everything possible to enhance your chances of success. Setting customer-friendly hours, presenting yourself appropriately on the phone and in correspondence, and staying organized won't in and of itself guarantee success, but it will set the stage for you to do your best work.

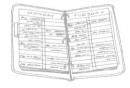

Phone Faux Pas

- **The Surly Busy Bee**—Overstressed and busy with something else, the proprietor answers the phone with a one-word "Yeah?"—as if to say to the caller, "This had better be worth my time, pal, 'cause I got bigger fish to fry." When the caller hangs up in disgust, this guy may have just lost a lot of business.

- **The Mumbler**—Not completely comfortable talking to others, the proprietor answers with an unintelligible "Heluh, this mmph. . . henrimph, can im oss grmmp?" forcing the caller to ask, "Is this Henry's Upholstery?" If you're going to have a phone, don't make the customer work hard to use it. Speak clearly.

- **The Shouter**—After an initial greeting, the proprietor says, "Hold on, will ya?" then shouts to coworkers or kids or barking dogs, "HEY, KEEP IT DOWN IN THERE I'M ON THE PHONE FOR CRYING OUT LOUD!" The customer, eardrum now ringing, is embarrassed for the proprietor and loses confidence in him as a businessperson.

- **The Challenge**—Often practiced by auto parts counter help and other "technical" business owners. Every phone call or approaching customer is viewed as an opportunity to show off how much more they know about the product. If you're in the know, the service is fine. But woe to the customer who doesn't yet understand the intricacies of the product. Humiliation is the only way out. Don't make your customer pay homage to your superior knowledge just to get courteous service.

- **The Cynic**—"We can't fix that, nobody can fix that. Within two weeks, are you kiddin'? Can't be done. You're wastin' my time." Yes, sometimes customers ask for what seems to be the impossible, but remember you're trying to develop a relationship with people who need your product. Look at this as an opportunity to talk the customer into something more realistic. "Well, my schedule is busy within that time frame, what if I were able to get it to you by Friday the nineteenth?" Be helpful, and your customer will respond positively.

- **The Invisible Man**—A frequent technique of various contractors. They're out on the job all day, don't get back until it's too late to return phone calls, and somehow forget to call back. During boom times, they have enough business to get away with this, but it's bad policy for the long term. Even if you're too busy to take more business, make a point of calling back prospective customers and letting them know you appreciate their call and that you'd love their business at another time. Help them out with the name of a colleague if you can. This simple courtesy will keep you going even when the gravy train runs dry.

- **The Chatty Cathy**—You wonder how they ever make any profit since they spend all day talking. There's nothing wrong with taking an interest in a customer and making polite small talk—you'll even make some great friends from your customers—but bring it back to business in a timely fashion and wrap up the conversation so you can get back to work—which is what the customer wants, too, ultimately.

CHAPTER FIFTEEN

Keeping the Books

Counting Your Profits

If you have a hard time forcing yourself to roll around in the numbers, think of it this way: you're counting your money. Presumably one of the reasons you started your business was to make a little dough—so don't you want to find out just how much you're bringing in? Well, record keeping and accounting is all about tallying up the pluses and minuses.

Of course, sometimes it's hard to face the fact that you're struggling financially, which might make it hard to study those income statements. Fair enough, but the sooner you recognize the problem and make some changes to fix it, the more likely you'll be able to turn things around. You don't want to be forced out of business, realizing that you'd have been OK if you'd paid attention and made a few changes six months before.

F or those of us who struggle to balance our personal checkbooks each month, the idea of bookkeeping for a home business may seem daunting. But there is good news—between relatively easy software programs and traditional bookkeepers, you can find ways to keep your books current without turning into a CPA.

Even if you do nothing more than hand over the bills and checks to someone else, it's a good idea to understand how basic accounting works. At a minimum, you'll want to be able to read your monthly statements and know how much you owe, what you're worth, what you have or need for inventory, and what your cash flow situation is. You'll want to be able to monitor revenue and expenses on a monthly, quarterly, and annual basis so you can make the best decisions for the future of your business.

Good records are also important when you have to deal with outside entities—like the IRS. You will have to pay taxes, and good record keeping helps you pay only what you really owe. Even the best tax consultant can't help you if you can't figure out where your money went.

And, of course, you may want to borrow money to help grow your business. Solid record-keeping will be a strong point in your favor when it comes to a loan committee making a decision. How you track your business finances is a strong reflection of how well you run your business. You may be the greatest cabinetmaker in the state, but sloppy books can make you seem less than a good risk.

You, the Computer, or an Accountant?

If you're comfortable with a computer and spreadsheet software, small business accounting packages such as QuickBooks or Peachtree Accounting make it astoundingly easy to do your own bookkeeping. In tandem with tax preparation software, it's no trick to do it all yourself if you're so inclined. Or you can use the software to maintain your records, then take a disk with the appropriate information to your accountant for creation of monthly, quarterly, and annual statements.

But don't decide to do your own bookkeeping and tax preparation simply to save money. The time you spend, the mistakes you make, and the tax savings you might miss are likely to cost you as much as what a competent accountant might charge.

Most important, make sure that you *do it*. Good accounting means regular accounting—it won't do to save all your receipts in a shoe box, then sit down the following April 14 and try to figure out how much money you made. Not only does the IRS require you to follow accepted accounting principles, but you'll need financial reports at least monthly to help you make the best business decisions.

If you enjoy doing your own bookkeeping, and if you find it a good way to keep a close watch on your business finances—not just monthly but weekly and daily—then by all means do it yourself. You may find it helpful, for example, to start out doing your own books, then hiring an accountant down the road. By that time you'll have a good understanding of your finances and might make better use of the advice an accountant can give.

If you've set up your home business as a corporation or if you have employees, the added complications may make having an accountant essential. After all, you need to spend most of your time generating revenue, not counting it!

Of course, you don't have to use a computer or an accountant. You can still maintain the requisite records by hand. The One-Write system, in which you make account entries as part of your check writing, has long been a popular option for small businesses.

Beginners' Bookkeeping

You'll need to make a few decisions about your accounting system up front. If you plan on working regularly with an accountant or bookkeeper, sit down with him or her ahead of time, discuss the needs and nature of your business, and make these choices together.

You'll need to decide on your *business year*. For most home businesses, the business year will be the same as the calendar

Divided We Conquer

Even though you are home-based, you'll need to keep your business and personal finances separate. Open up a business bank account as soon as possible, and route your income and business expenses through it. Set aside one of your credit cards to use strictly for the business, then pay it off using the business account. When you need to use personal money for business purposes, deposit that investment into the business checking account. If you buy something for the business out of your own pocket, reimburse yourself out of the business checking account so that you have a record of it. Better yet, establish a business petty cash account. And, of course, save all your receipts.

year, January 1 through December 31. As a sole proprietor this simplifies your taxes, given that as a self-employed person you'll be paying taxes based on the calendar year anyway.

The other option is to establish a fiscal year. Your fiscal year can start at the beginning of any month in the calendar year, ending the last day of the month prior—for example, July 1 through June 30. Of course, you can start your business any time and still use the calendar year as your business year.

Most of us use a *cash method* of accounting in running our households. Money is income when the paycheck arrives, and expenses are recorded when we pay them. This method will also work for many home-based businesses, especially service businesses. It's simple and straightforward.

If you have inventory, however, you will be required to use the *accrual method* of accounting. Income is recorded when an invoice is sent out, and expenses recorded when the bill comes. You'll have receivables (money owed to you but not yet received) and payables (money you owe others but have not yet paid) listed as assets and liabilities on your monthly balance statements.

Basic Records

You'll have to keep records of anything that involves spending or receiving money, recording the transactions in a revenue and expense journal. You'll record all revenue received and expenses paid, assigning each to the appropriate account. (The electric bill to the Utilities account, for example.) This should be maintained on a weekly basis.

Save receipts, check stubs, and deposit slips as backup evidence for your entries. Also maintain a mileage log for business use of your vehicle. (It's helpful to keep a record of your actual vehicle expenses, too, so you can determine the most advantageous way to deduct your automotive expenses.) A phone log, especially if your home phone doubles as your business line, will be helpful, as well as a petty cash log to track small cash purchases that are business-related.

For travel expenses, separate meals and entertainment costs and record the name of the client and the purpose of the trip.

You'll also want to keep a log of your fixed assets (such as vehicles, office equipment) that can be depreciated over time. If you purchase products for resale or if you buy raw materials to create a product, you need to maintain a record of your inventory.

Retailers with daily receipts should clear the cash register on a daily basis, tracking taxable sales in order to pay sales tax based on your state and city's regulations. Deposits should be made daily or weekly—don't let your revenue sit around the house to get lost or misplaced.

On a monthly basis, add up your revenues and expenses, create a profit and loss statement, and balance your checkbook. You should also update your cash flow projections and balance sheet.

A computerized accounting program can simplify the entire process. You enter every transaction once, and let the software create the individual logs and records.

Analyzing Your Progress

One of the most important reasons to maintain good records and use accepted accounting procedures is that you can use your monthly statements to analyze the health and progress of your business. If you've done your homework and created a business plan (see Chapter 7), then you know that there are several reports that you, your accounting software, or your accountant can prepare to help you understand how your business stands. They include a profit and loss statement, a cash flow statement, and a balance sheet.

A *profit and loss statement* (P&L) details your income and your expenses for a given accounting period. Each month, you will look at how you stand not only at the end of that month but year-to-date as well. You'll compare the current year's figures (monthly, perhaps quarterly, and annually) to those of the previous year.

A *cash flow statement* compares money coming in versus money going out. You cannot only look back to get a picture of

Picking an Accountant

When selecting an accountant or bookkeeper to work with, ask for recommendations from other home businesses in the area—it's always helpful to work with someone who is well informed about the peculiarities of a home-based business. Your Chamber of Commerce or Small Business Development Center can probably point you to some reputable accountants.

Make an introductory appointment with several, then interview them. Ask about their qualifications, how they charge, how they like to work with small business owners, and what you can expect from them monthly and annually. Are they qualified tax preparers as well, or will you also need a tax consultant? Do they have any experience in your specific industry? Ask for references.

your past cash flow trends but, more important, look forward to check your projected cash flow. This will answer the big question: Will I have enough cash to pay my bills when they're due?

A *balance sheet* details your business assets and liabilities. It will let you see how much your business is worth.

As you analyze these reports, compare your income and expenses to your projected budget. When you began the year, how much profit did you expect to have each month? Are you below your target? If so, is it a revenue problem (you're not making or selling enough) or an expense problem (you're spending too much)? If it's a revenue problem, maybe you need to increase what you're spending on promotion or have a sale. What part of the business isn't performing as planned? Perhaps you had planned on selling a certain amount of product to other retailers, but haven't yet found the time to find them. Well, now's the time. If you're spending far more than planned, it's time to review your expenses and find out exactly where the money is going.

Or perhaps it's simply a matter of having too much equity in your inventory—a quick check of your balance sheet will tell you. Make sure you're comfortable with your inventory level—if you're a retail business, for example, you don't want to get caught with out-dated inventory that nobody will buy.

How about your cost of goods? Is your gross profit margin high enough? If not, maybe you're pricing is too low. Or perhaps you need to look into other, less expensive suppliers. Or perhaps there's more waste of raw materials than you'd planned.

Look not just at the monthly figures but year-to-date figures as well. Look for trends. Are your overhead costs rising? Do you need to pass those costs on to your customers in the price of your goods or services? Or perhaps you need to look again at your phone, Internet, and overnight delivery charges and find a way to cut back.

If you extend credit to your customers, check your accounts receivable aging. Are all accounts current? How much of your accounts receivable is over 30 days? 60 days? Any over 90 days past receipt of the invoice? By checking this regularly, you can stay

on top of those clients who tend to be slow payers—and withhold further services to them if necessary.

The key to dealing with any business challenge is catching problems before they become insurmountable and acting quickly to reverse negative trends.

Getting Paid

With most home-based businesses, it's likely that you'll be doing the work or creating the product before you get paid for it. This is especially true for service businesses—whether you're cleaning houses, operating a kennel, or snowplowing driveways, customers will be used to either paying upon completion or being sent an invoice.

Included on the invoice will be the payment terms. Is the bill due in 10 days? 30 days? Send out invoices promptly—terms are usually from receipt of invoice, so you don't want to slow up payment by delaying the invoice yourself. All terms should be clarified before the work is done, but make sure you remind the client of the terms by stating them on the invoice.

With regular customers this is rarely a problem. They know your work, you come to trust that they pay on time, and their checks always clear. If you've planned your cash flow appropriately, you won't have problems.

With new clients, however, there can be risk involved. To avoid potential conflicts, make sure that you fully inform your customer about your rates or the cost of the job at hand—preferably in writing. Get them to sign a work order, agreeing to the work, the estimate, and acknowledging that it is only an estimate. Communicate with them if, in the middle of the job, it looks as if the job will cost more than your estimate. If your business involves purchasing parts or inventory for a specific job, ask for a deposit ahead of time to cover the cost.

In many cases in which customers won't pay the bill, it's the result of a misunderstanding rather than an inability to pay. Do your utmost to clarify the scope of work and the payment terms ahead

A Mouse Click Away

If you use an accounting software program and regularly input bills, payments, invoices, and checks as they're received, you're only a few mouse clicks away from an up-to-date picture of your current finances. With QuickBooks, for example, a pull-down report menu will not only lead you to a P&L, balance sheet, and cash flow statement for any accounting period you choose, but also to reports detailing accounts receivable and payable, sales, and inventory, among others. This can be extremely helpful when cash flow is tight, for example.

of time. If it's a large project, create a contract that outlines the obligations of both parties.

There are also those unfortunate times that the customer can't pay the bill. With some businesses, such as a car repair shop, you can always hold the customer's car until you get paid. But other businesses are left trying to collect with little or no leverage.

But don't let that stop you. Although you don't want to spend hundreds of hours and thousands of dollars collecting a $250 outstanding invoice, you do want to take reasonable steps to collect what is owed. Start with a few phone calls—be pleasant and polite, and ask for a specific date that you can expect payment. If you don't receive it on that date, contact them again. Send a letter, again pleasant and polite, insisting that you get paid—and set a specific date by which you expect payment.

If you still get nowhere, and if you have some faith in your customer, you might offer to set up a payment plan—an amount weekly until the debt is paid. Regular payments are what you're looking for here—if they owe you $500 and can pay $25 a week, take it—as long as they continue to pay.

If you still have problems, you can turn the account over to a collection agency, which will take a percentage of what's collected. Or you take the customer to small claims court.

Small claims court is exactly that—a court where you can use the system inexpensively to make a small claim—usually up to $1,500—against another person or business. If you have the paperwork to back up your claim, you'll likely win—though that may not help you if the customer simply has no money.

Paying Yourself

Many home businesses are bootstrap operations, relying on a lot of hard work and little up-front capital. Owners whittle their personal expenses down to the bare minimum and plow extra cash back

Dealing with the Big Guys

Home-based businesses are usually small businesses and often have clients or customers who are much bigger. Sometimes larger companies take advantage of this and use bureaucratic roadblocks to slow down payment. It can be frustrating dealing with a company that won't make paying your invoice a priority. "We only cut checks on the second Tuesday of the month," or "It's on the second assistant vice president's desk," may be a logical explanation for them, but doesn't help your cash flow.

In dealing with such companies, first make sure your paperwork is in order. Send an invoice, whether they ask for it or not. If your contact at the company doesn't handle payments, find out who does and address the invoice accordingly. Second, be reasonable. Don't expect the accounting department to turn around a check the next day. A check within 30 days is more likely.

Third, make friends. Enlist your contact to help push the payment process along internally. Follow up with the right person in accounting. Be a pleasant, persistent voice on the phone. Be sympathetic with his or her plight as a cog in the machine, and convince that person to help you out. Keep pushing. Ask what you can do to improve the turnaround in the future, and be glad you don't work in a place like that.

And if this doesn't work, stay professional and keep going up in the hierarchy. Eventually, you'll get to someone who can get you paid. It may take a letter to the CEO, but you should get a response eventually. And if you don't or can't, it may be time to find a new client.

Signs of Trouble

Regular, ongoing customers or clients are the backbone of any good home business.

But be wary when you start seeing regular customers taking longer and longer to pay. If you're used to getting paid in two weeks, and you begin to see the checks coming four weeks, then five weeks or more after receipt of the invoice, address the issue immediately. A friendly call to make sure they've received an invoice can let them know you're aware of the delay. Be wary of continuing to provide your products or services until they are current or on a regular payment plan. You don't want to find yourself with a significant bad debt six months or a year down the road because you were too lenient with a friendly customer, or you may find yourself in line behind them in bankruptcy court.

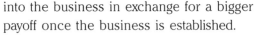

into the business in exchange for a bigger payoff once the business is established.

But that doesn't mean you shouldn't pay yourself. Psychologically, it's important to feel that the business is providing you some income. You may decide to put that money right back into the business, but plan for at least a small, regular owner's draw—monthly perhaps—so that you can feel the satisfaction of getting paid.

As a sole proprietor, you are not an employee of your business. You don't write yourself a paycheck. Instead, you will take an owner's draw, which is recorded as a payout of equity as retained earnings. The owner's draw is not a business expense.

Determine the amount of a monthly draw based on your projected annual profit. If Lenora's Cake Decorating expects to make $10,000 in profit by the end of the year, Lenora may decide to write herself a check for $400 every two weeks. Or, knowing that her business is strongest during the wedding season in May and June, she may decide to take a draw of only $200 every two weeks in the first quarter and then boost her draw later in the year, in order to help her cash flow.

For more information on this topic, visit our Web site at businesstown.com

CHAPTER SIXTEEN

The Personal Side

In Chapter 1, you took an inventory of your personality traits and decided that, yes, you do have the ambition, initiative, resourcefulness best suited for home-based business ownership. But once your business is up and running and the excitement of start-up starts to calm down, a new phase of your work life begins to settle in. You are beyond the stage where you are doing concrete and exciting things such as choosing a name, buying furniture, and collecting your new business cards from the printer. Now, you may start finding you need a little extra push to get into the office in the morning. When there's no boss waiting for you to fill the seat at your desk, this can be a bit of an obstacle.

If you think back to any job you've had in the "regular" workaday world, you probably will have seen the same kind of pattern. Remember starting a new job? Before your first day, you buy a few new items of clothing to suit the atmosphere of your new office. Your first week is spent setting up your personal work space, meeting your colleagues, getting to know your way around the building. By the end of the first month, you've met everyone, including those stragglers who were on vacation when you started or the people you deal with only during a certain monthly financial cycle. It's all new and constantly changing in the first month, right down to finding the best places to get lunch.

But somewhere between three to six months, the newness wears off. Then it takes a different type of stimulus to get you excited about work—your boss starts you on a new project, the department hires a new colleague, you take on a new client. Some people thrive on the day-to-day routine of the job, but if you are entrepreneurial enough to be setting up your own home-based business, chances are that the same old thing is not what gets you up in the morning.

With your own business, it is entirely up to you to find ways to keep motivated. Besides that, you need to combat the added feeling of isolation. For those who can get fired up over the smallest things, finding motivations will be easy; for others who look for the larger things, it is more difficult. But it can be done.

Staying Motivated

The first step to staying motivated is to understand what it is that actually motivates you to begin with. The list of motivating factors can be as varied as there are home-based business owners. One of the first things to consider is: Why did you start your home-based business? Was it . . .

- **Control?** Did you want to start a business because you wanted complete control over your work life? Over the way you spend your day? If control over your day was your main motivation, be sure you are taking control. Did you leave a nine-to-five job to take charge of your own workday only to find yourself working nine-to-five from your home office? Change that—you can do it, because you are the boss! Maybe in the summer you can set your work hours from 7:00 A.M. to noon and go to the beach for the afternoon, then pick up a few extra hours in the evening. You no longer have to go to the fitness center with the crowd that works nine to five—fit in your workout during the off-hours when the weight room or the pool is empty. Save your bookkeeping for two hours in the evening when your favorite classical music show is on the radio. Straighten up your office and clear your desk on Saturday mornings while you listen to "Car Talk" and the kids are at basketball practice. Quit the week at 3:00 P.M. on Fridays. Take a woodworking class or horseback riding lessons on Monday mornings so you never have to have the Monday morning blues again. Don't just remember that you're now in full control—do something with it!
- **Money?** Did you leave a job and start up on your own because you felt as if you were spending your time making someone else rich? Because you'd rather be lining your own pockets with the profits from your hard work? Did you determine that the only way you were going to considerably expand your income was to go into business for yourself? Because we all need to eat, shelter, and clothe ourselves,

and we like a little fun to boot, money is a key motivating factor in anything that relates to work and business.

If money is your motivation, perhaps until business catches on you might need an extra push here and there. Maybe it would help to find the money-making angle for everything you do, even if at first it doesn't seem the task is directly related to the bottom line. Or sign up for a class that is specifically geared toward increasing sales, bringing in new clients, or even cutting costs. Until you are making deposits as often as you are writing checks for your business account, these money-oriented motivations may be just the ticket.

- **Creativity?** Were you feeling less than creative in your old job? Maybe you felt as though your talents could be better used, better developed, and that your employer wasn't helping you expand your horizons—sometimes for obvious reasons, such as you'd use your increased skills to get a new job or open a home business!

- **Innovation?** Did you always feel there was a better way to do something? Or a particular business intrigued you and you knew if you opened your own, your approach would be an automatic hit in the marketplace. Many people dream of inventing that better mousetrap, but you've actually decided to give it your best shot. Innovation is exciting, and this combination of excitement, creativity, and challenge is what got you started tinkering in your basement in the first place.

This may be one of the tougher motivations to keep fresh. Unless your business is innovative by nature, set up to create new things all the time, not just one new-and-improved mousetrap, you may need to be creative in your extra push. Attend conferences for inventors and get yourself out among people being as creative as you are. Talking with others about innovation and invention will reignite your enthusiasm. And while you're out there, ask other entrepreneurs how they stay motivated.

Whether or not any of these motivations are good reasons to open a business doesn't really matter—it is the factor that motivated

JD Designs: Creativity-Driven

Jill, a graphic designer, worked for a marketing firm designing clients' brochures and other materials. Over the course of her employment, she saved and bought herself a nice computer system that she set up in a sunny room in her home.

While still employed, Jill took some evening courses to expand her graphic art abilities and met someone in class who worked at a book publishing firm. When he asked her to work freelance designing a book cover, Jill's life changed. Working on the book cover made her realize that her office job wasn't allowing her the creativity she craved. Within a year, she quit her full-time job, started up JD Designs, and now works from her sunny home office for all sorts of different clients, including her former employer. Some days she's working on book covers, other days advertisements, recently she even did a design for the packaging of a soap product. When she gets up to go to her office, her motivation is that she can be as creative as she likes, her days are never the same, and she decides what projects she works on and what just doesn't seem interesting to her. She's had to learn a little bit about selling herself, and sometimes it's an effort to pick up the phone and reach out to new potential clients, but she can do it as long as she keeps her original motivation—spending her days being creative—in mind at all times.

you to start your business that matters. Now that you've put your finger on what got you going in the first place, you need to find ways to use that motivating factor or factors to reinvigorate your enthusiasm for your business, to keep you making the calls, sending letters, perhaps even to get you to climb the stairs to your second-floor office each morning!

How you do that is almost as personal a choice as your motivating factor itself. Maybe a quote from a successful businessperson has always gotten you revved up—frame the quote and keep it near your computer or phone. Better yet, stencil it on the wall! If your motivation is to double your number of clients from 6 to 12 in a year, get an easel and a white-board, write numbers 1 through 12 on it, and fill in the clients as they come in. When you get to number 8 or 9, you'll probably become extremely motivated to fill in the rest of the blanks. Or, if your motivation is more concrete, such as saving enough to buy a classic Porsche in cash, tape a photo of the car to your computer monitor or near the phone. That will keep you going!

Setting Goals

One of the best ways to stay motivated is to set goals. And once you have accomplished those, or better yet before, set some more. You can set different kinds of goals:

- Short-term goals: "I'm going to make six calls a day to new clients, every day this week," or "By the end of the month, I want to have my entire client list on this new database program I bought."
- Long-term goals: "By this time next year, I will have tripled my sales," or "In five years, I'd like to be out of this small former laundry-room office and build a new addition off the back of the house."

You can set goals based on revenue or goals based on tasks you want to accomplish. If you're running a newsletter or magazine, perhaps your goal is to increase your publishing cycle from four times a year to six. If you are running an online retail business, maybe you'd like to have doubled your product offerings by the next Christmas selling season.

Whatever the goal, the point is that goals give you something to look to the future for. And the future is what makes you get out of bed in the morning. If you miss your goal, it's not the end of the world. Being realistic in goal-setting is a time-honored skill and something one learns by doing.

Feeling Swamped

Running a home-based business can be overwhelming. Not only do you have to do the work itself, you're responsible for all the administrative tasks. And guess what, you're probably also the official sanitation engineer!

Once business gets booming, it can swamp you. Different people react to such stress in different ways—some might become workaholics, others tend to shut down and become less efficient. However you react, realize that it's not uncommon to lose your motivation when things seem to have grown beyond your control.

First thing to do is to organize and prioritize your tasks. Break down the seemingly overwhelming projects into bite-sized chunks. Do you feel hopelessly behind in your filing? Will it take a solid week just to catch up? Are you also behind in sending out invoices? Which is more important? Right, your plan will be to move on the invoices first.

And though you probably can't take a week away from the rest of the business just to organize your files, you may be able to spend 30 minutes a day for a week. That will give you an idea of how bad the problem really is, and you can plan for the time it will take to finish up.

If upon organizing and prioritizing all your tasks you conclude that "it just can't be done by one person," then get help! You can hire a temp for a day, right? Or maybe you need to turn your record keeping over to a bookkeeper on a regular basis so you can

Ready, Set, Go!

Goals are the carrot on the stick to the rabbit, or they can be the rabbit to the hound. In other words, the goal that motivates one person isn't necessarily what motivates another. Figure out what goals, long and short term, you want to strive for with your company and get up each morning ready to reach for them.

focus on the revenue-producing part of the business. There are always solutions, and by taking control you'll stay motivated.

Overcoming Isolation

With all the motivation in the world, running a home-based business can still be a lonely endeavor. First off, since you work where you live, you can go days without ever leaving your property. Most of the time that's good news—but there are days when you've just got to get away.

Few home-based offices are set up for employees so you will mostly be working on your own, day in and day out. Proprietors of retail businesses and some service businesses will interact with customers, but the business-customer relationship is unique and doesn't always provide you with the relaxing social interaction you may crave. Even if your family is around, effectively providing you with "company," chances are you will still feel somewhat removed from the world of colleagues who can empathize with your particular industry's ups and downs and peculiarities.

The solutions are fairly simple—phone, e-mail, go out to lunch—but you need to consciously set out to do these things. Here are some ideas to make sure the four walls of the home office don't close in on you:

- **Run errands.** A quick trip to the bank, post office, or copy shop can be just the tonic you need. Of course it's possible to do your banking and buy postage over the Internet, but sometimes just getting away from your office is a better side benefit.
- **Go to business events.** Join the Chamber of Commerce, or just check the local paper regularly for business events in your town or any other town in your business reach. Often these will include speakers who can offer motivation, inspiration, or information to help you in your business. Whether it's the Rotary Club, Lions Club, or other community service organization, find a compatible group and interact. Breakfast

meetings provide you a chance to sit and chat with a table full of people before the speaker appears. Besides the opportunity to socialize, don't underestimate the contacts you can make at these gatherings.

- **Improve your skills.** You can't possibly know everything there is to know about your business. Check your area's community colleges, the local university, and other educational outlets for classes that may help you in accounting, marketing, or computer-related subjects. Looking forward to a class that meets once or twice a week is a great way to feel less isolated. Fellow students can become lasting friends. And while you are creating more life outside your office, you'll also be learning how to better run your business.

- **Take classes for fun.** Maybe you are a home-based business owner who tends to spend all waking hours working. Take a break from your business—if you've always wanted to learn French, go for it. No one is telling you that you can't take a class during "normal working hours." Even if the class doesn't allow for much socializing, seeing some different surroundings can help you feel less isolated.

- **Go out to lunch.** You have to eat lunch, so why not give it a dual purpose? Find an inexpensive lunch spot and meet a friend there every Thursday. Or every Tuesday after the mail delivers that weekly trade magazine, take it with you to your favorite eatery and read it over lunch break.

- **Join a volunteer organization.** It's hard to overemphasize how important it can be to make use of the fact that you no longer punch an actual or imaginary time clock. Do things you could never do before, such as volunteer during daytime hours. These are the times that are most difficult to get volunteers for, because most of the world is at work. Allow yourself to feel enriched by the great opportunity you have given yourself to work from home, for yourself, and donate some of your good fortune to your community.

Overwhelmed?

A common reaction to feeling overwhelmed is to shut down—there are so many things to do that your brain gets in sort of a traffic jam and you can't do anything. Combat that overwhelming feeling by being proactive about not getting to that point to begin with. Keep lists of things to do, and prioritize the list. Work on things that have a concrete deadline, but don't ignore all the non-deadline things that also need to be done. When you get things done, cross them off the list—and then congratulate yourself and treat yourself to a small reward!

Positive Self-Esteem

Maintaining positive self-esteem is an ongoing life challenge, whether or not you work from home. In many ways, working in your own home-based business can be an uplifting experience for your self-esteem. In other ways, you'll have to remember to pat yourself on the back, since you don't have a boss to do it for you (or to reprimand you, which is the other side of the coin).

If you came from a "regular job," your self-esteem can suffer from losing that impressive job title beside your name on the business card of an international company. That's OK—if you've been careful in naming your business, give yourself an impressive title and slap it on a business card. Who but you and your closest acquaintances need to know that Midwest International Freight is operated out of the corner of your living room, and that yes, you are the CEO—and the CFO, and the secretary, and that you clean the office, too?

Or maybe your self-esteem is depreciated on those trips to the bank when you're no longer depositing tidy sums of money in the form of biweekly paychecks but instead are withdrawing weekly sums for bare-bones living expenses. Get back to your list of goals! If your goals are too lofty to allow you some short-term success that makes you feel better about yourself and your current situation, then concentrate on breaking those big goals up into smaller steps.

Self-esteem is a very individual thing and you need to address it before you start feeling too negative. If you have friends who make you feel less than adequate because you are no longer the foreign marketing guru for a well-known company, maybe you should spend less time with those friends until you feel more accomplished. Most likely, you will find that most of your friends are so impressed with your bravery in starting your own business that you'll be amazed at their sincere praise for your new venture.

And don't hesitate to bring up self-esteem issues with a small business counselor or even a therapist. Your personal feelings about what you're doing will have a great bearing on the success of your business, so you want to give yourself every chance you can. Plus, you want to be proud of your new life and your courage to take the step that many people only dream about.

Shake Up Your Workday

Maybe one day a week you want to play all afternoon and put in your hours in the evening. Go for it! Although the fact remains that even with a home-based business you are still at the mercy of the workday hours in which the rest of the world does business, with some common sense you can still set your own lifestyle in a way you never could while working for someone else. If you can't bring yourself to quit for the day at one o'clock, then quit at noon and get back to your desk by four, when there's still time to return any calls that came in while you were gone.

CHAPTER SEVENTEEN

Problem Solving

Running your own business will certainly be gratifying, but it will not be problem-free. In fact, there may be days, weeks, or even months when you seem to spend more time "fighting fires" than planning ahead and charting your course for success.

Fear not. Successful problem solving can be a great source of a sense of accomplishment in your business. Keeping a positive attitude and greeting each problem as a challenge is helpful.

Recognizing Problems Early

Nearly any problem can be tackled effectively if you recognize it sooner rather than later. In fact, minor challenges often turn into major problems simply because the person in charge wasn't willing to face it down early enough. But how do you recognize a potential problem soon enough?

Sometimes you are smart and honest enough with yourself to know that there's a problem with your business, but you're just too close to it to see exactly what the problem might be. There's nothing wrong with calling in an outsider.

Your accountant can be invaluable in helping you understand what's really happening in your business. Use him or her, especially if divining profit and loss statements is not your strong suit. Accountants are particularly good at foreseeing financial struggles. If you work with your accountant to determine typical financial ratios within your trade, he or she can help you measure your own business against the norm and identify trouble spots.

A word of caution, however. At the risk of unfairly generalizing an entire group of professionals, remember that accountants deal in realities. Theirs is a world of hard numbers—one and one always equal two. Entrepreneurs often find success by figuring out some seemingly impossible way to make one and one into three. Listen to your accountant in order to understand clearly what is going on in your home business, but don't be afraid to trust your own instincts as well. Have your accountant show you what you have done so far, but make up your own mind about what can be done in the future.

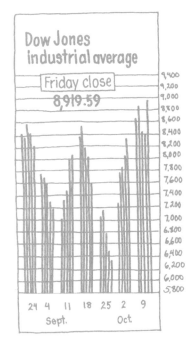

Cash Flow Problems

One of the most common problems small entrepreneurial businesses face is cash flow. Sure, there's money coming in, but there always seems to be money going out, too. At the risk of stating the obvious, successful businesses have more dollars coming in than going out and carry a cash reserve to cover those temporary times when the opposite may be true.

The easiest way to avoid cash flow problems is to maintain a high enough reserve—or, simply put, to have enough in savings to cover yourself. But not everyone can do that. Home businesses in particular are often started and operated on a shoestring—which is all the more reason to watch your cash flow closely.

That's why nearly every small business book stresses the importance of a business plan, including a cash flow analysis. These tools are not meant for use once and then put away in the files. Review your cash flow statement often. In these days of inexpensive computers and software, you don't need to be a trained accountant or information technology nerd to update a cash flow statement on a regular basis.

Revise your future income and expense estimates regularly. When you created your annual budget in November, you may not have forecast every expense accurately. Make a point of reviewing your projections for the rest of the year at least quarterly, and if money is tight, do it no less than monthly. That way you can revise future expenditures based on real, year-to-date numbers. Every month you go into a fiscal year, your budgeted numbers are further from the date you created them—and are possibly less accurate as a result.

You can also stay alert to what may be coming down the road. Keep an eye on the economy overall, and the trends within your trade. If you're a plumber or electrician, you'll want to watch new housing starts in your area and the pace of new and old home sales—those numbers will tell a story that effects your business. Over the years, you'll garner enough knowledge and insight to know almost exactly how a rise in the unemployment rate might change the pace of your own small business.

Reach Out

Two public service organizations can help in recognizing and solving problems. Small Business Development Centers (SBDCs) are associated with colleges and universities located across the country and offer a wide variety of programs and advice for small businesses. Check your local listings to find the nearest SBDC office.

Another resource is the Service Corps of Retired Executives. These retired execs act as consultants to help you analyze your business and discuss problems and solutions. If you are matched with a former exec with a world of experience who is happy to help you out, it works. The success of the program depends on finding a good match, however. Sometimes SCORE volunteers come from a corporate world and their advice doesn't quite mesh with an entrepreneurial or home business issue.

Monitor the Competition

One of the dangers of operating your own business is that daily operations keep you so busy that it can be difficult to keep your head up, looking out for trouble down the road.

Let's consider an example: you own and operate Tip Top Tack Shop, a retail business based in a small barn on your property. You sell horse paraphernalia to the many horse owners in the immediate, 100-square-mile area. Your home-based business is now 18 months old, and business has grown steadily. You invested most of your available capital in inventory to start the store, and you have good credit terms with a number of vendors.

But with the work it takes to maintain your own horses and tending to the store, you don't get away from your property as much as you used to. At the end of one particular quarter, you notice that sales have slowed—in fact, your sales are down in each of the last three months. Curious, you look over some specific sales information and discover that one of your biggest customers, the owner of a commercial horse farm, hasn't bought anything during that time. Without her, your business is marginal at this stage in its development.

You find a good excuse to drop by her place the next day. In chatting, you learn what you came to learn—and it's not good news: a large tack retailer and pet supply house some 100 miles away has started an online catalog, offering deep discounts on numerous items. Even with shipping charges, your largest customer can save money buying online, and she likes being able to place an order late in the evening from her computer.

Are you sunk? Not by a long shot. First, make a simple list of your options.

1. Cut expenses.
2. Find more customers or another large customer.
3. Start your own Web site.
4. Woo back your old customer.

Do You Have an Advisory Board?

Many entrepreneurs understand that along with their strengths as businesspeople, they also have the occasional weakness. To offset those weaknesses and to provide insight, alternative points of view, and much needed moral support, an advisory board can be great.

Ask a few acquaintances if they'd be willing to serve on such a board. Three to five is a good number. They needn't be close friends—in fact, it might be better if they weren't your best friends—but they should be people you trust and whose opinion you value. (This does not mean that you always have to agree with each other!) Ideally, among them will be people who run their own small business or have done so in the past, as well as people with experience in your industry or trade. You may even want to consider paying them a modest stipend for their efforts—as a gesture, but also as a way to keep the relationship semiformal. You want their counsel first, their friendship second.

Set up a regular meeting time—say quarterly. You might consider meeting for lunch (you pick up the tab) or for dinner. Create an agenda for those quarterly meetings. You might start off with a report on how the business is faring, including specific sales and expense figures. Share your projections for the next quarter. Next on the agenda may be discussion of specific goals for the next quarter or next year. Another agenda item may be a particular problem you're encountering. Explain your view of the problem, some ideas you had for solutions, and seek their counsel and input.

Don't do all the talking yourself! You've gathered this group together to help you make the best decisions. Give them your best assessment of where you are and where you're going, then ask a lot of questions. *And listen*. The answer you're looking for is probably there, but you've got to be willing to hear it.

On a less formal basis, make use of your board of advisors when you need another perspective or a moral boost between your quarterly meetings. You don't want to be a pest, but a quick call to bounce an idea or two off someone who knows your business can be a huge advantage.

Hiring Help

Many home businesspeople enjoy not only being the sole proprietor of their business but the sole worker as well. As their business grows, the idea of hiring employees, and dealing with taxes, insurance, and other paperwork is counter to what they want their home business to be.

But that doesn't mean you can't hire help. Perhaps you have an accountant, but still do your own bookkeeping. Why not engage a book-keeper (maybe even another home businessperson who understands your needs) to free up more of your own time for generating revenue. Hiring a house cleaner may seem like an extravagance, but consider the value of your own time—you may be wasting valuable, money-

(continued on next page)

Cutting back expenses is certainly an option, but in the long term, your business needs to grow to survive. It's not really the long-term solution needed for this problem. Finding other customers should be an ongoing part of your business plan—but sometimes it's tough to predict when that will happen. Starting your own Web site is certainly something to consider—if you have the capital, if it fits your business plan, and if you think you really can compete with a large retailer in the e-commerce arena. Without the volume the larger retailer has, it's not likely you'll be able to go head-to-head with them.

But perhaps there are ways you can woo back your previous customer. She may get good prices, but what about emergencies? You have stock on hand, and you probably don't mind a late-night call if she needs something quickly. Perhaps if she guaranteed you a minimum amount of business each month, you could offer her a discount—and if she can predict when she'll need certain supplies, maybe you can deliver. Sell your ability to provide better, personalized customer service and work to meet her needs, and you have a good shot at getting your biggest customer back. Then concentrate on finding a few more like her, so that next time one of them bolts for a new kid on the block, you aren't affected as dramatically.

10 Common Mistakes
1. Undercapitalization

In other words, you don't have enough money. It's one thing to cut back on personal expenses and live off a small salary temporarily as you start your business, but when your lack of capital seriously compromises the service you're able to provide your customer, you're headed in the wrong direction. For example, if your lawn care business is behind schedule because you don't have the money to buy and maintain the equipment you need, you're stuck.

2. Too Much Debt

A related problem to undercapitalization is having more debt than the business can handle. Say your Great Aunt Goodheart loans

you the $15K you need to start TeeHee T's, a business creating and selling T-shirts with funny slogans on them. You invest in equipment and inventory. The money starts coming in, but you promised to pay Aunt Goodheart back at a rate of $1,000 per month—and you know she's counting on the money. But your initial revenues are only in the $2,000 per month range—which would work fine if you just didn't have to pay back the original loan so quickly. You pay it back anyway, but are not left with enough to reinvest in inventory and other business expenses needed for growth.

Some small businesses start out with a reasonable debt, but continue to borrow during cash flow crunches and end up accumulating more debt than they can manage to pay off. As a home business entrepreneur, watch your personal credit card balances.

3. Poor Customer Service

You may be the greatest roofer, accountant, or resume writer in the county, but if you treat your customers with disrespect, you'll find it more difficult to stay in business. Yes, there are nightmare customers who push the limits. But you can be fair and direct without being unpleasant. Every customer deserves to have calls returned, appointments kept in a timely fashion, and paperwork in order. Respond to complaints quickly—often customers just want to be heard, and ignoring them only makes the problem worse.

4. Looking Too Much Like a Home Business

You've taken all the night courses needed to be an income tax preparer and consultant. You worked for one of the national tax preparation firms to get experience. Now you've gone out on your own, running a tax preparation business out of your home. But when clients come to your place of business to meet with you, you sit around the kitchen table. Dirty dishes are stacked in the sink. The kids' toys are strewn about. Customers are not going to take you seriously.

5. Poor Planning

Even the most brilliant businessperson will have a tough time making the best decisions without a road map. A business plan

Hiring Help

(*continued from previous page*)

making hours behind a vacuum when you could be paying a maid service to help out. Are you spending too much of your time sorting out computer problems? More than likely there's a local computer whiz with a home business of her own who will, for a modest fee, provide technology support and keep you up and running.

Don't go overboard—look carefully to see what your business can afford and what it can't. But remember that the most important thing you can do for the progress of your business is generate revenue, and paying another person to handle some of your support functions may pay off.

focuses your efforts, helps you measure your progress, and keeps you on budget. Don't start a home business without it.

6. Waiting Until It's Too Late

You know you have problems, but you just can't make yourself face them. When you finally do dig into the numbers to analyze the depth of the crisis, it's too late to save yourself. If only you'd tried to reverse the negative trends a few months before . . .

7. Unrealistic Expectations

This common problem is related to poor planning and research. Sure, it seems as if every one of those tourists who drive by your house all summer would be willing to drop $50 to $100 on items in your craft store, but since you renovated the garage and opened the shop, only some stop and only a few of those actually buy something. What's wrong?

Nothing at all, perhaps. You may be doing quite well given your location, product line, and pricing. Your only problem may be that you expected to generate $100K selling wooden candlesticks out of your garage, and it just isn't going to happen. A little market research ahead of time could have told you exactly that.

8. Defeatist Attitude

Just as unrealistic expectations can sink your ship, so can a defeatist attitude. When things aren't going as planned, try to be invigorated by the challenge. Keep things in perspective (it's only a business, after all, and you can always start another one, right?), and look for the solutions. You're the owner, the inspiration behind this venture. If you give up in your own mind, the end is nigh.

9. Poor Time Management

You're busy all the time, but most of your customers are still waiting. What the heck's the deal? Well, maybe you have more customers than you can handle. If so, great, but maybe you're not scheduling

Trapped in Inventory

Retail businesses are particularly sensitive to cash flow interruptions because they effect what inventory they do or don't have to sell. Small retailers often have much of their capital and/or available credit tied up in the inventory that's on the floor. It's not earning interest, and after a while customers get bored with it.

Managing inventory levels is a critical skill for a small home business. Check with the trade organization covering your kind of retail business to find out the average "turn" rate—how often you expect inventory to move in and out the door. If you've got things for sale that are hanging around too long, then return them or put them on sale, but get them off the shelves and replace them with something else. You don't make money having items sit on display forever.

Watch and track sales by inventory type. Not everything will sell at the same rate, and some higher margin, high-price items might take longer to turn and make a profit for you. But customers vote with their dollars, and if you're stocking an item that's finishing last in the money polls, it's time to exchange it for something new.

If you find yourself trapped in an inventory deadlock—you can't sell the stuff you've got, can't return it, and don't have cash or credit to buy in new inventory—then it's time to wheel and deal. Call your suppliers. They're in the business of selling things to you for resale, and they won't make more money off you until reorder. Convince them to work with you—by sharing a markdown on the retail price so you can put the item on sale or by allowing you to return items for credit on new inventory. If they're good distributors or vendors, and you're a good customer who usually pays the bills, then they are likely to listen.

See if you can unload the inventory you have to someone you know can use it. Call up the customers who bought some before and offer them a deal on the rest.

The important lesson here is that the longer inventory hangs around your retail store, the harder it is to sell, and the less likely you'll be able to sell it. It makes the rest of the inventory look stale to repeat customers—who notice these things! So get rid of it, and find a way to get fresh goods on your shelves.

your available time as well as you could. Spending a few too many minutes on the phone perhaps?

10. Cash Flow

Yes, we discussed cash flow already. Well, here's a reminder— fewer dollars are coming in than going out and no reserve. If your expenses are fixed, then you're in a fix without a sizable reserve. It's not uncommon for viable businesses to lose money during start-up or expansion. Some businesses are seasonal and have to plan for covering costs during the off-season when there's little or no revenue. If you've planned for it, you'll survive. But if you can't keep the creditors at bay or meet payroll, then it's only a matter of time.

For more information on this topic, visit our Web site at businesstown.com

PART IV

Promotions and Sales

CHAPTER EIGHTEEN

Creating a Marketing Plan

L ike a business plan, a marketing plan is important first because of the process. Creating the plan itself forces you to ask and answer key questions about the focus of your business, so that as you go forward, you have refined your goals and have a road map to reach them.

Once the plan is on paper, it serves its second purpose as a tracking device. Rather than creating a marketing plan and tossing it into a drawer never to be seen again, it can and should be referred to frequently. It can help you stay focused, stay on track, and change directions in the most intelligent ways when necessary.

Elements of a Marketing Plan

A marketing plan can be long or short, but ideally it should answer questions about who will buy your product or service and how you expect to get them to do it. It will also discuss who your competitors are for those customers and how you plan to make the customers come to you instead of the competition.

Some marketing plans will be relatively complex and citing "core competencies" and "distribution channels." That's fine for some, but don't be intimidated if you didn't go to business school and aren't familiar with these terms. What you do need to find out and need to be able to express is what business you're in, how big the market for it is, and how you can attract the customer base you need to succeed.

An outline of a typical marketing plan might look like this:
Mission Statement or Statement of Purpose
Executive Summary or Description of the Business
Overall Market Analysis (including Competitive Analysis)
Goals
SWOT Analysis
Marketing Strategies
Target Market Analysis (including Customer Needs and
    Characteristics)
Implementation Plan
Review and Evaluation Plan

Don't get too hung up on one form or another. Remember, the key is the process of asking and answering the right questions and then getting that information down on paper in a way that will suit your needs.

Keeping It Simple: Reliable Jon's Mowing

Let's start by considering a marketing plan for a lawn care business run by Jon, a teenager who isn't yet old enough to drive. His mission is to generate $200 weekly mowing lawns in his immediate neighborhood.

Overall Market

Jon researches the overall market and determines that in an area with upper-middle-class demographics such as his, about 35 percent of households hire someone to mow the lawn on a regular basis and about half of the remaining households hire someone once or twice a year during vacation. Using a survey of one sample street in his area, he determines that, of those who hire help to have lawns done regularly, half use a commercial lawn care service and half hire a local kid like himself to do the work.

Jon walks around the neighborhood and estimates how far he would be willing to push his mower to get to a potential customer and discovers that there are 260 households within his market. Using that number, he estimates the following:

Total Households: 260
Households that hire regularly (35% x 260): 91
Households that use commercial services (50% x 91): 45.5
Households that use kids like himself (50% x 91): 45.5

Households that don't hire regularly (65% x 260): 169
Households that hire once or twice a year (50% x 169): 84.5

Use It or Lose It

Regardless of whether your marketing plan is a simple document of a few pages or a more complex analysis designed to support a plea for loans or investment, make it useful. No amount of market research will help you if a marketing plan stays in a drawer or gets relegated to the circular file once it's done. Create a plan that you can refer to frequently, checking off each step of your plan as it's accomplished and reviewing your assumptions and projections.

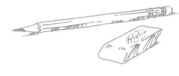

Using the above, he estimates the size of his market to be 45.5 potential regular jobs plus 84.5 once- or twice-a-year jobs with "vacation" households.

From a financial standpoint, he estimates that on average homeowners pay $25 to have their lawns cut. The season in his part of the country starts in April and goes through the end of October, and Jon guesses that, on average, regular customers would need their lawns cut 15 times a year. From that, he figures the overall market to be worth:

Regular customers: 45.5 x 15 = 682.5 mowings x $25 = $17,062.50
     per year
Vacation customers: 84.5 x 1.5 = 126.75 mowings x $25 = $3,168.75
     per year

Jon wants to average $200 a week for 30 weeks, for a total of $6,000 for the season. With a total estimated market of around $20,000, he needs to capture 30% of the market ($6000 ÷ $20,000 = 30%).

Competitive Analysis

Jon knows a couple other kids who mow neighbors' lawns, but they aren't really looking to do much more than that. Using the Yellow Pages he discovers that there are a half-dozen commercial lawn care services listed, but only one is located within five miles of his neighborhood. He looks in the local weekly newspaper and sees that another lawn care service company is located about eight miles away.

He also checks the bulletin boards at the local supermarket and diner to see if anyone has advertised there. Plus he keeps his eye out for lawn service trucks in his neighborhood.

Jon calls all the commercial services and asks what they charge. All but one have a $40 minimum no matter how big the yard. The other simply says he would have to see the yard to give an estimate. He asks each company if they have any customers in his neighborhood so that he can look at the yard and see how good a job they did. Of the seven, two say it's too far away and they wouldn't want the job anyway, two say they have no customers in that area, one says he "did a couple lawns around there" but refuses to name them, and two give him an address to look at. He checks them both out: They are huge lawns, well over an acre.

Jon also asks the guys he knows who mow lawns for their neighbors how much they get. One gets $25 and the other $20. In both cases, the neighbors are elderly people.

From this survey, Jon has learned:

- The commercial services do not seem to have a particularly high penetration into his market.
- It would take a little work for a prospective customer to get a quote from one of the commercial services.
- It would likely be a minimum of $40 per lawn to hire a commercial service.

Goals

Jon knows he needs a 30 percent share of the market, or about 15 regular customers who will pay on average $25, 15 times during the season, plus another 15 vacation customers who will pay him an average of $25 to mow their lawns at least once. If he works five days a week, that means he has to do at least three lawns a day.

SWOT Analysis

To help determine the best way to go about achieving their goals, businesses sometimes will do a "SWOT" analysis. SWOT stands for the Strengths, Weaknesses, Opportunities, and Threats of the business. Outlining his SWOT may be overkill for a summer lawn mowing service, but Jon sits down and goes through the process just to see if there's something he hasn't considered.

Strengths—What does his business have going for it?
Pleasant outgoing personality
Known in the area as a responsible young man, knows many
    families
Strongly motivated to save money to buy a new mountain bike

Aiming at a Moving Target

When you're hunting customers, you're pursuing a moving target. The key is to constantly refine your knowledge of the market and become more accurate over time about how your business will grow. That way, you'll recognize fundamental market changes sooner than your competition, and can adapt to new customer demands quickly.

Weaknesses—What does his business have going against it?
Limited to area where he can push his mower
Limited labor, only one person

Opportunities—What can he take advantage of in the market?
Competition isn't as focused on his market
Could offer to water indoor plants and take care of pets for customers on vacation

Threats—What might make things difficult for his business?
Only one mower, might break down
Weather unpredictable, extended rainy period could cause problems

Marketing Strategies

Given his understanding of the overall market, his goals, his strengths, and weaknesses, where does Jon start in his quest to find 15 households as regular customers? First, he determines his target market—those customers he can appeal to most based on the services he can provide.

Target Market Analysis

Although Jon doesn't have the figures to back it up, he's guessing that the older the customers, the more likely they are to pay to mow the lawn. He knows that if he charges by the hour, larger lawns could be mowed more efficiently by riding lawn mowers, and people with larger lawns might more likely either own a rider or have the lawn done commercially.

He also knows that it would take as much effort to get a regular customer for the season as it will to get the once- or twice-a-year customers.

Consequently, Jon concludes that his target market consists of older homeowners with medium-sized lawns who won't want to pay $40 or more for a commercial service but will be pleased to help out a local teenager by paying $20–$30 for the job on a regular basis. As a secondary market, he would go

after people on vacation or business trips who needed their lawn cut once or twice a year.

Knowing he wanted to appeal to older homeowners, Jon called his grandparents and asked them what was important to them when it came to hiring someone to mow their lawn. Did they have any complaints about people who had done it for them in the past?

He learned that they valued reliability. They were accustomed to their schedules, and if it was arranged that the lawn would be mowed on Friday morning, then they expected it to be done Friday morning. They also told Jon that they were more comfortable if the person doing the work was dressed neatly and appeared trustworthy.

Based on this information, Jon decided to call his business "Reliable Jon's Mowing."

Jon's next step was to figure out how to reach his target market. He needed to move fast, focus his outreach, and keep his expenses down, all of which eliminated traditional advertising media such as newspapers. He decided he would use direct mail to reach his senior customers (thinking that a mailed flyer would have more credibility among seniors). For his target "vacation homeowners," he planned to canvas the neighborhood door-to-door with a flyer: once at the beginning of the season and once around July 1 as a reminder before the peak vacation months.

He then went to the local senior center and asked if they had a mailing list of seniors in his neighborhood. They did, and since he was such a nice young man and only wanted names from a few streets, they let him copy them off the main mailing list. He was pleased to discover that of the 260 households in his market, 75 were listed as seniors.

For his direct mail campaign, Jon made flyers promoting his reliability and reasonable prices. He scanned in a photo of himself and put it on the flyer so that potential customers could see his clean-cut, trustworthy face. At the bottom of the flyer, he put a cartoon character who was saying to himself, "Terribly hot out. I think I'll call Jon . . . "

For his door-to-door campaign, Jon altered the flyer to promote both his regular service as well as his vacation services, including extras like indoor plant care. He left a blank space on the flyer,

Smart Fixes

Once you've identified a weakness of your business, can you fix it? In Jon's case, he approached his friends who were mowing their neighbors' lawns and told them that if they ever wanted extra work to check with him, he might be able to help. He also volunteered to cover for them if they couldn't get to their neighbors' lawns in time. By establishing this relationship, Jon had a source of casual labor (with their own lawn mowers) to help him out if he got behind or if his own mower was being repaired.

and as he went door-to-door to drop off the flyers, he wrote in what he would charge for that particular household's lawn.

In addition to his direct mail and door-to-door campaigns, Jon knew that word-of-mouth would be important. He made a list of everyone he could think of to tell about his new venture. He created business cards to hand out to those people as reminders. Among the people he told were his mailman, the minister at church, and the electric meter reader, all of whom were out and about in the neighborhood frequently.

The final part of Jon's plan was to post flyers and/or business cards in various key places around the community, including the supermarket, a small engine repair business, the senior center, and the public library.

Jon's plan was to be fully employed by the time school let out for the summer in early June. He planned to sign up five regular customers each in March, April, and May, with leads for vacation customers as well.

Review and Evaluation

Jon started his campaign in March and planned to review his progress every two weeks for the first two months, and then monthly after that. Initially it was slow going—March was apparently too early to get people thinking about mowing lawns, and if he were to do it again, Jon would hold off on his flyer campaign until early to mid-April.

At the end of April, Jon had only five regular customers and was slightly discouraged. But within two weeks, he had signed up five more, and by the end of May another four, for a total of 14 regular customers—very close to his goal of 15. He considered canceling his plans for a follow-up flyer in early July for vacation households, but when a dry weather spell in June slowed his overall business (grass just wasn't growing fast enough), he went ahead with it.

Needless to say, Jon's biggest problem the rest of the summer was remembering to have some fun, since he had all the work he could handle. In fact, as the season wound down, he was working on a business and marketing plan to expand his business using additional workers.

Though Reliable Jon's Mowing is a simple example, it shows every step of the market planning process—identify the market, look for ways to penetrate that market, create a plan to do it, and review and evaluate as you go.

Before you spend time and money promoting your business, you need to have a clear idea who you're trying to reach. A realistic and well-researched marketing plan will help you focus your resources on the market that will most benefit your business. By reviewing and updating your plan regularly, you can do the best job possible of hitting that always moving target.

For more information on this topic, visit our Web site at businesstown.com

CHAPTER NINETEEN

Sales Basics for the Home Business

E ver hear the old cliché, "Plan your work and work your plan"? As timeworn as the saying may be, it's still true. Jumping haphazardly from one sales effort to the next is not the best way to go about selling your product or service. You need to create a plan that helps you identify your target market, prioritize your leads, and track your success.

Your marketing plan should identify your target market (see Chapter 18). If you're running a pet grooming service out of your home, your target market is likely to be those people with dogs and cats who live within an easy drive of your house. Easy, right? But are you looking to go after dog show contestants who demand very specific services and are willing to pay dearly for them? And if so, how many of those kinds of customers are within driving distance? Or are you more interested in the average dog owner who wants a professional to groom her pet a few times a year? Knowing the answer to these questions will help focus your sales efforts.

Sometimes it's as easy as hanging out a sign, putting a small ad in the newspaper, and waiting for business to roll in. If so, then you've picked the right business to be in!

More likely, though, you've developed a good reputation for pet grooming among friends, and you've recently decided to make it more of a full-time business. Now you need to sell your services to a few new customers. Certainly advertising is a part of the promotional mix. But how do you create a plan to build your business through sales?

Let's go back to our neighborhood dog groomer. Who would be the best customers? Presumably those households with lots of hairy, unkempt dogs, right? Maybe. More likely it is people who are already grooming their dogs or getting their dogs groomed—they're already convinced that pet grooming is worthwhile, which makes your sales job easier. All you have to do is convince them that you're the right person for the job!

Making a Sales Plan

According to your business plan, you know you need to generate $30,000 in revenue to meet your goals for the year. You've called around to other groomers, and you know that the average rate per grooming session is $40. That means you need 750 grooming sessions annually, or 14 to 15 per week. If the average pet owner has his pet groomed three times a year and half of the pet owners have at least two pets, then you'll need around 175 different clients. Sounds like a lot, doesn't it!

Let's say you're starting with a dozen clients for whom you've been grooming pets for years. Where do you go for more? One of the best ways to generate sales leads is through your current satisfied customers. If they're your friends, ask them to help out by recommending you to their friends, coworkers, and relatives. Don't be shy—ask for names and addresses or phone numbers and the best way to approach these potential customers. Offer a free grooming session to any current customer who brings in another customer for the first time. Give current customers half-price coupons to hand out to other pet owners they know.

Let's return to our sales plan. If you've got a dozen current customers, could you generate a "lead list" of 25 more potential customers from them? Probably, if you're aggressive. And if you continually mined your regular customers for new leads, you might, over a year's time, come up with ten times that many leads.

OK, so you figure you can generate 250 leads just through current customers. Will those leads all become customers themselves? Not likely. Your success rate will depend on many factors—the demographics of your area, the strength of the competition, how well you sell your services—but let's say you're good at what you do and you're able to convert 25 percent of those good leads to actual customers. That's around 63 new customers you can plan to add to your original 12, leaving you with 75 at year's end.

So where are the rest of the customers going to come from? You still need another 100 clients—which will need to be converted from as many as 400 or 500 leads.

Think about other noncompetitive businesses that serve the same market. For a pet groomer, that could be veterinarians, kennels, pet stores, and pet supply stores. Can you access

their customers? Perhaps one of the businesses has a mailing list they would rent to you for a direct mailing. Such businesses often have bulletin boards for posting services offered. Maybe one of them has a flyer or mailer and would allow you to advertise, especially if you offer a discount to their customers. Or perhaps you could give a grooming workshop at one of their places of business which would help them while promoting your own business.

For your plan, let's say you discover that the local pet supply store is willing to rent you their mailing list of 500 names. Once you sort them out by zip code, you find 250 that are likely candidates, geographically, for your pet grooming services. You're halfway to the rest of your goal.

You live on a relatively busy street, and you're planning to hang out a sign. You figure that you'll get at least five people a month who'll stop in to find out about your services. That's 60 in a year, all at a relatively high conversion rate—they took the time to stop by, so it will be easier to sell them on the quality of your service.

Although it's expensive, you feel it's important to be in the Yellow Pages. You figure a small listing will generate another 10 calls a month, or 120 annually.

Let's add up your leads so far:

Lead Source	No. of Leads	Est. Conversion Rate	No. of Customers
Word-of-mouth recommendations	250	25%	63
Other related businesses	250	10%	25
Drive-by inquiries	60	75%	45
Yellow Page inquiries	120	30%	36
Original customers			12
Totals	680	35% (avg.)	181

You now have a plan for generating enough leads to end up with an appropriate number of clients within a year. Will it work? Who knows? You might get more or fewer leads or end up with more or fewer clients per lead. The important part of this process is that you create a plan, on paper, for going out into the market and generating business.

Timing

For your pet grooming business, you now know with your plan where your leads and customers will come from. Don't forget, you aren't likely to follow up on everything at once. After all, you still have to leave time for grooming a dog every now and then.

Work out a reasonable schedule for each of your sales initiatives. You can get started right away on the drive-by traffic—as soon as your sign is ready, hang it up and wait to see what happens. The inquiries you get shouldn't overwhelm you—as long as you're ready to do business. If you hang your sign before you're ready to take clients, make sure you add a temporary "Coming Soon" banner, since you want to avoid disappointing a potential customer. If someone sees your sign, stops in, and is told that you'll "be opening soon, not sure when, maybe a month, maybe more," you're in danger of turning him or her off. A few days early is OK—even a few weeks—but have a definite opening day in mind and be ready to take appointments. Then, if someone stops by before you're ready to go, the conversation can be more positive: "We'll be opening on the fifteenth, and I'm taking appointments now. What days are good for you? I have some openings on Thursday the eighteenth."

Similarly, your word-of-mouth advertising via your current clients can start right away. It will take time and ongoing effort to build the business this way, but it's effort well spent. Your current customers will lead you to others like them—reliable, repeat clients who love to talk about what a wonderful job you do.

On the other hand, your Yellow Pages advertising will depend on the annual deadline in your area. If the deadline has just past, then you may have to wait a year to get that Yellow Page listing and may have to consider a different print advertising plan in the meantime. As you put together your sales and promotion plan, call

Web-Based Directories

An alternative to the Yellow Pages are Web site-based business directories. Many local Internet Service Providers, newspapers, and Chambers of Commerce maintain Web sites that enable local businesses to be listed as part of a town or city directory. And the good news is they're often free or inexpensive.

and find out the deadlines and publication dates of the various Yellow Pages and similar business directories in your area.

As a home business pet groomer you next need to decide when to initiate the direct mailing to the list rented from the local pet supply store. There are many variables to consider, but it would be wise to get the business up and running before you take on a sales initiative that may generate (you hope!) a flood of inquiries. Make sure you're ready to follow up on the leads you get and can handle the business they generate. To quote another timeworn cliché, "You only get one chance to make a good first impression!"

For simplicity's sake, let's say you're opening for business January 1. It might then make sense to begin your sales push in February, with the idea that business will start to really pick up in March. That gives you plenty of time to work out the bugs of your daily business regimen with current customers. Based on the response you get in this initial sales push, you can then fine-tune your budget for additional sales initiatives later in the year.

Needs-Based Selling

So now you have people calling you and stopping by your home business to find out more about the new dog groomer in town. They've responded to your sign, direct mail, or other advertising. You can assume that they have a dog or cat and are interested in grooming. How do you complete the sale?

Good salespeople like to focus the potential customer's attention on the benefits of a product or service. So what are the benefits of a well-groomed pet? A cleaner house, perhaps—less time spent vacuuming up dog or cat hair. Pride, as other pet owners admire the owner's pet. The pet's health, as it's easier to spot skin problems or other maladies when the dog is well groomed. The pet's happiness—as grooming will make them more comfortable, especially in the summer heat.

OK, you've got them hooked. Who could resist making their beloved pet happier and healthier, while keeping their house

cleaner and spending less time vacuuming? Now let's sell the advantages of your specific services.

Again, focus on the customers' needs. Are they busy people (who isn't?)? Your convenient location and flexible hours (after all, you're a home business) lets them easily drop Fido off on the way to work and pick him up later on. Are they concerned that Fido will get only the best care? A quick tour of your immaculate facilities (invite them in!) and your warm interaction with your own pets will quickly convince them that you're trustworthy. Are they concerned about whether you'll do a first-class job? The sheet of glowing praise and recommendations from current customers, not to mention your money-back guarantee on the first visit, will boost their confidence.

And yes, some customers may be price-conscious. Your market research has told you what competing groomers charge. If you're a bit more expensive, you'll calmly point out the "little extras" that you offer that make your rate worthwhile (and which no self-respecting pet owner would want to deprive their beloved companion of). After all, you use only the finest pet shampoo, you use only the best towels and blow dryer, your holding pens are cleaned after each client, and you insist that every pet that enters your business is given a flea bath. Your standards are high because your customers demand it—and you charge appropriately.

Of course, if you're prepared to compete based on price, then charge $5 less than the other guy—and make a big deal of it! That other guy is a good fellow and all, but your overhead is lower and you can do the same (or better) job for less.

Face-to-Face Selling

If you're a consumer, then you've been the victim of good salespeople and bad salespeople. Bad salespeople have a way of making you hate the product even if you do want to buy it, because you hate them. They demonstrate zero understanding of your concerns or situation, don't listen, and often rattle off a prepared speech or list of the features of whatever it is they are trying to sell. They

Projecting Revenue

As you consider the timing of your sales plan, you'll want it to coincide with your revenue projections in your business plan. If you're planning on a major promotional and sales push in April and May, then your business plan should show a corresponding jump in revenue as a result of that push. If you're a retailer, that revenue increase will be immediate—in April and May. If you're a contractor, you may not see a revenue jump for several months after you make the sale. Whatever your business, your sales plan should go hand in hand with your revenue (and expense) projections.

have a set selling style that works with a certain percentage of customers. They miss a lot of sales because they annoy too many qualified customers.

Bad salespeople also often have irritating habits. They don't look you in the eye, they interrupt, they fidget, they look over your shoulder to see if a better prospect is coming along. They dress poorly. They ignore you to answer the phone or deal with a colleague on a minor matter. They are pushy rather than helpful. They make you, the customer, feel unimportant.

Good salespeople, on the other hand, are good listeners. They want to hear about your needs, and they look for opportunities to point out how their product or service meets those needs. They are well groomed, present themselves professionally, meet your gaze, and tell you what you want to know. They make themselves available, at your service, but they also give you room to consider and decide on your own if you prefer. They do well in business because they make customers feel special, as if they are making the right decision in buying their product or service.

When you're selling face-to-face, let your pride in your work show. If asked to compare your product or service to a competitor, take the high road: Stress the positive aspects of your product rather than bad-mouthing your competition. Talk to your customers; establish a relationship. Smile and be happy to see them. Listen to their problems or needs. Ask leading questions to get them to tell you more. Acknowledge and support their needs. Give good advice based on your knowledge. And show them how your product or service will fill their needs and benefit them.

Phone Sales

Phone sales are more difficult than face-to-face selling because it's harder to gauge a customer's reaction. But the phone is a valuable tool, and the better you can get at projecting confidence and developing a pleasant phone manner, the more you'll sell based on incoming or outgoing calls.

Try not to sound rushed. If a customer took the time to look up your number and call you for information, then they are likely a

good lead and thus valuable. Try to remind yourself that every call could be your next big customer—and treat the caller with the respect you would give someone who represented a large chunk of your business. Keep your voice bright and friendly—you should sound as if you're happy to hear from them.

Your job on the phone is to find out what customers need and quickly let them know how your product or service can help. If it's a complex need, invite them to stop by. Ask for their address in order to send them printed information. Be helpful.

This is not to say that there aren't some callers who are a waste of time, and after a while it's easy to recognize someone who is just fishing for information, isn't really committed, or just wants to chat. And though you do need to manage your time well and bring those conversations to a timely end, remember your dependence on good word-of-mouth. Be courteous at all times, tell the chatty caller that you'll "let them get back to work," and give them a cheery good-bye.

Telemarketing

Using outgoing telephone calls to generate business is a tough way to go these days. It works, of course—otherwise you wouldn't get the myriad telemarketing calls you do. But telemarketing of this sort is a percentage game—call 1,000 people, and you'll get some to part with their money. That's a hard game to play for most home-based businesses.

What might be more worthwhile for a home business owner is a telemarketing program to call highly qualified potential customers or past customers on a regular basis. Do you have a list of customers who haven't made use of your services in a while? Why not spend a few evenings calling them, reminding them of what you offer, and find out if there's any particular reason they haven't used you. You'll garner some valuable feedback, and you'll no doubt scare up a few customers who just had been too busy to think about it.

You can also use telemarketing as a follow-up to a direct mail campaign. If you create a response card that is sent to a geographic area, you may be able to follow up by phone with those

Track Your Success

Not every plan works out. The goal with any sales plan is to maximize the return on your efforts. In order to refine your future efforts and keep sales costs in line, make sure you track the results of every sales promotion you try. How many calls did the ad in the local weekly generate? How does that compare with your radio campaign or your special offer? Which offers seem to work best? A direct mail campaign might generate a lot of leads, but how many of those leads were you able to convert to paying customers? How much did those paying customers cost to get? How does that cost compare to other lead-generating techniques?

As you plan your future sales, have your past results—in terms of customers, cost, and revenue generated—at your fingertips in order to aim your efforts in the best direction.

who return the card. That way you're spending your phone time with good leads rather than getting hung up on by irritated people who have no interest in your service.

Direct Mail

One of the most common methods to reach your target market is by direct mail. Mailing list companies—or "list brokers"—have become more and more sophisticated in their ability to target certain demographic and niche groups. With intelligent list rental and management, you can get a lot for your money with a direct mail campaign. That said, direct mail can be expensive. It's easy to waste a lot of hard-earned cash on a poor direct mail campaign.

There are two keys to success using direct mail: Know your target market, and create a marketing plan. Do the research a marketing plan requires so that you feel confident you know who your customers are. Then test the mailing lists that you think include those potential customers before you spend a lot of money.

There are three basic costs to direct mail:

1. The cost of the printed piece you mail
2. The cost of the names on the list
3. The cost of postage

Fear of Willy Loman

For some people, selling almost comes naturally. They've never met a stranger. For others, especially those who like the idea of being on their own in a home-based business, the idea of becoming a proactive, outgoing salesperson is intimidating. Although you should always be yourself, if you create a sales plan and follow it, listen well, and point out the benefits of your product or service and how they meet the needs of the customer, you too will become a good salesperson. And no longer fear turning into Willy Loman!

The list broker will often offer "one-stop shopping," and will help you design your direct mail piece and arrange printing and mailing.

If you try a direct mail promotion for your home business, develop an offer that requires or encourages an immediate response. A free quote or giveaway, a deep discount, or a good offer with a deadline will help prompt a quick response. Once you get the potential customers to contact you, you can then work on converting them from potential to actual paying clients.

Internet Sales

Many home-based businesses can take advantage of selling over the Internet. The Internet is a viable, cost-effective way to reach out beyond your local geographic area to qualified customers around the world.

Many Internet Service Providers have access to basic electronic catalog software and can help you create an online catalog, complete with "shopping carts" and security for credit card numbers, relatively simply. And though it's certainly easy to spend tens, even hundreds of thousands, on a comprehensive online catalog, it can be relatively inexpensive, too.

The challenge for those interested in e-commerce is competing with the millions of Web sites already out there, especially companies that have spent a lot of time and money building their brand through more traditional advertising media or that already have a category-leading brand. But if you have a niche product and can make yourself known to the small target market of potential customers who are willing to buy off the Web, then you can add sales.

Some specialty product makers may be able to join a cooperative e-commerce effort. Depending on your business, there may be a group already selling online to your target market, and you can add your product to the existing online catalog. The best situation will have you dealing directly with the customer—that way you can get their mailing address and add them permanently to your customer base.

Practice Your Pitch

If selling on the phone is a big part of your business, don't be shy about practicing. Ask a friend to pose as a potential customer and call you with a zillion demands. Practice asking probing questions, taking an interest in the customer's needs, and telling the customer about your services. You might even want to write down some notes on selling or turns of phrase that work to keep by your phone to help out when you get a real business call. By practicing in a low-pressure situation, you can improve your skills for the time when it counts.

CHAPTER TWENTY

Promoting Your Home Business

Promotion is important for any business, but it can be critical for many types of home-based businesses. Typically, your home is assumed to be just that—a home. So you've got to work a little bit harder to make the right people—your potential customers—know that your business exists and you want their patronage.

Paid vs. Unpaid Promotion

One way to think about the various ways you can promote a business is paid versus unpaid. Paid promotion is usually some sort of advertising that you pay to run on a planned schedule. Unpaid promotion would be publicity, such as when you send a press release to the local newspaper announcing the opening of your business, and the newspaper then runs as a news story. Unpaid promotion still may have costs associated with it, but you aren't paying the media (newspaper, radio or television, trade journal) to run it.

At first glance, unpaid promotion might seem better, since it's free, right? Not necessarily. There are advantages and disadvantages to both.

The advantage of paid promotion is that it's predictable. You can place advertising in the medium you choose, when you choose. This is particularly important if you're planning a grand opening sale or some other time-sensitive event. If the sale starts on Thursday, you can count on your advertising running in the newspaper on the days you choose, say Tuesday, Wednesday, and Thursday. If you've determined that the local weekly newspaper is the best way to reach your target customers, you can arrange to have your ad run in that paper when you want it there.

With unpaid promotion, you are often at the mercy of whatever space may be available in a given issue of your chosen medium. If the local weekly has space that week, they may run your press release. Then again, they may not. If you've planned your grand opening and the press release doesn't run, you're out of luck.

The disadvantage of paid promotion, of course, is that it can be expensive. In major metropolitan areas, the leading newspapers, radio stations, and television stations are often out of reach for most home businesses. And without a well thought out plan, any business can blow a wad of cash on advertising that doesn't generate the response you want.

However, by using a carefully crafted combination of paid and unpaid promotions, just about any business can get its message out. And with some basic market research, you can get that message to the people that matter—your target customers.

Creating an Image

The first thing you must consider as you begin to look for ways to promote your home business is how you want your customers to perceive your business.

One of the reasons you start a home-based business is to be able to do things your way. That includes creating an image for your business that suits your tastes and your vision. Of course, that vision also needs to appeal to the target market. If you're so unique as to be considered weird by the very people you want to do business with, you might have gone too far.

Do you make and sell teddy bears? Well, a "cute" image might work. Do you haul away junk cars? Then cute might not be quite right—unless you use it to advantage. Do you operate a septic service? Sometimes humor works well ("We're number one in number two!") and serves to make your business stand out. Are you an accountant? Humor might not work as well in a profession dealing with people's hard-earned money. Try to create an image that will give your business appropriate credibility.

That said, there's an advantage to standing out from the crowd. By pushing the limits and creating an image that's a little different from the norm, you may help your business stick in the minds of potential customers.

As discussed in Chapter 6, your business name is often the first impression a customer gets of your business. As you develop an overall image for your business, try to make sure that the name fits the picture and supports your promotion efforts. If it takes you five

minutes to explain what your business name means, it's probably not helping you. Pick a name that communicates clearly to potential customers the product or service you provide. Don't let clever wordplay get in the way of the essential message.

Image at Home

If you are inviting customers into your home for your business, you have quite a challenge. It's like trying to be ready to receive guests at a party, all day long. The guests don't care how busy you've been, how many school projects your children are working on, or that the washing machine broke down. When they arrive at your home business doorstep, they begin making conscious and subconscious judgments about your business and its suitability for them, the customer.

- Think carefully about your signage. Business signs need to be easily seen and easily associated with your property. In winter, darkness often intrudes into the business day, so you may want to consider outdoor lighting for your sign (as well as the entrance), assuming it's permitted by your zoning ordinance. A customer who has to work hard to find you comes to your door with a negative impression.
- Make sure there's appropriate parking. Make sure it's clear where they are supposed to park and where the entrance to the business is located. By making it easy, you create a positive image of your business even before the customer steps across the threshold.
- Consider using a separate entrance for your business area. As discussed in Chapter 8 on setting up your home business office, the more separate the space, the easier it will be to keep the occasional chaos of family life out of the business environment. This is especially true for a retail home business, in which the way you display your merchandise will impact sales. If you create a comfortable space that encourages customers to shop, with lighting that shows off the product and

leads the customer through the store logically, you'll be creating a positive image—and you'll sell more to boot.

- Be dressed appropriately. Sure, you're working out of your home and nobody but you is determining the dress code. But your appearance is part of the image of your business and needs to match. Nobody minds a mechanic with a few grease spots, but if you're running a yarn shop and you greet a customer fresh from weeding your garden, you run the risk of forming the wrong image.

- Make sure there's an appropriate space to meet with customers. Supply comfortable chairs and a desk or work surface to spread out paperwork. The kitchen table might work in a pinch, but most customers will feel more comfortable if a separate space is set aside especially for such consultations.

Image Away from Home

Many home-based businesses, indeed many regular businesses, never have cause to invite their customers to their offices. This might be true of the home-based plumber or electrician, the consultant, or the small manufacturer who only sells wholesale.

So how does the customer develop an image of your business? Any time a customer interacts with you, one of your vehicles, or your work site, they are making a judgment about the business. It starts with the first phone call. Your professionalism and phone manner immediately tell the customer something. Is your phone a separate business line? Do you answer the phone with a simple hello, or do you use a businesslike greeting? Do you keep advertised hours? Does your van, truck, or car have a professional-looking sign or does it look as if it was tagged by delinquents with multicolored spray paint? Are your tools organized? Do you wear appropriate clothing for your service, or did you throw on whatever was on top of the pile that morning?

All of these elements will be part of the image of your business in the eye of the customer. Before you start spending money on

Negotiate!

Advertising rates are in part set by publishers and broadcasters based on their costs, but more on what the market will bear. In almost every case, make an attempt to negotiate a better rate than what's being offered. Many times—even in a strong economy—your advertising rep will find a way to cut you a break. They want to keep your business.

advertising, make sure the rest of your business is ready to support the image you're trying to create.

Stationery and Logos

An image of your business is also created by your letterhead and business cards. Ideally, any printed piece of paper coming out of your business should work to reinforce the image you want to promote.

You are likely to adopt a logo for your business. It may be as simple as a clipart character supplied by the local business card printer, or it may be a custom abstract design created by a graphic artist. As you might imagine, the former is cheaper than the latter. But creating a unique image for your business can be helpful, so consulting a graphic artist to help you create a logo especially for your business is a good idea. Of course, if you're graphically inclined, home computers make creating your own logo easy and fun.

When it comes to logos, simplicity is usually best. As with business names, what may seem clever to you may be unreadable to a customer. As you develop your logo, look around and compare. Virtually every company has a logo—even if it's nothing more than the name of the company in a distinctive type style.

It's important that a logo is versatile. You'll want to use it on letterhead, envelopes, business cards, and invoices, and possibly on bags, packaging, signage, advertising, etc. Make sure your logo works well in one color—four-color logos look great in four colors, but when they run in a black and white newspaper ad, they sometimes lose their luster and become unrecognizable. And, if you're having a letterhead printed, one or two-color printing will be significantly cheaper.

All of the basic printed pieces used by a business—letterhead, envelopes, business cards, notes—are available in blank form that can be printed on a computer printer at home. Especially for a start-up, it may make more sense to buy a small package of ready-to-print business cards at the local office supply store, rather than running off 1,000 units at the local print shop. Similarly, you can create a template as your letterhead and print out one sheet at a time as you need it.

You'll need to choose paper for all these printed pieces. All sorts of colors, weights, and textures are available. Pick something that appeals to you, but matches the image of your business. "Bargain Betty's" won't require a fancy card, whereas "Anthony's Fine Antiques" might want something a little distinguished.

Web Sites

More and more home-based businesses are using the Internet to promote their business. Many Internet Service Providers (ISPs) make a limited Web page available as part of the monthly fee for Internet access. Local newspapers and Chambers of Commerce frequently will make hosting a simple home page (a single Web document) or entire Web site part of the services they provide. With the Web design software available for any good home computer, creating and updating your home page or full-service Web site is relatively easy.

From an image standpoint, you'll want to make sure that your Web presence echoes the rest of your business. Most important, make sure that it's easy to access and understandable. If your home page is a mess, a potential customer won't blame the host or the Web designer, they'll chalk it up to you and your business.

One frequent complaint of Web users is that businesses fail to update their home page or Web site. The Internet is a fast-changing environment. Don't set yourself up for an impossible task by promising regular updates and new information if you can't keep up with it. It would be better to simply create an informational home page, with e-mail addresses, phone, and "snail mail" addresses to contact for further information.

Advertising Basics

Advertising works. Just ask any one of the dozens of advertising sales representatives who'll contact you once they figure out that you

Buy What Works

Although keeping your advertising budget in line is critical, it makes no sense to buy a bargain ad if it's not going to bring in business. Although it's fine to try new media and new publications in search of additional customers, beware of buying an ad just because it's cheap. Even an inexpensive ad is wasted money if it doesn't reach your target customers.

Get Credit Due

Whenever you place an ad, ask to see it before it runs. Make sure your phone number, address, and opening hours are correct. If you're having a sale or a special offer, make sure those details are correct. But don't leave it there—make sure you get a copy of the publication when the ad is running and double-check your ad. Mistakes can happen—an ad can run in the wrong section of the paper, upside down, or an older ad is run instead of the new one. If a mistake was made, contact your ad rep immediately so he or she can correct the problem and give you credit for the ad that ran incorrectly. If you wait two or three days to notify the publication, they may only credit the first insertion—the rest of the run will then be your problem.

have an ad budget of any kind. From weekly newspapers and flyers to the Yellow Pages to the latest in Internet ads, they'll all be happy to spend your time convincing you that new customers and big growth is just around the corner if you'll only advertise with them.

And in the right circumstances, not all of them will be wrong.

Setting an Advertising Budget

How much you spend on advertising will depend considerably on the type of business you operate and its location. It's often said that the true cost of a business location is equal to the cost of rent plus the cost of advertising to get your customers to come to that location. An ice cream shop on the main drag across from the beach isn't likely to have as big an advertising budget as an ice cream shop on a back street six blocks from the beach.

Home-based businesses that are located off the beaten track may need to spend a little extra on advertising to keep themselves in the eye of the market. If you're a custom fence builder whose market consists of households within a 50-mile radius, a good portion of your potential customers will never drive by your house to see your wonderful "Custom Fence" sign out front—you'll need to reach out to them one way or another.

If you're just starting up, you can assume the need to budget some money to help get the word out about your new business. Then you'll want to consider an ongoing annual advertising budget to generate ongoing business.

Small business consultants will sometimes suggest a figure such as 2% to 4% of your gross annual sales as a reasonable advertising budget. But it's difficult to make a sweeping generalization like that— your budget will depend on any number of factors, not the least of which will be available working capital. If you want a guideline that might be accurate, contact the trade association for your business, and ask them for some average percentages for a business your size.

Newspapers

The most common advertising media for small businesses in the last two centuries has been the local newspaper. Traditionally

these have a high penetration in the market—75% of households may get the paper—and reasonable ad rates.

Newspapers usually sell advertising based on a price per column inch. The rate will depend on the market, the circulation of the paper, and the competition. A small daily newspaper might charge $15 to $20 per column inch. A weekly in the same market might charge less.

A *broadsheet*, which is the typical full-sized newspaper, is divided into six columns across the page. In general, an advertiser is charged for each inch of each column their ad takes up. On a six-column page, one column is 2 ¼ inches wide, so an ad measuring 4 ¼ x 2 would be a total of 4 column inches. A *tabloid* newspaper is smaller in size, but operates in the same way, with fewer columns.

In the variety of kinds of newspapers, there are paid-circulation papers, free newspapers that are delivered to every household in a town or region (sometimes called shoppers), and free newspapers that have bulk distribution only. Daily newspapers are typically paid circulation, weeklies are sometimes paid and sometimes free, and shoppers are usually free.

When deciding whether to use newspapers to advertise your home business, you'll want to first consider whether it reaches your target market. You can always ask the advertising representative for a copy of their *media kit*, which will show you the demographics of the newspaper's readership. Of course, the rep will be doing everything possible to convince you that the high-income readers they serve are exactly what you need. What you want to look for instead is specific circulation info—how many people in your target area actually get the paper? If it's free, how many read it? Will the ad you can afford stand out? How much of the circulation you're buying is wasted? That is, if you're advertising in a 25,000-circulation paper to get to the 1,000 households in your market, is this publication worth it or would something else be more cost-effective?

Look at the other advertisers that use the paper. Are they going after the same customers? Call a noncompeting business and ask them if they're pleased with the results of their ad. What kind of response do they get from the ads? Can they quantify it? How fre-

Track the Competition

If you have competitors in your area who advertise, you can track their advertising and guess how much they spend. It'll take some time, but go to the local library, where you'll find several months' supply of local newspapers. Scan each one and make note of the size and frequency of your competitors' ads. Check the Yellow Pages and other media, such as local radio or bus advertising. Once you talk to the advertising reps for each of these outlets and learn the advertising rates, you'll know the cost of your competitors' ads. Tally up the figures, and you'll have a good idea of their ad budgets.

Ad Reps

Good advertising representatives can be incredibly helpful, especially on the local level. They spend their day talking to small business-people like yourself and often have a good sense of how the local economy is faring. Creative ad reps can help you design ads, make constructive suggestions, alert you to when the medium they represent has a good deal going, and help you stay within your ad budget and build your business.

On the other hand, bad ad reps can be extremely annoying. They never consider the needs of your business, get details wrong in creating and placing your ads, and constantly pester

(continued on next page)

quently do they advertise? What section of the paper do they find most effective?

If you conclude that your local weekly paper reaches your target market, consider the different possibilities within it. You could buy a "run of paper" (ROP) ad that would be placed somewhere within the news pages. Often you can request up-front positioning or sports page positioning, but most papers won't guarantee placement unless you're buying a back page or similar premium placement. As with anything, the more money you spend with someone, the more your requests are granted. Another option would be to buy a classified ad. In theory, classifieds get a more focused audience because the ads are "classified" by subject—automotive, home and garden, items for sale, etc. Of course, then you may miss the potential customer who didn't know they needed your product or service! Many service businesses and contractors will go into a directory—often around television listings or similar—which is priced to meet the needs of those businesses.

Inserts

One way to get a lot of information out to a targeted area is through newspaper inserts—those preprinted flyers that grocery stores and other large retailers pay to have inserted with the rest of the newspaper. A newspaper will charge a price per thousand, say $25 to $100, depending on the frequency and quantity. The client is responsible for the cost of printing the insert. The client can then pick, by zip code or by community, which households will receive the insert.

If your newspaper has a circulation of 35,000, but you only want to reach 5,000 households in your immediate area, you could print 5,000 flyers and then pay, for example, $50 per thousand, or $250, to have it delivered to the 5,000 households in your target market.

Many free newspapers and shoppers go to every household. Most paid circulation newspapers offer the opportunity to reach all households in an area via a shared mail package or direct delivery. Ask the ad rep about the options.

Some readers consider inserts junk mail and immediately consign them to the recycling bin. Others are coupon junkies who go

straight to the inserts and only occasionally read the front section of the paper. Who is your customer? What image do you want to project? You'll have to decide whether an insert is right for your business.

Yellow Pages

Do you have to be in the Yellow Pages? Well, certainly a Yellow Pages ad rep will tell you that your business is doomed without a quarter-page Yellow Pages ad.

The advantage of the Yellow Pages is that virtually every household has a copy, because it's handed out free of charge. The rep will point out that with a Yellow Pages ad you will get 24-hour-a-day coverage 365 days a year. Compare that to newspapers or radio, in which your ads are here now and gone, the rep will say.

The truth is, of course, that no one uses the Yellow Pages every hour, every day of the year. But when people do, they are prime potential customers—they're looking to buy.

The disadvantage of the Yellow Pages is that once you place an ad, you're committed for the year. There's no opportunity to reduce your ad to save money. You are charged on a monthly basis, but you can't change your ad for a year. And with the proliferation of different telephone books, the Yellow Pages, while still the most prevalent, no longer holds the monopoly on business telephone listings that it once did.

For most home-based businesses that cater to customers in their immediate area, the Yellow Pages is a reasonable component of the media mix in any advertising program. If you offer a service, whether pet-sitting, plumbing, or a product, a Yellow Pages ad is good to have. But be wary of taking out large display ads—especially if there isn't much competition for your business. The money spent on a large Yellow Pages ad might better be spent elsewhere.

Radio

Radio stations charge by the length of the ad spot, the frequency, and the time of day. You'll pay more for your ad to air during "drive-time" (morning and evening rush hour) than you will at 2:00 A.M.

Ad Reps

(*continued from previous page*)

you to buy ads you don't want or need.

Don't be bashful about calling the advertising manager and requesting a different rep if you're not comfortable with the one who's calling on you. If you're a good advertiser, the manager will listen. If you've got a good rep, use him! A good rep will go beyond the call of duty for a regular advertiser who pays the bills. She may be able to help you get a press release into the paper, create a special ad campaign for you, and will work with you to get the most for your money.

Radio stations are often segmented demographically by virtue of their format. Is your target customer a rock-and-roll listener? A country fan? A news junkie? Perhaps your customers are office workers who listen during the workday. If your business happens to appeal to listeners of one format over another, buying radio time might be a smart option for you.

Local AM stations can provide an inexpensive link to a target market. Focusing on local news and talk shows, these stations often appeal to an ultra-local listenership that is ideal for home-based service businesses, for example.

The disadvantage of radio is that the ad is so ephemeral. Your target customer has to be listening—actively—at the exact moment the ad airs in order for the message to be delivered. In addition, it's difficult to get details to sink in—phone numbers, exact name of a business, the specifics of a sale or promotion.

Remember that your advertising budget is there to help you build an image and establish credibility among current and future customers. The right kind of radio campaign can help you establish name recognition and credibility in your market. A customer hears your ad on the radio, thinks nothing of it, but recognizes the business when he or she looks in the Yellow Pages.

Television and Cable

The growth of cable has changed television advertising considerably. Network TV was once a legitimate mass medium, like a major metropolitan daily newspaper. But the penetration of cable now rivals or exceeds most newspapers, and with cable comes a great proliferation of channel choices. For the home-based business, this can be an advantage.

Advertising costs on cable are based on the length of the ad spot, the frequency, and the time of day it runs. Often, however, the big hurdle for small businesses is the cost of production of a 15- or 30-second television ad. You can get away with something cheap, of course, but consider your image—does a cheesy TV ad help or hinder the image you're trying to project?

For many home-based businesses, the best value on cable may be the crawler ads shown on the local access channel or program-

Ad Agencies

Most large corporations use advertising agencies to create and place their advertising campaigns. These may be independent agencies that serve a number of clients or may be an exclusive in-house agency dedicated to the one big account.

Why use an agency? First, an ad agency works for you, the business owner. Consequently the agency is presumably better suited to offer unbiased advice on where to spend your advertising dollars. Second, the agency will have creative people available to help you design your campaign. And third, generating a significant campaign is a lot of work—by using an ad agency you can focus more of your time on satisfying the customers your ads should be generating.

The disadvantage of an agency is that it costs more. Agencies will charge you the full rate of the ad placement, though they'll be getting a discount from the media in which the ads are running—not unlike travel agents. For the average home-based business, you will probably be able to save money by going directly to the newspaper or radio station and working out an annual contract rate.

ming guide channel. Usually consisting of text only, these can be inexpensive and effective. It's not like buying a 60-second spot during the Super Bowl, but for your needs, it is probably more valuable.

Some markets still have local television channels that, whether delivered via the airwaves or by cable, may present a cost-effective advertising medium for a small business. Check the rates and the cost of the production of the commercial.

Sure, it's neat to see yourself or your business on television in your commercial, but ask yourself how many of your target customers will see it if you can only afford to run it at 3:00 A.M. You may be the only one in your neighborhood catching those *Gilligan's Island* reruns at that hour.

Community Advertising

Once you establish your business and people in your area see that you advertise, you'll be inundated with requests to advertise in any number of community outlets: school play programs, local sporting event programs, newsletters of the local Lions Club, Rotary Club, and so forth. In most cases, those asking you to advertise will be appealing more to your sense of community support than to your business acumen.

Some of these requests will come in the form of sponsorship. For just $500, you can be the main sponsor of the Littleville Community Theater production of *Oh, Calcutta*, with a full-page ad on the back of the play program as part of the bargain. If your research and instincts tell you that you can get adequate response, then consider it. If not, then realize that it's just a charitable donation, not good promotion. If you can afford charitable donations, then do it. But do so understanding exactly how and whether it helps your business.

For some home businesses, community ads will be opportunities to reach your target audience for a reasonable cost. But advertising works best when it's part of a plan. If you believe that placing an ad in the local fire department newsletter is a good idea, make it part of your annual advertising plan. Track the results. If it doesn't work, try something different the following year.

One good way to contribute to various community activities is by donating a product or service to be used as prizes. Have the winner come to your business to pick up the prize. That way you'll have a chance to build a relationship with a potential new customer.

Set aside a budget for this type of expenditure and stick to it. Don't feel bad about saying no. You're running a business, and the community will be better off if you stay in business as a productive, taxpaying citizen than if you go bankrupt from buying ads in every community-based promotion that comes along.

Direct Mail

A popular and often effective way to reach your customers is via direct mail (also discussed in Chapter 19). Mailing list rental is big business these days, making it relatively easy to find list brokers in your area. They can provide you with names and addresses (or labels) of your target customer—by age or income demographic, by interest category, by zip code—you name it, they have it.

When using direct mail, create a promotion that encourages quick response, such as a sale with specific dates or a coupon that expires. You're trying to get potential customers to make a special effort to spend money in your business—make it worth their while to do so quickly.

Direct mail can be expensive. Even assuming that you take advantage of postage discounts, postage alone will likely cost you in the $200 per thousand range. But if the list is closely aligned to the customers you want to reach, it can be well worth it. For example, if you have a small list of regular customers who have requested to be on your mailing list, it may be worth direct-mailing them even if you're paying first-class postage rates: 33 cents or $330 per thousand.

Typically, a list rental company will take your mailing piece and send it for you in order to avoid people "stealing" their lists. Begin building your own list from the responses you get from the mailing.

The movies are the only business where you can go out front and applaud yourself.

—WILL ROGERS

Coupon Mailers

One way to use direct mail less expensively is to consider a coupon mailer, in which your coupon is included in a packet along with anywhere from a dozen to four dozen other companies' coupons.

If you've received one of these promotions yourself, look at the different companies that have coupons in it. Are they targeting your same customers? Would your business seem out of place in this mailing? Call a noncompeting business that participated and ask about their response rates. How much business did they get from the coupon? Would they do it again? If so, would they change what they advertised on the coupon?

Web Site Ads

While you may not be ready to host your own Web site, you can still advertise on the Web. If you're already Internet-savvy, you know about advertising on the Web in its many forms.

The value of Web advertising is still unknown. If your business needs to attract customers with a narrow interest focus from a wide geographic area, the Web might be right for you. For example, if you provide products and services to quilters, you're probably not relying on your immediate geographic area for your customers. If you're set up for selling via mail order, the Web may work. Consider placing ads on sites for publications related to your business: trade, special interest, and business-to-business publications. Or, you might consider running a contest in a Web ad to drum up new business.

Trade Shows, Consumer Shows, and Fairs

Annual trade shows, consumer shows, or other events are for some home businesses excellent showcases for your products or to promote your services. There you can expose your business to new potential customers face-to-face. You'll get a chance to try out a few new sales pitches, ask a lot of questions to get a sense of customers' needs, and check out your competition in the next aisle.

On the other hand, you also might spend a lot of time and money only to watch people completely uninterested in your product or service file by without a glance. Like any form of promotion, it only helps if you're pitching your story to the right audience.

Lots of opportunities are out there: home shows, business-to-business expos, country fairs, Chamber of Commerce events, etc. It's always better if you can attend the event as a spectator first before signing up to be a vendor or exhibitor. If that's not possible, ask to see the previous year's program and call a few of the exhibitors listed to see if they are going back this year and what they thought of the turnout. Did they book any business at the show? Were they able to successfully follow up on leads they got at the show?

Be aware of all the costs of participating. Large trade and consumer shows involve not only booth or space rental costs, but may require you to rent fixtures and furnishings at high rates.

Be aware of your image. Sure, you may be able to get away with a cardboard sign and single table and a paper table covering, but how will your business be regarded in comparison with competitors at the show? Find a way to display your business that makes your small size a benefit for the customer. Don't look cheap; look cost-effective.

And finally, do what you can to get names, addresses, and phone numbers of interested potential customers at the show. Follow up. You paid good money to get those leads, use them!

Unpaid Promotion

There are a lot of ways to promote your business without buying advertising space. Promotion you don't have to pay for is less predictable, but it is part of any good promotional strategy. But just because it's free doesn't mean it won't cost you anything. At the very least, it will take up your valuable time.

Press Releases

The most common form of publicity for the home-based business is the press release. A business has an announcement, writes it up, and sends it off to various media. Ideally, an editor or

Your Ad on a Billboard?

Most outdoor display advertising will be beyond the means and needs of the average home-based business. But you might look for opportunities to advertise on billboards at local school sports complexes or Little League ballparks. Depending on your business and the cost, this may be for you.

reporter receives it and sees a good story in it, calls you up, and bingo—you're on the front page of the business section. Or, the press release is run more or less verbatim in a "Business Shorts" section of the local paper.

Though it can be that easy, dealing with newspapers is often a frustrating experience. Reporters are often on deadline and overworked, and they are inundated with hundreds of press releases, phone calls, faxes, and e-mails letting them know about the next great story idea of the century. Even the cheeriest reporter develops a cynical veneer over time. Consequently, you will need to be persuasive to get their attention.

Keys to getting the most out of your local newspaper:

- Take a moment to find out the newspaper's standard policy regarding news releases. Local weeklies are often willing to run press releases and photos when a business first opens. How far in advance should these be sent? If you include a photo, can it be a color print or must it be black and white? Good newspapers will have their policies printed, occasionally run them in the paper, or have them posted on a Web site. Otherwise, call the editor and find out. If you're already an advertiser in the newspaper, ask your ad rep to tell you the policy regarding press releases. Pay attention to what kinds of press releases run in the paper.

- Find out the name of the person you need to contact. If you want to announce the opening of your business, who do you speak to? A small weekly may only have one full-time editor, but there may be a local freelance columnist that helps out. A daily may have a business editor, a reporter, or other staffer whose job includes typing in press releases. In many cases, the names are listed in the paper along with e-mail addresses or phone extensions.

- Write up a press release and send it or fax it to the appropriate person. You can call first, but guess what? They're just going to ask you to send them something. Have that something ready.

- Generate a list of story ideas relating to your business. Is your business part of a growing trend locally or nationally? Does it require unique training or knowledge that would be of interest to readers? Is your personal background particularly interesting? Do you have a fascinating or famous customer who would be willing to be interviewed? Could you offer a reporter an opportunity to personally experience some aspect of your business? There's a story in every business, but you often have to dig for it.

- Be prepared to follow up. Once you've sent your press release, don't assume that the appropriate person has received it. Call and find out. If you aren't able to speak directly to the appropriate person, call back later. Find out the best time to call—reporters and editors often work odd hours and won't take calls when on deadline. Don't expect a callback—it may happen, but more than likely your call was one of at least dozens, and a press release just isn't very important in the grand scheme of things.

- Once you do reach the appropriate person, make the most of your call. Ask if he or she has any questions. Ask when she expects the press release to run. Try to engage her in conversation. If she's a reporter, compliment her on a story of hers you read and liked. See if she'll listen to a few of your story ideas.

- Don't be put off if you get put off. It may take you a dozen or more calls to get to the right person, and even then that person may tell you he or she doesn't have time to talk. Stay cheery, and call back at a more convenient time. Be pleasantly persistent.

Ways to Get Attention

There are many ways to put yourself in the public eye. But the most consistent involves a little work: follow up, follow up, and follow up some more. Other ways to bring the spotlight your way include:

- Get with the mayor—or any politician. Politicians love publicity and are good at getting it. Often newspapers can't help

Check Your Ego

Starting your own home business is a source of great pride. Like an impressive job title, your business can become a symbol of your success. You want to shout to the world, Look at me! I own and operate Vince's Va-va-va-voom Vacuum Repair!

But be careful not to let your ego dictate your advertising budget. It's a kick to see your name or the name of your business in the paper or see it on television, but it only makes sense to spend the money if the ads are generating customers.

Is building up name recognition part of your marketing plan, or are you doing it because it makes you feel good? You don't want to be known far and wide as Vince, the guy who went bankrupt after spending his savings on TV ads that didn't work.

PR Specialists

One way to help boost your business profile is to hire a public relations (PR) firm. PR professionals will have the mailing addresses of all local media outlets, and perhaps have personal relationships with many of the writers, editors, television producers, and other decision makers within the media. They know how to tell your story in a way that will get the attention of the targeted media.

Such services cost money. But, as with advertising agencies, sometimes paying someone else is worthwhile, either because you don't feel you have the skills or because your time is better spent on the core activity of the business. And hiring a PR firm doesn't have to be expensive. For a reasonable fee, you may be able to hire someone local to write a press release, send it to the appropriate places, and follow up with phone calls.

but send a photographer down to a ribbon cutting if the head of the city is there. After all, they want politicos to give them the straight dope when it comes to what they consider a real story.

- Provide photos. Don't expect the newspaper to send out a photographer unless you're in a car wreck. Anytime you can provide photos, do so. But if they're just "grip-and-grin" shots of you in front of your business, they won't be high priority. Try to get an interesting shot.
- Do something a little bit wacky. Want to promote your U-Pick Blueberry Farm? Send the newsroom some fresh-baked pies, then call to follow up. You'll get heard.
- Become a source. When you call the local news editor, don't always pitch a story about yourself; instead have a hot tip on another story in town. It doesn't have to be controversial. Even good feature stories are welcome.
- Network. Though sole proprietors are usually busy people, the more you can be involved in your town, the more opportunities you'll find to promote your business. Whether it's involvement in the Chamber of Commerce, Little League, or Rotary Club, the relationships you'll develop will help promote your business.

You will have to work a bit harder when you're promoting your home business, especially if you're hidden away from a well-traveled road. But with a savvy combination of paid advertising and free promotion, you can reach your target customers and get them to beat a path to your door—or at least get them to call you on the phone. Promotion takes a little creativity and a lot of work, but it can be the fun part of running your own business.

For more information on this topic, visit our Web site at businesstown.com

PART V

Resources

Glossary of Basic Business Terms

Account balance. The amount of a particular account at a given time.

Accounts payable. Amounts you owe vendors for supplies or services already provided.

Accounts receivable. Amounts owed you for products or services already provided.

Administrative expense. Those expenses for managing the business, as opposed to sales expense or cost-of-goods expense. Commonly referred to as "admin."

Aging. The length of time from when an invoice was generated.

Amortization. Paying a debt over time.

Annual report. A summary of the yearly finances of a business.

Appraisal. An estimate of the value of an asset.

Appreciation. The increase in value of an asset over time due to economic conditions; typically, real estate will appreciate over time. The opposite of depreciation.

Arrears. Past due amounts. Often used with taxes, as in "in arrears."

Asset. Something of value that is owned by you or the business.

Bad debts. Amounts owed that are not collectible. If a regular customer who owes you $1,000 for a job already completed declares bankruptcy, then it's likely the $1,000 is bad debt.

Balance. The summary of an account.

Balance sheet. A summary of assets and liabilities.

Bill of sale. A receipt stating what was sold, to whom, when, and for how much.

Bottom line. Net profits; what's left over in revenue after cost of goods and overhead are deducted.

Break-even analysis. An estimate of revenues and expenses that projects the point at which a business will make as much as it spends, or "break even."

Budget. Projected income or expenses.

Business plan. A document describing your business and its projected growth, including projected revenues, expenses, and profits. Often used as support in seeking financing for a business.

Capital. Money invested in a business.

Capital equipment. Equipment used in a business that usually depreciates over time.

Cash discount. A discount offered to a customer in exchange for paying immediately.

Cash flow. Money coming in and going out of a business. Important to small businesses, which need to make sure that income arrives in time to pay expenses.

Collateral. Something pledged to a lender in order to secure a loan. For home businesses, a home is sometimes used as collateral to borrow money.

Commission. A percentage of the sales price paid to a salesperson.

Corporation. An incorporated business, a type of business organization. Corporations are separate legal entities from their owners.

Cost of goods sold. What it costs to buy the products you sell, or the cost of the ingredients or parts of the product you manufacture for sale. Often referred to as COGS.

Current assets. Cash, inventory, or other things that will be used up or converted to cash in the short term (within a year).

Current liabilities. Amounts due (payable) by a business, including outstanding bills, loan payments, taxes, etc.

Current ratio. The comparison of current assets and current liabilities.

Debt. Borrowed money the business owes.

Depreciation. The decline in value of a fixed asset over time.

Direct mail. Selling products or services by mail.

Distributor. A business that buys products from manufacturers for resale to retailers.

Entrepreneur. Someone who starts a business.

Equity. The value of the business after liabilities are subtracted from assets.

FIFO. First In, First Out; a way of accounting for inventory.

Franchise. A business that involves an ongoing relationship with a parent company, usually including a shared trade name and a franchise fee.

Gross profit. Sales revenues less the cost of goods.

Income. Money you receive from the operation of the business.

Income statement. A summary of income and expenses for the business.

Interest. A percentage you pay in return for borrowing money.

Inventory. Goods purchased for resale but not yet sold, or raw materials to be used for making a product for resale.

Investment. Money (or other assets) put into the business.

Liability. Any debt or unpaid bill the business owes.

Liquidity. How easily a business can convert assets to cash.

LIFO. Last In, First Out; a way of accounting for inventory.

Limited liability company. An LLC, a kind of business organization similar to an S-corporation, in which the business exists separate from the owners, limiting their liability for the corporate debts.

Limited partnership. A kind of business organization in which one or more partners is solely an investor and whose liability is limited to the amount invested.

Loan. Money a business borrows.

Loan agreement. The written terms of a loan, including the amount, term, and interest rate.

Market niche. A small part of a customer base that a business might go after. For example, a carpenter might go after the niche of customers interested in custom kitchen cabinets.

Market research. Finding out how big the market is for your business—how many potential customers, how much they spend, and what the competition may be.

Market share. A business's share of the total market for a product or service. If there are 1,000 potential customers and your business regularly caters to 250, then your market share is 25 percent.

Marketing plan. A plan that identifies the market for a product or service and the methods by which the business will approach and sell to that market.

Merchandise. Product for sale.

Net sales. Sales revenues less discounts and returns.

Net worth. What you or your business is worth when you subtract your liabilities from your assets (what you owe from what you own).

Operating costs. What it costs you to administrate the business on a day-to-day basis.

Overhead. Ongoing administrative costs of the business that typically stay the same.

Partnership. A kind of business organization involving two or more people. Like a sole proprietorship, partners are owners (not employees) who are fully liable for the debts of the business.

Payables. Money due to vendors of products or services.

Principal. The amount of a loan that is borrowed.

Product. An item a business might manufacture or sell.

Profit and loss statement. Also known as the P&L.

Pro forma. A projected estimate, as in pro forma income statement.

Projections. Estimates of future sales, expenses, or profits.

Publicity. News about your business, such as sending out a press release to local newspapers.

Receivables (see Accounts Receivable). Money due from a customer for services or products.

Residential zone. An area of a community set aside for homes.

Retail sales. Sales to the public.

Retailing. Selling to the public.

Revenue. Money coming into the business.

S Corporation. Or S Corp, a form of incorporation providing tax and liability benefits, often used for small businesses.

Sales lead. A potential customer.

Sole proprietorship. The simplest form of business organization, in which one owner is personally liable for the debts of the business.

Target market. The specific group of customers to which a business expects to sell.

Telemarketing. Selling by telephone.

Trade organization. A group dedicated to serving a particular trade or kind of business.

Turn rate. The frequency an inventory item "turns over," or sells, in a year.

Venture capital. Investment in a business.

Wholesale. Selling (or buying) for resale.

Working capital. The money needed to operate your company on a day-to-day basis, usually the difference between current assets and current liabilities.

Zoning. The division of a community into zones set aside exclusively for a specific use, typically residential, commercial, or industrial.

Resources for the Home-Based Business

Home Business Books

Accounting for the New Business. Christopher R. Malburg. Adams Media.

The Best Internet Businesses You Can Start. Marian Betancourt. Adams Media.

Business Planning Guide. 8th ed. David H. Bangs, Jr. Upstart Publishing.

Easy to Start, Fun to Run, & Highly Profitable Home Businesses. Katina Z. Jones. Adams Media.

How to Become Successfully Self-Employed. 2nd ed. Brian R. Smith. Adams Media.

How to Incorporate and Start a Business In. . . . Adams Media publishes these guides with specific information for 30 different states.

Marketing for the Home-Based Business. 2nd ed. Jeff Davidson. Adams Media.

Selling 101. Michael T. McGaulley. Adams Media.

Streetwise Complete Business Plan. Bob Adams. Adams Media.

Streetwise Small Business Start-Up. Bob Adams. Adams Media.

Home Business Magazines Online

Entrepreneur's Home Office
www.homeofficemag.com

Home Office Computing
www.smalloffice.com

HomeBusiness Journal
www.homebizjour.com

HomeBusiness Magazine
www.homebusinessmag.com

Inc.
www.inc.com

The Small Business Journal
www.tsbj.com

Home Business Organizations

American Home Business Association
www.homebusiness.com
4505 S. Wasatah Blvd.
Salt Lake City, UT 84124
(800) 664-2422
Offers a variety of benefits to members, including health insurance, discounts, newsletter.

Home Office Association of America
www.hoaa.com
133 East 58th St., Suite 711
New York, NY 10022
(800) 809-4622
Another membership organization offering a variety of services, including insurance and advice.

Internal Revenue Service (IRS)
www.irs.ustreas.gov
U.S. Dept. of the Treasury
1111 Constitution Ave. NW
Washington, DC 20224
(202) 622-5164

National Association of the Self-Employed
www.nase.org
P.O. Box 612067, DFW Airport
Dallas, TX 75261-2067
(800) 232-6273
Membership organization that offers a variety of services, including health insurance. Also lobbies on home business issues.

Service Corps of Retired Executives (S.C.O.R.E.)
www.score.org
(800) 634-0245
Retired execs provide free advice, face-to-face or even via e-mail.

Small Business Administration (SBA)
www.sbaonline.sba.gov
408 Third St. SW
Washington, DC 20416
(202) 205-6600
Offices in every state; check your local phone book's government listings to find the one near you.

Small Business Development Centers (SBDC)
These centers assist small businesses, especially start-ups. Associated with colleges and universities. Check local listings for the center nearest you.

Home Business Web Sites

Business Planning Resource (*www.bplans.com*) A site for a business planning software program; among other information, it offers sample business plans.

Entrepreneurial Edge Online (*www.edgeonline.com*) A commercial site for the entrepreneur.

Entrepreneurial Parent (*www.en-parent.com*) Geared toward home-based entrepreneurs who have children.

Home-Based Business Resource Center (*www.be-your-own-boss.com*) Another commercial site offering advice for the home business.

LIST International (*www.teleport.com*) A how-to site for home-based businesses.

The Marketing Resource Center (*www.marketingsource.com*) Marketing information for small businesses.

Small Business News Online (*www.sbnonline.com*) An online magazine for small businesses.

Your Home Business (*www.discribe.ca/yourhbiz/yourhbiz.htm*) Directed at current and prospective home business owners.

www.bizproweb.com Features resources for the small business owner, including links to shareware (low-cost) business software.

www.onvia.com An online store selling services such as credit cards and long-distance plans to small businesses, the site also offers news and advice articles of interest.

www.smallbusiness.suny.edu This site, sponsored by the State University of New York SBDC, has a terrific research network with numerous links to other small business resources on the Web.

For more information on this topic, visit our Web site at businesstown.com

Index

We Have EVERYTHING!®

Available wherever books are sold!

Everything® **After College Book**
$12.95, 1-55850-847-3

Everything® **Astrology Book**
$12.95, 1-58062-062-0

Everything® **Baby Names Book**
$12.95, 1-55850-655-1

Everything® **Baby Shower Book**
$12.95, 1-58062-305-0

Everything® **Barbeque Cookbook**
$12.95, 1-58062-316-6

Everything® **Bartender's Book**
$9.95, 1-55850-536-9

Everything® **Bedtime Story Book**
$12.95, 1-58062-147-3

Everything® **Beer Book**
$12.95, 1-55850-843-0

Everything® **Bicycle Book**
$12.95, 1-55850-706-X

Everything® **Build Your Own Home Page**
$12.95, 1-58062-339-5

Everything® **Casino Gambling Book**
$12.95, 1-55850-762-0

Everything® **Cat Book**
$12.95, 1-55850-710-8

Everything® **Christmas Book**
$15.00, 1-55850-697-7

Everything® **College Survival Book**
$12.95, 1-55850-720-5

Everything® **Cover Letter Book**
$12.95, 1-58062-312-3

Everything® **Crossword and Puzzle Book**
$12.95, 1-55850-764-7

Everything® **Dating Book**
$12.95, 1-58062-185-6

Everything® **Dessert Book**
$12.95, 1-55850-717-5

Everything® **Dog Book**
$12.95, 1-58062-144-9

Everything® **Dreams Book**
$12.95, 1-55850-806-6

Everything® **Etiquette Book**
$12.95, 1-55850-807-4

Everything® **Family Tree Book**
$12.95, 1-55850-763-9

Everything® **Fly-Fishing Book**
$12.95, 1-58062-148-1

Everything® **Games Book**
$12.95, 1-55850-643-8

Everything® **Get-a-Job Book**
$12.95, 1-58062-223-2

The ultimate reference for couples planning their wedding!

- Scheduling, budgeting, etiquette, hiring caterers, florists, and photographers
- Ceremony & reception ideas
- Over 100 forms and checklists
- And much, much more!

$12.95, 384 pages, 8" x 9¼"

Personal finance made easy—and fun!

- Create a budget you can live with
- Manage your credit cards
- Set up investment plans
- Money-saving tax strategies
- And much, much more!

$12.95, 288 pages, 8" x 9¼"

For more information, or to order, call 800-872-5627 or visit everything.com

Adams Media Corporation, 260 Center Street, Holbrook, MA 02343

FIND MORE ON THIS TOPIC BY VISITING
BusinessTown.com
The Web's big site for growing businesses!

- ☑ Separate channels on all aspects of starting and running a business
- ☑ Lots of info on how to do business online
- ☑ 1,000+ pages of savvy business advice
- ☑ Complete web guide to thousands of useful business sites
- ☑ Free e-mail newsletter
- ☑ Question and answer forums, and more!

http://www.businesstown.com

Accounting
Basic, Credit & Collections, Projections, Purchasing/Cost Control

Advertising
Magazine, Newspaper, Radio, Television, Yellow Pages

Business Opportunities
Ideas for New Businesses, Business for Sale, Franchises

Business Plans
Creating Plans & Business Strategies

Finance
Getting Money, Money Problem Solution

Letters & Forms
Looking Professional, Sample Letters & Forms

Getting Started
Incorporating, Choosing a Legal Structure

Hiring & Firing
Finding the Right People, Legal Issues

Home Business
Home Business Ideas, Getting Started

Internet
Getting Online, Put Your Catalog on the Web

Legal Issues
Contracts, Copyrights, Patents, Trademarks

Managing a Small Business
Growth, Boosting Profits, Mistakes to Avoid, Competing with the Giants

Managing People
Communications, Compensation, Motivation, Reviews, Problem Employees

Marketing
Direct Mail, Marketing Plans, Strategies, Publicity, Trade Shows

Office Setup
Leasing, Equipment, Supplies

Presentations
Know Your Audience, Good Impression

Sales
Face to Face, Independent Reps, Telemarketing

Selling a Business
Finding Buyers, Setting a Price, Legal Issues

Taxes
Employee, Income, Sales, Property, Use

Time Management
Can You Really Manage Time?

Travel & Maps
Making Business Travel Fun

Valuing a Business
Simple Valuation Guidelines